The Hospital and Clinic Improvement Handbook

The Hospital and Clinic Improvement Handbook

Using Lean and the Theory of Constraints for Better Healthcare Delivery

Boaz Ronen, PhD

Joseph S. Pliskin, PhD

Shimeon Pass, MSc, MBA

OXFORD
UNIVERSITY PRESS

OXFORD
UNIVERSITY PRESS

Oxford University Press is a department of the University of Oxford. It furthers the University's objective of excellence in research, scholarship, and education by publishing worldwide. Oxford is a registered trade mark of Oxford University Press in the UK and certain other countries.

Published in the United States of America by Oxford University Press
198 Madison Avenue, New York, NY 10016, United States of America.

Library of Congress Cataloging-in-Publication Data
Names: Ronen, Boaz, author. | Pliskin, Joseph S., 1946– author. | Pass, Shimeon, 1947– author.
Title: The hospital and clinic improvement handbook : using lean and the theory of constraints for better healthcare delivery / Boaz Ronen, Joseph S. Pliskin, Shimeon Pass.
Description: Oxford ; New York : Oxford University Press, 2018. |
Includes bibliographical references and index.
Identifiers: LCCN 2017041985 | ISBN 9780190843458 (pbk. : alk. paper)
Subjects: | MESH: Delivery of Health Care | Hospital Administration | Quality Improvement
Classification: LCC RA965.6 | NLM W 84.1 | DDC 362.11—dc23
LC record available at https://lccn.loc.gov/2017041985

9 8 7 6 5 4 3 2

Printed by Sheridan Books, Inc., United States of America

CONTENTS

FOREWORD

More than a decade has passed since I wrote the following foreword to these authors' earlier book, *Focused Operations Management for Health Services Organizations*. When they honored me by asking for an updated foreword to this new work, I began by reviewing the original foreword and was immediately struck by its continuing relevance. My first line then ("Health care badly needs this book") is my first thought now. And the full, original foreword follows these introductory thoughts.

What has happened in the intervening years in the world of healthcare quality has been progress, without doubt. Boosted by the Institute of Medicine reports, *To Err Is Human* (1999) and *Crossing the Quality Chasm* (2001), the awareness of defects in care soared in the United States, and in many other nations. Patient safety became the flagship dimension for improvement, but the evidence base and enthusiasts for five other dimensions specified by the Institute of Medicine (effectiveness, patient-centeredness, timeliness, efficiency, and equity) also grew rapidly.

My colleagues, Tom Nolan and John Whittington, and I broadened the terrain of concern in 2008 with the promulgation of the Institute for Healthcare Improvement "Triple Aim" (better care for individuals, better health for populations, and lower per capita cost through improvement) as the proper set of goals for a socially relevant health and healthcare system.[1] Within a few years, many organizations and even nations worldwide were mapping "Triple Aim" objective into their strategic plans.

Quality sciences advanced in parallel, especially with respect to measurement. And as attention to improvement grew, so did examples of success—local breakthroughs on individual projects and dimensions of performance.

This news was good—but it was not great. The problems were ones of pace and scale. Good ideas and new models were born, but they generally

1. Berwick, D. M., Nolan, T. W., and Whittington, J., 2008. The Triple Aim: Care, Health, and Cost, *Health Affairs*, 27, 759–769.

failed to grow or spread. Healthcare delivery improvement showed nothing like the viral spread of new information technologies and devices. The status quo systems remained the dominant ones, and they still do today. And, consequently, overall health system performance has not achieved Triple Aim breakthroughs anywhere yet.

Worse, on the heels of the Great Recession and in the subsequent waves of governmental and private austerity, healthare systems have been squeezed hard between their own rapidly rising costs and the severe budget pressures that nations have introduced in public-funded care and that the private sector has increased in privately funded care. Rather than energizing systematic quality improvement as the best source of efficiency, these pressures have diverted the attention of governing boards, governments, and managers from improvement investments. Pressure, not improvement, has been the plan.

Here, in sum, is what has happened in the intervening decade since *Focused Operations Management for Health Services Organizations* appeared: Awareness of the need for improvement has grown, metrics have developed, prototypes for new care have appeared, and the urgency for change has increased. What has lagged behind are results at scale, and, in my view, the main reason for that is that the most powerful, scientifically grounded methods for system design and redesign have not yet been adopted or mastered by most healthcare organizations and leaders. Exhortation cannot do what is needed. Only science can.

That is what this new book offers, just as the earlier one did. *The Hospital and Clinic Improvement Handbook: Using Lean and the Theory of Constraints in Healthcare Organizations* is full of ideas that, if mastered, can help craft a route to excellence on all components of the Triple Aim at once. It is not easy, but it is right. My hope is that those who lead and fund the pursuit of health and healthcare will give this book the attention it warrants.

FOREWORD TO THE FIRST EDITION

Healthcare badly needs this book.

The century of proud progress that marked the 1900s placed medicine securely on its proper scientific platform. Unparalleled growth in subject-matter expertise brought to the bedside the benefits of pharmacy, surgery, diagnostic tests, and images in accelerating frequency, and that progress continues. The engine of those gains has been largely the wedding of clinical sciences with other sciences—molecular biology, physics, material sciences, and genetics, for example. The application of new knowledge gained new footing in the later decades of the 20th century thanks to deep interactions between medicine and statistics, epidemiology, decision analysis, and emerging evaluative methods of clinical epidemiology. In public policy and care design, econometrics and psychology also gained footholds, with the landmark Rand Health Insurance Experiment ushering in a new era of health services research.

The pattern can be interpreted thus: healthcare has made progress on two routes—within disciplines and at the intersection of disciplines. Both forms of progress have mattered a great deal, but anyone familiar with these intellectual advances knows that in many ways the development of science on the second route—at intersections—has been the slower and more difficult of the two. To bring molecular epidemiology, statistics, and economics, for example, into the service of healthcare has required vision, strong leadership, and a willingness to take risks. Bridging between intellectual pursuits previously unfamiliar with each other requires translation, patience, an attitude of respect among strangers, and foundations and other funders willing to offer some venture capital to the meeting places.

I recall clearly that I first met Professor Pliskin, one of the authors of this book, under the auspices of then-Dean of the Harvard School of Public Health, Howard Hiatt, who must rank in any accurate healthcare history as one of the most courageous and successful intersection builders of our time. Although his formal background had been deeply rooted in classical research in clinical oncology and molecular biology, by the 1950s well-honored terrain for formal research, Dr. Hiatt had come to feel that progress for healthcare as a system—a system deeply troubled by defects, excess cost, irrational clinical practices, and, most urgently, social inequality—would depend on new interactions, between healthcare knowledge and other domains of knowledge that, until then, had not had much to do with clinical care. As Dean at the Harvard School of Public Health, Dr. Hiatt created a new Center for the Evaluation of Clinical Practices and attracted the interest and attention of some young and some not-so-young mavericks, some of the stature of Professors Fred Mosteller, Benjamin Barnes, and Howard Frazier, and others who were still finding their way into their academic niches, such as Milton Weinstein, Harvey Fineberg, Duncan Neuhauser, Shan Cretin, Emmett Keeler, Mark Rosenberg, and me. Joe Pliskin, ready and able to try to forge new links between operations research and healthcare, was soon interacting with us.

The new Center and its senior sponsors cut the risks of exploring new terrain together but not quite to zero. It still took a modicum of risk-taking for young statisticians or economists to migrate away from their disciplinary departments enough to work steadily and productively with young clinicians equally willing to engage in research that was hard to explain to their clinically based colleagues. But it was fun enough to thrive, and from that era at Harvard and elsewhere came the foundations of a new wave of clinical epidemiology, cost-effectiveness analysis, decision analysis, and health services research that matured fully in the few decades that followed.

One such intersection, however, did not, in my opinion, flourish as it should have. For reasons unclear to me, operations research—the types of quantitative and systems methods so ably explored in this book—did not quite find the traction in healthcare that other, related sciences—economics, statistics, and even psychometrics—more rapidly did. As a result, we have today widespread use of valuable psychometric surveys (like the SF-32 and its progeny), widespread commitment to, or at least awareness of, evidence-based medicine, and strong centers of health economics around the United States. The equivalent realization regarding operations research and its related disciplines—that these hold the seeds of crucial understandings and a foundation for change—did not then fully blossom.

Luckily, systems scientists like Ronen, Pliskin, and Pass, absolutely experts in their disciplines and unwilling to give up their firm interest in healthcare, continued to pursue their mastery of their fields and their explorations of how healthcare could benefit. Equally important, new waves of theorists in systems science advanced their basic work and began to explain their rather complex insights in ways that less technically proficient communities could understand—Goldratt, Senge, and others.

Meanwhile, healthcare has continued to advance on many fronts but to get into deeper and deeper trouble on others. Soaring costs, fragmentation of care, discontinuity, and a growing sense of frustration in the workforce have become symptoms not only in the United States but also in almost all developed nations. These authors have aptly subtitled their book, "Doing More with the Same Resources," and that, exactly, is the heart of the matter that faces almost all healthcare systems and organizations as the 21st century gains momentum.

And, it is the disciplines they have mastered and present here that have the greatest possible future leverage on that very issue. The concepts we need in healthcare to "do more with the same resources" are not simple. To explain them to people like me takes the elegance of thinking that Ronen, Pliskin, and Pass have refined in decades of teaching. But the news is good—the concepts are mature, the teachers are in hand, and the need has crested. It will take only one more step—a giant one, but not impossible—for healthcare leaders to recognize that, as responsible clinical care required their interest in and use of evaluative clinical sciences in recent times, so will the proper and prudent design of the systems they must now create require their interest in and use of the very best of modern systems sciences—ideas like the theory of constraints, the focus on cycle times, and totally new views of waste and efficiency as presented in this book. Ideas whose time have come are delivered here by teachers ready to help us meet them. One must not underestimate the daunting managerial challenges that the needed changes will bring with them, but the potential payoff is immense.

My close colleague and friend, Tom Nolan, PhD, a master systems thinker himself, has spoken for several years of the need to "dignify" systems sciences in healthcare, so that we can take advantage of them on behalf of patients and communities. Interested leaders will find no resource to study modern systems theories more dignified or comprehensible than this one. It is time to use what they know.

Donald M. Berwick, MD, MPP
Newton, MA
May 28, 2017

PREFACE

The healthcare sector faces challenges that are constantly escalating. Populations are growing worldwide and so is the share of the elderly in society. There is a constant proliferation of new medications, diagnostic methods, medical procedures and equipment, and know-how. This huge progress greatly improves the quality of medical treatment but at the same time increases its costs. Governments and authorities are allocating ever-growing budgets to healthcare systems, but the increased budgets do not cover the increased costs of providing quality healthcare to the public.

In this book, we present methods that can ease these challenges to some extent. Throughout the book, we will provide answers to questions like:

- Can our hospital reduce the response time of the emergency department (ED) substantially (e.g., by 40%) and increase the clinical quality with existing resources?
- Can we increase the throughput of the operating rooms (ORs) substantially (e.g., by 20%) without additional resources?
- Does reliance on traditional cost accounting methods lead us to make wrong managerial decisions in pricing, costing, investment justification, and make/buy decisions? If this is true, then what are the alternatives for better decision-making?
- Why do inadequate performance measures undermine value creation?
- Can we increase throughput, reduce response time, and increase quality by well-made addition of inexpensive resources to the right areas?
- Why is the undifferentiating addition of resources not the recipe for improvement in healthcare organizations?

These topics are addressed in this book along with many more managerial issues of high relevance and impact for healthcare systems and healthcare provision. The methodology presented in the book is intended to help managers of healthcare systems to be able to better deal with these challenges.

The book should be of value to all executive and managerial personnel in every healthcare organization including hospitals, HMOs, laboratories, ministries of health, clinics, health insurance establishments, and government agencies. The book offers practical knowledge and effective tools for people in managerial as well as staff positions. We made special effort to present this important content in a very fluid and simple (but not simplistic) way for the benefit of a very broad audience. As a matter of fact, this book is equally useful for nonprofit and for-profit organizations, in diverse sectors such as public and private service and industry.

The main theme of the book is that one can do **much more** with the **same resources** in terms of throughput, response time, and quality by using practical tools and techniques. It provides a system view and touches on issues of performance measures, operations management, quality, cost-accounting, pricing, and, above all, value creation and enhancement. We hope that on reading the book, every person within a healthcare organization will be able to implement immediate actions resulting in relatively rapid improvement in most performance aspects of the organization. The book focuses on reducing waste and avoiding nonvalue-adding activities. This is the essence of the Lean concept. Lean is a philosophy. Several books dealing with Lean in healthcare have emerged in recent years (Albanese et al., 2014; Black & Miller, 2008; Zidel, 2012). The virtue of the current book is that it provides a series of tools that are simple, easy to comprehend and use, and have already achieved amazing results in many healthcare organizations. It is the use of the theory of constraints (TOC) along with other focusing tools that provide the high added-value of this book. The current book is a revised and updated version of our previous book (Ronen et al., 2006).

The book also presents methods like the TOC that yields fast improvement in systems such as ORs and emergency departments. For example, the book demonstrates how simple tools like the focusing table, the focusing matrix, the complete kit concept, and Pareto analysis can increase throughput, reduce response time, and create value in the healthcare industry.

Based on our vast experience in implementing the methodology presented in this book for improving healthcare systems as well as on our observations of the most recent improvements in dozens of organizations, wards, and clinics, the use of these methods can increase throughput in areas like ORs by 10% to 20% and reduce response time in places like EDs and clinics by 20% to 40% while using only existing resources.

Various chapters present simple tools for more effective management. These tools are accompanied by dozens of real-world examples of their successful use. Chapter 19, for instance, helps to identify value drivers and guide decision makers on *where* and *when* to implement various components of value creation. The *how* is highlighted in the specific preceding chapters. Chapter 20 presents real-world successful applications of the various tools in a variety of hospitals and healthcare organizations.

Naturally, this book is also intended to be a text and reference in teaching management of healthcare organizations, especially operations management in healthcare management and public health programs, both for graduate and undergraduate students. It will also be very relevant to related fields such as social work, psychology, and all allied health professions.

The book is based on our own extensive experience in using and successfully implementing all components presented in the book in healthcare settings. It also reflects our rich teaching experience with managers and students in various settings such as MBA programs, executive MBA programs, healthcare management programs, and schools of public health. Our experience encompasses Harvard University (School of Public Health), Columbia University (Graduate School of Business), New York University (Stern School of Business), Tel-Aviv University (Coller School of Management), Boston University (School of Management), Ben-Gurion University of the Negev (Faculty of Health Sciences, School of Management), in various Northwestern University Kellogg programs throughout the world, and in SDA-Bocconi University in Milan, Italy. We plan to use this book as the only textbook in our courses.

Thousands of executives and students were exposed to these methods over the last decade by actively implementing the methods described in the book, taking our courses, or participating in our workshops. Many successful implementations occurred thanks to this exposure. We have led projects where the methods were successfully implemented and achieved both short- and long-term results. Our book presents many case studies and real-world applications that had a strong positive impact in many organizations.

Our approach is very applications-oriented using new managerial approaches. On the one hand, it is not the typical quantitative operations management book, and on the other hand it is not an organizational behavior one. It is mission/business-oriented, targeted to achieve immediate and substantial improvements in healthcare organizations.

Boaz Ronen
Joseph S. Pliskin
Shimeon Pass

CHAPTER 1

The Modern Healthcare Environment

OBJECTIVE

- Why is there a need for new managerial approaches?

For more than 20 years healthcare systems of most Western countries have been faced with the challenges stemming from massive increases in healthcare costs in real terms and as a percentage of GNP. As a result, they have been obliged to cut expenses in other sectors to provide their people with a reasonable healthcare system. Classical breakdowns of healthcare system costs can be shown in either the supply part or in the demand part. During this time, the business environment in many sectors has been characterized by rapid changes. The customers gained much more power and are now very demanding. They are seeking better quality, shorter response times, and lower prices. They are pushing their caregivers to use every new technology that can help them and resolve their problems.

This trend is the result of international revolutions and macroeconomic, technological, political, and social changes. This environment is characterized by:

- The high-tech revolution and the use of high-technology products and services.
- Globalization of the world economy.
- Fierce competition among organizations within and across countries.
- Global excess capacities in production, services, and some areas of development.

- Internet availability and accessibility of data and knowledge.
- Cheap and rapid communication.
- Timely availability of materials and services.
- Ease of global travel and conveyance.
- Extensive use of advanced information technology.

A similar situation exists in the healthcare market:

- The customers demand more.
- The customers have more and better information.
- Technologies (equipment, medications, devices, and procedures) develop rapidly while budget growth cannot keep pace.
- People have longer life expectancies.

In nonprofit organizations, including government agencies and hospitals, recent years have brought an **increase in demand** for services on the one hand and **budget reduction** on the other. This situation results in much higher pressures on management. Using new managerial approaches and philosophies enable these organizations to extract additional output without increasing resources. For example, in one major hospital, operating room output has increased by 20% with the same personnel and with better clinical and service quality.

This situation can nicely be described by the scissors diagram of Figure 1.1 where budgets increase in time relatively slower (if at all) than the need for quality healthcare services.

THE REMEDY—ADOPTION OF NOVEL MANAGERIAL APPROACHES

Advanced technology, professional personnel, and powerful information systems do not guarantee survival in the highly competitive and challenging

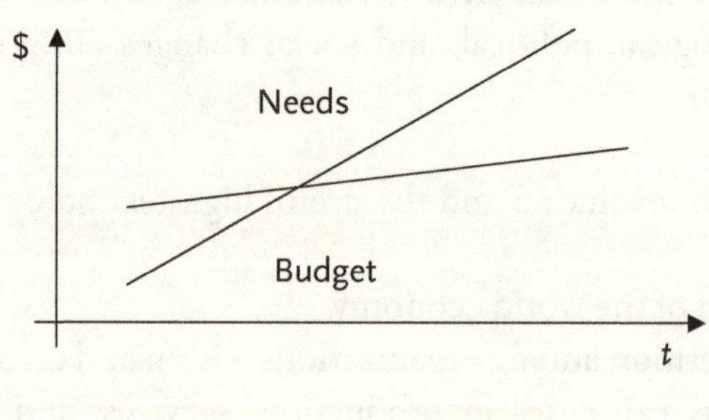

Figure 1.1:
The scissors diagram

healthcare market. They are perhaps necessary or supportive conditions but definitely not sufficient. The main determinant in the ability to survive the competition is the adoption of advanced managerial approaches that are compatible with the new business environment.

In today's businesses and healthcare systems, three main managerial methods can make a difference once implemented in the organization. These are the theory of constraints (TOC), the Lean managerial approach, and the quality methods known as the Six Sigma approach.

TOC was developed by Eliyau M. Goldratt, author of the breakthrough book, *The Goal* (Goldratt and Cox, 1992).

The Lean approach has emerged from the fundamental rules of the just-in-time (JIT) approach (Schonberger, 1986). The quality revolution and the Six Sigma approach have developed on the roots of giants like Deming and others (Deming, 1986). These approaches have been developed and successfully implemented in many organizations. Moreover, in many instances managerial decision-making has changed. The foundation for the development of these new approaches is the desire to be compatible with a new business reality and to engage relevant value drivers to improve and enhance the value of these organizations.

Value Enhancement—increasing the value of the organization to its owners, its workers, and the community. In for-profit organizations, the value of the organization is the discounted cash flow. In nonprofit organizations, increasing value means continuously improving the key performance measures.

Management teams of most organizations have come to realize that to succeed in the global competitive environment, it is not enough to revert to technological innovation or to use cheaper resources and materials. It is essential to see the whole picture and manage differently. The new managerial approaches result in enhancing the value of the organization.

The new managerial approaches have several characteristics:

- They are based on common sense.
- These approaches evolved out of practice; only later did they receive academic and scientific validation.
- They are simple and use the KISS ("Keep it simple, stupid") approach.
- They break down the myth of the naïve input–output model.

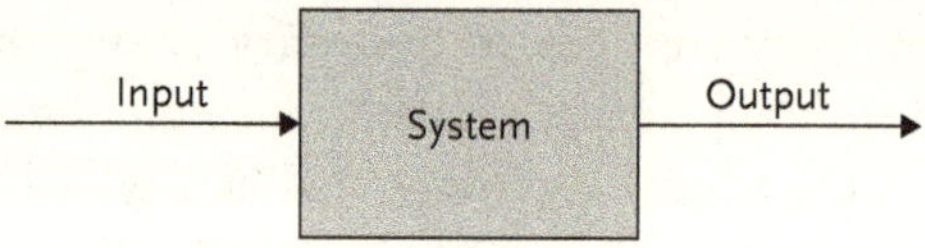

Figure 1.2:
Input–output model

The input-output model is described in Figure 1.2.

The naïve input–output myth implies: "If we want to increase system outputs, we must increase inputs." This rationale implies, for example, that if we want to increase patient throughput in a clinic by 20%, we may request more input in the form of personnel, space, advertising, and so on. Similarly, if we want to decrease waiting time for patients, this rationale calls for requesting more personnel and equipment. The modern managerial approaches show that this myth can be broken. We can **increase output** without increasing input, just by changing the managerial approach. Evidence for better management of **existing resources** can be found in Mabin and Balderstone (2000), Cox et al. (2016) and in Coman et al. (1996). As will be seen in the sequel, in these cases an additional managerial "input" has been added—a different managerial approach.

LEAN AND SIX SIGMA

The healthcare world has been accustomed to various buzzwords and acronyms over the years. A common acronym was TQM (total quality management), then replaced by CQI (continuous quality improvement) and more recently the concepts of Lean and Six Sigma.

Let us examine the last two.

Lean

The concept of Lean emerged from studies of the Toyota manufacturing methods back in the 1980s, and was termed "Lean manufacturing," "Lean production," or simply "Lean." It represents a management philosophy of reducing waste within a system or process. By reducing waste, one can focus on other elements that can add value to the product and service the customer of the organization.

The first to coin the term "Lean" was John Krafcik (1988). We also refer the reader to systematic review of the literature of Lean management in healthcare (Lawal et al., 2014).

Back in the 1960s, the Japanese developed a management philosophy, JIT, based on three rules:

- Rule 1 of JIT: Work only as needed in terms of timing, quantity, and specifications.
- Rule 2 of JIT: Work in small, appropriate, and smart batches.
- Rule 3 of JIT: Avoid wastes and activities that do not add value to the organization.

The concept of **Lean** is exactly **Rule 3 of JIT**, only the name has changed. Avoiding wastes and activities that do not add value are the essence of this book.

The concept of JIT was widely accepted in industry but did not make it into the healthcare industry. Ironically, the concept of Lean, is one of the hottest items in today's healthcare industry.

Six Sigma

Six Sigma is a set of techniques and tools for quality improvement. It was first introduced by Motorola in 1986 and has spread around the world quite quickly. It usually goes hand in hand with the Lean system. Its origins are in Dr. Deming's work back in 1980s (Deming, 1986).

Six Sigma is based on process improvement by removing causes for defects and reducing variability. It uses dozens of tools such as the Pareto diagrams (see chapter 3), control charts, and statistical methods that aim toward stabilizing and controlling processes. The main philosophy is that the product or service is as good as the process by which it was made.

The term "Six Sigma" represents a 99.73% probability of a part or a service to be within accepted limits (or 2.7 parts per thousand to be outside accepted limits). The term "Sigma" symbolizes the statistical term of "standard deviation."

Six Sigma has emerged in healthcare following the 1999 report of the Institute of Medicine showing that nearly 100,000 people died every year in the United States from medical mistakes made by healthcare professionals. Six Sigma is also associated with reducing variability, which is extremely important in healthcare. We address the issue of variability and controlling it in chapter 14.

THE THEORY OF CONSTRAINTS (TOC)

The theory of constraints (TOC) was developed by Goldratt (Goldratt and Cox, 1992). The theory claims that the attention of management should be focused on the few constraints that prevent the organization from achieving its goal.

TOC is an innovative and very effective approach, and we consider it a managerial breakthrough. It is a focusing method that provides simple tools, focusing techniques, and a managerial global view. One of its best tools, **the seven focusing steps**, as we will see in chapter 4, is based on the conceptual foundations of operations research methods such as linear programming (Ronen and Starr, 1990).

TOC's main tools are the seven focusing steps (Ronen et al., 2001), the drum–buffer–rope scheduling mechanism (see chapter 5), identifying the core problems using the current reality tree (chapter 7), and the conflict resolution diagram (chapter 8).

TOC is gaining increasing acceptance among practitioners as well as academics (Gupta, 2003). Its application provided thousands of organizations worldwide with significant performance improvements, such as increased throughput, reduced inventory levels, and shorter lead time (Mabin and Balderstone, 2000). While reports of successful TOC implementations are mainly from manufacturing organizations—especially aerospace, apparel, automotive, electronics, semiconductor, steel, and heavy engineering (Mabin and Balderstone, 2003)—TOC has also been implemented in diverse nonmanufacturing industries including financial institutions (Smith, 2004) and in the public sector (Shoemaker and Reid, 2005). Schragenheim et al. (1994) applied TOC in the process flow industry. It was also applied to project management (Goldratt, 1997) and to the adjudication system (Maayan, 2012). Last but not least, it was applied to health services (Knight, 2014; Ronen et al., 2006; Cox et al., 2016).

Our experience shows that the integration of these three management philosophies, accompanied by other tools (the complete kit concept, global decision-making, etc.) maximizes the value of healthcare organizations.

CHAPTER SUMMARY

The market for healthcare organizations is not only the region or the country in which they operate but rather the whole world. On the one hand, this creates a threat from organizations outside the country, but on the other hand it opens opportunities to penetrate huge outside territories. Management has become more difficult and more demanding considering the fierce competition, the increasing complexity and diversity of products and services, and the need to implement advanced technology. Past achievements are becoming obsolete because of competitors' improvements. An organization that does not improve will be driven out of the market. Technology, skilled personnel, and information systems are necessary but not sufficient conditions for survival. In addition, there must be the important component of managerial approaches that are congruent with the competitive environment of today.

Nonprofit organizations, hospitals, government agencies, and community healthcare systems face increased demand for their services along with the pressure for containing costs. Implementation of new managerial approaches will improve their performance.

The objectives of management are to enhance the value of the firm (in business firms) or to improve organizational performance (in nonprofit organizations). Many organizations are fighting for their survival. They need to identify relevant value drivers and improve them using innovative approaches based on common sense. The bottom line of these approaches is "doing more with what you have."

CHAPTER 2

Principles of Management in the Dynamic Healthcare Environment

OBJECTIVES

- Why most healthcare organizations resort to suboptimization and how a global view can avoid this.
- Why the optimizer approach may interfere with healthcare organizations achieving their goals and how the satisficer approach is an answer.
- Why focused management.

WHAT IS A SYSTEM?

A system is a collection of interconnected components acting together toward a common goal. It is a complex and **holistic** entity. It can be a biological system, an engineering system, or an organizational system (business, goal-oriented, or nonprofit). A system has a **goal** that drives its activity. The overall goal generates defined **quantitative objectives** that must be achieved as well as a set of **performance measures** that enable management or owners to exercise control and judge whether they are on the right track to achieve the goal. The system has boundaries within the environment it operates. The system consists of **subunits with hierarchy and interaction.** The system has a **process** that **converts** the **inputs** it receives from the environment into **outputs** the environment receives from the system. Some organizational systems have a **feedback** process by

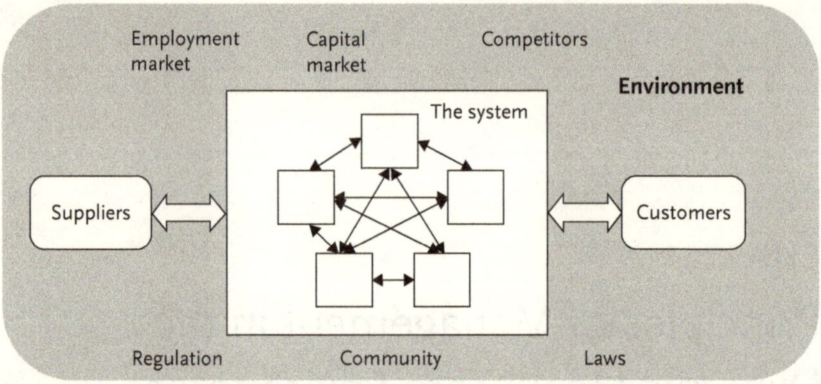

Figure 2.1:
The classical organizational system

which the system corrects its activity and adjusts itself to environmental changes (see Figure 2.1).

W. E. Deming (1986), one of the pioneers of quality management, is responsible for the change in the modern perception of the organizational system. He emphasizes the "people" element in the system, and he includes suppliers and customers within system definition. Including suppliers and customers indicates that they are partners of the effective operation of the system. Hence, without a full dialog between the organization and its customers on the one hand and between the organization and its suppliers on the other hand, the system cannot improve performance. Without such a dialog, the system cannot comply with its customers' needs and will not receive adequate responses from its suppliers for its needs. This modern outlook is depicted in Figure 2.2.

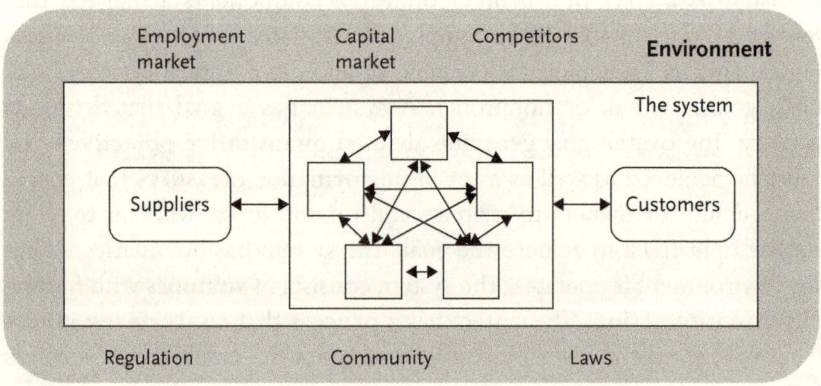

Figure 2.2:
The modern organizational system

Goldratt has added an important layer to system theory (Goldratt and Cox, 1992) by proposing to simplify the way we perceive the system and focus on its constraints. For instance, the performance of the whole system depends on **a few** factors, designated as the **system constraints** (see chapter 4). Thus, in a hospital, for example, the operating rooms (ORs) are usually the system constraint (the bottleneck). The performance of a system depends mainly on the efficiency and effectiveness of the bottleneck. This simplification along with the focusing approach helps us to better understand the system and improve it.

SYSTEM OPTIMIZATION AND SUBOPTIMIZATION

A major managerial failure emanates from the approach that "if every subunit in the system will operate optimally, then the whole system will be optimal." However, an organization where every subunit is striving to improve its own performance without examining interaction with other subunits, or without examining the relation between these activities and the overall objectives and performance of the whole organization, may find itself with adverse effects on organizational performance. This phenomenon is referred to as suboptimization or local optimization.

Suboptimization of a system: separate optimization of every subsystem that results in **underutilization** of the performance potential of the whole system and may result in a deterioration of overall performance.

Suboptimization is usually caused by a local focus of the suborganization. This phenomenon also results from ignoring interactions among subsystems, from improper performance measures or from the fact that a local objective function of a subsystem is not necessarily congruent with the overall objective function of the organization.

Example: The purchasing department in a hospital was measured by purchasing costs and discounts obtained from suppliers. The desire to minimize costs drove purchasing managers to buy inferior quality products. The poor quality caused clinical and service failures and an increase in repeat hospitalizations of many patients. Overall, the hospital's performance was compromised.

Example: In a large hospital's surgical ward, most attention was given to optimizing performance and tight scheduling in the ORs. Because of the reduced attention, the ward suffered from many cases of infections, thus negatively affecting the ward's performance and achievement of goals.

THE "SATISFICER" VERSUS THE "OPTIMIZER"

Nobel laureate H. A. Simon recognized many years ago a managerial situation that causes decision-making hardships. As a result, he suggested a different approach that revolutionized management. Simon (1957) claimed that executives, engineers, and decision makers of all kinds are trying to become "optimizers" while making decisions.

Optimizer—executive, engineer, or decision maker who wants to make the **best possible decision** without consideration of time constraints.

To achieve the **best possible decision**, the optimizer must generate all the alternatives, gather all the information, and build a model that will evaluate the alternatives and choose the best among them. All this requires time, effort, and money. In the real world, there is no limit to the number of alternatives one can generate and evaluate. We are all familiar with the situation where a group of executives and professionals gather and someone claims, "We have not yet examined all the possibilities." With every set of alternatives, there will always be the one person that will claim that there is a need to invest more time in additional options.

Information retrieval may not be easy. If it is mostly external to the organization, it also costs money. In addition, the information that is available inside the organization is not error- or bias-free. In fact, decision makers never have all the needed information on hand to evaluate any given alternative.

Building the "optimal" model to evaluate alternatives is also time- and labor-intensive. Finding an optimal solution to problems necessitates much preparation: defining all the decision variables, collecting all the relevant data (time studies, demands, labor resources, suppliers, customers, competition, quantities, costs, batch sizes, delivery times, orders, inventory, etc.), building a model that will describe the real situation, selecting optimization and calculation methods, and searching for software and hardware to perform the optimization.

The perfect solution sought by the optimizer may potentially bring about a better decision, but it usually comes too late. In a dynamic world, changes are frequent, and it is of utmost importance to make timely decisions with fast response to market situations. Thus, optimal solutions, even if attainable, become **irrelevant** as they are obsolete: The environment and the competition have changed, as have prices, laws, and regulations. Trying to behave as an optimizer, results in analysis-paralysis. In the medical world, "by the time the doctors decide, the patient will die." Similarly, there is a common wisdom among engineers and software professionals: "The enemy of 'good' is 'better.' "

Simon (1957) proposes an alternative approach and suggests that decision makers behave as "satisficers" (a term coined by him). Namely, decision makers should aspire to reach a "satisfactory solution" and not necessarily a perfect one (the "optimal" one).

Satisficer—an executive or decision maker who is **satisfied with a reasonable solution** that will significantly improve the system and does not strive for the optimal solution.

The satisficer sets a **level of aspiration**, a threshold he aspires to achieve (see Figure 2.3). The objective is no longer to maximize or minimize some performance measure but to achieve a solution that will improve that measure beyond the predefined level of aspiration. The satisficer need not examine all the alternatives. He can examine some of them until he finds one alternative that brings him over the threshold. At some point in time after the level of aspiration has been met, the satisficer may set a new aspiration level. This iterative process is one of continued organizational improvement. This approach is very efficient. The satisficer does not waste precious efforts and time in search for the ultimate solution. He or she rather quickly identifies steps that may significantly improve his or her current situation.

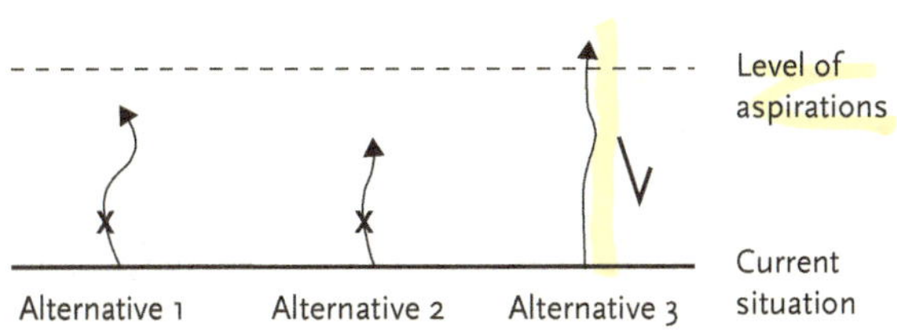

Figure 2.3:
The satisficer approach

The satisficer will achieve excellence by complying with two principles:

1. Setting a high enough level of aspiration that is compatible with market conditions, competition, or investor expectations.
2. Adopting an approach of continuous improvement.

The level of aspiration is set according to management expectations (e.g., reducing waits for an MRI), the performance of the best competitor, market conditions, necessary conditions for survival, and so on.

Continuous improvement is essential for the sustainable enhancement of the value of the organization. A one-time improvement gives the firm a temporary relative advantage over competitors. Without a process of continuous improvement, this relative advantage will be lost.

While the optimizer uses optimization techniques, the satisficer uses heuristics, which are decision rules that are not necessarily optimal but yield improvement (see Figure 2.4).

Example: Management of a hospital wanted to computerize patient records. A consulting firm was hired to analyze the whole system and its needs and to design and implement a new computerized system. The process took six years. After an additional two years, the technology changed and the system was rather obsolete. A competing hospital in the same city adopted a computerized patient record system used in other hospitals. The system was installed and slightly adapted to the specific needs of the hospital. Within one year the system was fully operative with concurrent development for more specific needs. The first hospital obviously tried to achieve the *optimal* solution and was left without a medical records system for six years while incurring very high development and consulting costs. The latter hospital settled for some satisfactory level of aspiration and had a *satisfactory* working system within one year at considerably lower costs.

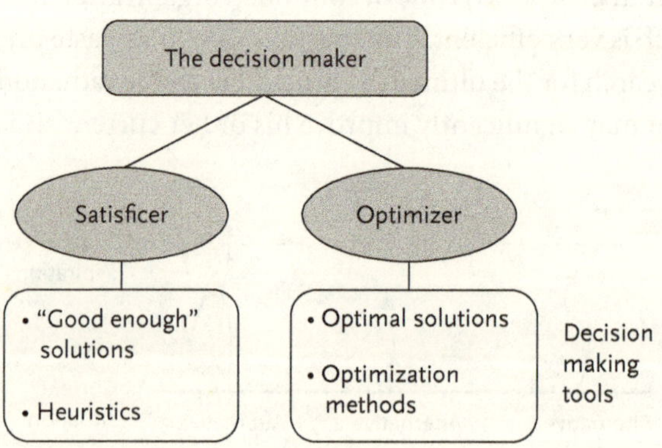

Figure 2.4:
Decision-making process—optimizer versus satisficer

The managerial approaches presented in this book are based on the saticficer approach and on heuristics, hence their suitability for the dynamic managerial environment of today. We are not providing problem-free "perfect" solutions. However, there is no doubt that the suggested solutions are good and bring upon significant improvement. On a philosophical level, the organization need not be perfect; it only needs to perform better that its competitors.

The optimizer approach may generate better solutions to some problems. However, the assortment of approaches and solutions presented in the book passed market and reality tests and are ready for immediate implementation.

ELEMENTS OF FOCUSED MANAGEMENT

To survive the fierce competition of today, any healthcare organization must continuously enhance its value and improve performance—"doing more with the same resources." Organization performance can be enhanced by improving its value drivers using appropriate managerial approaches. Choosing and implementing a mix of managerial approaches in accord with the specific organizational culture and business environment does improve the chances for better performance and value enhancement. The following managerial approaches characterize focused management:

- Constraint management using the theory of constraints (TOC).
- Lean approaches to reduce response time.
- The compete kit concept.
- Value-focused measurement and control.
- The global decision-making (GDM) three-stage model for decision making (determining transfer prices, make/buy decisions, etc.).
- Value-focused management approach.
- Methods for quality improvement and process control.

All these approaches will be discussed in subsequent chapters.

Focused management aims at improving organizational performance by identifying the relevant value drivers and focusing on them during the implementation.

Value drivers—parameters whose improvement will significantly increase the value of the business firm or significantly increase the performance measures of a nonprofit organization.

In a business organization, value is defined as the discounted cash flow (see chapter 1).

Examples of possible value drivers:

- Increasing throughput.
- Reducing response times.
- Improving performance measures.
- Quality improvement.

Experience (including numerous organizations where the authors were involved) demonstrates that using a variety of managerial approaches and adapting them to specific needs bring about significant performance improvements.

THE FOCUSED MANAGEMENT TRIANGLE

The focused management triangle is presented in Figure 2.5.

The focused management triangle reflects the basic principles of focused management.

A Global-System View

Management must consider the effect of a current decision on the whole system and not only on the single unit or subsystem. A global-system view will reduce organizational suboptimization.

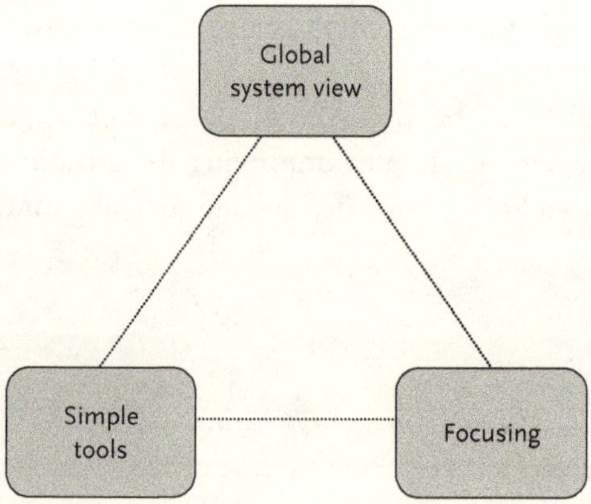

Figure 2.5:
The focused management triangle

Analysis of management and decision-making should consider the **whole** system and the impact of decisions on the system holistically and not only on subsystems.

Global vision requires expanding the system approach in two dimensions:

- Expanding the system scope.
- Expanding the time frame.

Expanding the System Scope

Example: In a private hospital, there was an effort to increase OR capacity. Personnel and equipment were added but throughput (the number of patients operated on) did not improve. By examining the larger system, it was discovered that the recovery rooms did not have sufficient capacity to contain the increased throughput of the ORs.

Example: A hospital acquired an additional MRI machine due to excessive long waiting times to get an MRI scan. A technician was added as well. However, patients had to wait much longer to receive the MRI results, so the overall time from making an appointment to getting results was unchanged. The problem was that nobody thought about the interpreting process and it became the bottleneck. This is another example that one should always look more globally.

Example: Many emergency departments experienced long waits and frustration. Some EDs made efforts to streamline their operation. However, they did not look beyond the ED. Patients were discharged or admitted faster than before. However, because the internal medicine wards remained congested, patients were boarded for long hours in the ED. One should not locally improve processes and management without looking into more global effects.

Example: In a cellular phone company, sales personnel were rewarded by the number of new subscribers they brought in. This reward parameter led sales force to heavily recruit customers that contributed very little to profit and presented high risk in bill payment. This inadequate performance measure also led them to sell new lines to existing customers who were kindly requested to silence their existing lines. Sales persons were rewarded for generating new lines that in fact did not generate any new calls volume. The bottom line result was increased costs to the company without addition of real sales.

In the decision-making process, every manager of a subsystem must evaluate everything from a global perspective to avoid suboptimization.

Expanding the Time Frame

Example: One of the departments of the Ministry of Health prepared medical emergency kits. Every item in the kit was chosen from a cost-effectiveness perspective. Within a short time, it was realized that one of the items, a low cost tourniquet, had a very short shelf life of one year, while all other items had a shelf life of four years. The tourniquet was plastic and was very cheap (2 cents each). This situation required refreshing the kit every year with a new tourniquet, necessitating disassembly of the whole kit and then reassembly. This annual maintenance was very costly. After some consideration, they decided to purchase a more expensive high-quality elastic tourniquet with a shelf life of at least four years. This resulted in a longer shelf life of the whole kit and drastically reduced maintenance costs. The original approach looked at the very short-term purchasing costs, without considering the longer life cycle cost of the whole kit.

Another case of expansion within time is the concept of the life-cycle cost (LCC), which considers the total life cycle of the product and, in addition to the purchasing price of the product, includes costs associated with infrastructure, maintenance, checking, failures, and more. When purchasing materials and components or when choosing and buying equipment, one must globally evaluate the LCC of the component, product, or equipment to make better decisions for the whole system. This is very important when purchasing medical equipment, or information technology, where LCC is referred to as total cost of ownership.

Example: A hospital was considering the purchase of a CT scanner. There were price differences in the quotations with no apparent differences in performance. The temptation was to purchase the cheapest unit. However, when the entire LCC was evaluated, the decision was altered to buying the scanner with the lowest LCC, which was the most expensive one, price-wise. In subsequent purchases, suppliers were required to provide full LCC figures.

Example: A large public hospital received a donation to build an additional, high-class building. The building was constructed and is now functioning. However, it is clear to management that the maintenance costs are excessively high and the hospital will not be able to maintain the building beyond its first few years.

Example: A health maintenance organization (HMO) adopted a global view in the time dimension, which resulted in a shift to invest more in disease prevention rather than disease treatment. This change of mindset led to better health for the insured customers and a drastic reduction in costs as a result of the decrease of utilization of medical services. This HMO recommended and offered free flu immunizations to members over age 55. They started to monitor the percentage of vaccinated customers in this group for each clinic and provided feedback to the primary care physicians. The number of pneumonia hospitalizations during that year dropped significantly when compared to previous years.

In the decision-making process, a manager must consider not only the short term but also the medium- and long-term issues.

It is obvious that every system is actually a subsystem of a larger system. As such, it is vulnerable to suboptimization. Working together and using global measures of performance can certainly reduce suboptimization.

FOCUSING ON ESSENTIALS

The time of executives and managers is scarce. The organization is continually struggling with daily crises and the time devoted to "extinguish fires" does not leave much room for change and improvement. Even for routine operations, it is difficult to find the time to deal with all issues. However, every issue that management wants to advance will get priority and consideration and will usually also be implemented. Hence, management focus on a small number of important topics yields significant improvement.

Focusing on essentials is one principle of successful management. The problems and tasks of a manager can be classified into four types, based on the Pareto principle (see chapter 3). This classification is presented in Figure 2.6.

- Type A problems: very few but important problems; **solving them will contribute much to the organization.** These are usually difficult problems that require time and management resources.
- Type B problems: several problems with medium importance; solving them will contribute to the organization.
- Type C problems: many routine problems that are easy to deal with; solving them will contribute little.
- Type D problems: numerous problems that are easy to deal with but spending time on them brings **negative** impact by taking up valuable management time that could have been used in solving important problems.

Many executives spend much of their time dealing with type C problems rather than type A. This happens when the urgent (C) pushes aside the important (A). Management must **focus on type A problems of the organization**. In other words, focus on those issues where a relatively small effort can have a big leverage on organizational performance. As we

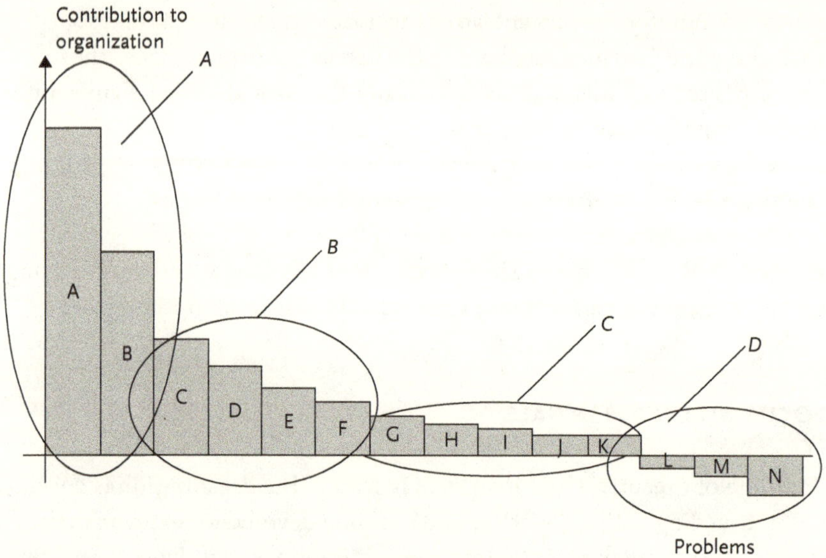

Figure 2.6:
Problem classification by contribution to the organization

shall see in the sequel, the manager must focus on system constraints, its bottlenecks, critical tasks in projects, risk factors, and more. Leading management to deal with the "important" requires a uniform language, determination, and managerial maturity.

Due to the complexity of day-to-day management and the obstacles facing the manager, she does not have more than 10% to 15% of her time to deal with essentials and improve value drivers whose outcomes will be realized only several months down the road. Therefore, she must commit herself to devote this little time to deal with the **real problems** that will enhance organizational value and improve its performance.

The world of management seems complex and complicated. But, as we shall see in future chapters, it can be made simpler if we focus on a few points whose improvement will improve the system as a whole.

Example: In a large hospital, the purchasing manager realized that the purchasing personnel need not be involved in every purchase. He realized that 70% of purchases are for less than $200. He changed policy so that every purchase for less than $200 can be authorized by the department managers using a "small purchases" budget. Such purchases could be made directly over the phone (according to a predetermined list of suppliers who agreed on reduced prices). The purchasing officers dealt only with large orders. This enabled the hospital to free valuable time of purchasing directors to deal with other important issues.

The following chapters will examine various focus areas: type A items using Pareto analysis, constraints, and bottlenecks; the critical chain in project management; and root problems in the organization.

SIMPLE TOOLS

Complex managerial tools are not usually utilized in organizations, and the ones that are used do not significantly contribute to enhancing value: "What will not be simple, will simply not be." Using such complex managerial tools has not brought remedy to managerial pains. The following chapters will present simple tools that can be implanted in various managerial environments: The seven focus stages of management by constraints, the focus stages of the Pareto principle, the focusing table and focusing matrix, a focused current reality tree, a conflict resolution diagram, and additional tools.

CHAPTER SUMMARY

- Today's business environment is dynamic, complex and difficult to manage.
- The manager faces fierce competition and uncertainty.
- To reach effective decisions, the manager must view the system globally, focus on the essentials, and use simple tools.
- The manager of a subsystem can apply a global system view by considering a **broader** system than the one he is heading and by considering a **longer time horizon.**
- Focusing on essentials will be through focusing on system constraints, type A items in the Pareto analysis and the root problems of the organization.
- Implementation of simple tools has a better chance for success. The three-stage focusing approach and the focusing table help managers to focus on essentials and work more effectively.
- Modern managerial approaches benefit from:
  - The satisficer way—striving to achieve good solutions and avoiding the endless search for the perfect (optimal) ones.
  - "Doing more with what you have"—increasing output using existing resources.
  - Applying common sense and daily experience.

CHAPTER 3

The Pareto Rule, the Pareto Based Methodology, the Focusing Table, and the Focusing Matrix

OBJECTIVE

- Know how, when, and why to use the Pareto methodology, the focusing table, and the focusing matrix.

THE PARETO RULE

Only a few of the principles of management have the potential for enormous contribution to value through intelligent use. Among these, the Pareto rule deserves special attention as it is one of the most important and simple principles of management.

Vilfredo Pareto was an economist of Italian ancestry who lived from 1848 to 1923. He discovered that roughly 20% of the population possesses 80% of world wealth. This is today referred to as the 20/80 rule or the "principle of the vital few and the trivial many."

Many management phenomena demonstrate the Pareto rule:

- 20% of the patients in a hospital ward consume 80% of caregivers' time.
- 20% of patients consume 80% of medications budget.
- 20% of medications account for 80% of pharmaceutical costs.
- 20% of patients in the ward require 80% of the staff's attention.
- 20% of laboratory tests account for 80% of laboratory costs.

- 20% of stores in a supermarket chain account for 80% of the chain's profits.
- 20% of suppliers supply about 80% of the purchasing budget.
- 20% of hospital inventory items constitute about 80% of the total inventory value.
- 20% of the sales force are responsible for 80% of company sales.
- 20% of failure reasons in an operating room constitute about 80% of all failures in surgery.
- 20% of a firm's customers generate 80% of the firm's revenues.

In the 1940s the 20/80 rule was expanded to the three-way classification known today as the A/B/C classification as follows:

- Group A—the 20% of phenomenon factors that are responsible for 80% of phenomenon outcomes.
- Group B—the 30% of phenomenon factors that are responsible for 10% of outcomes.
- Group C—the 50% of phenomenon factors that are responsible for 10% of outcomes.

For example:

- Group A—20% of patients in a ward account for 80% of ward expenses.
- Group B—30% of patients account for 10% of expenses.
- Group C—50% of patients account for the remaining 10% of expenses.

THE PARETO DIAGRAM

A Pareto diagram visually displays the Pareto rule. It facilitates communicating the classification and analysis. It is a simple and clear instrument with excellent field experience.

To derive the Pareto diagram for a managerial situation:

1. List all the sources/factors of the phenomenon along with their contribution to the phenomenon.
2. Sort the sources by descending order of contribution, from the most to the least.
3. Draw a histogram of all situation sources, as shown in Figure 3.1.

Consider this example of Pareto analysis of drug use in a hospital. Twelve popular drugs are consumed in a hospital ward. The data are presented in

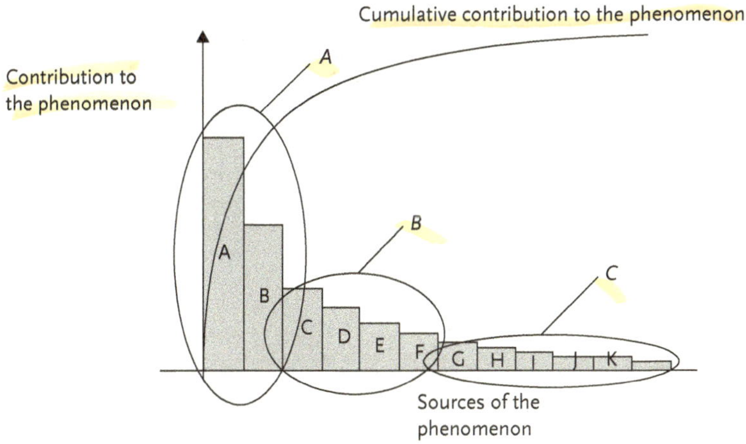

Figure 3.1:
Pareto diagram

Table 3.1. Each drug will be evaluated by its monthly cost; that is, the cost of every unit multiplied by the number of units used in this month.

Let us now sort the data in Table 3.1 from the drug with the highest dollar cost to the drug with the lowest cost. This result is presented in Table 3.2.

We are now ready to prepare a Pareto diagram (Figure 3.2) for the data in Table 3.2.

The Pareto diagram as described in Figure 3.2 enables the Pareto focusing, which includes two additional focusing steps: differentiation and appropriate resource allocation as outlined in the following discussion.

Table 3.1. EXAMPLE OF DRUG USE VOLUME AND COSTS IN A HOSPITAL WARD

Drug	Cost per unit ($)	No. of units consumed per month	Total costs ($)
A	180	361	65,000
B	250	160	40,000
C	950	347	330,000
D	90	389	35,000
E	75	267	20,000
F	560	89	50,000
G	1350	11	15,000
H	650	169	110,000
I	220	114	25,000
J	15	1333	20,000
K	56	1518	85,000
L	150	1367	205,000

Table 3.2. CLASSIFICATION BY DRUG COSTS

Drug	Costs ($)
C	330,000
L	205,000
H	110,000
K	85,000
A	65,000
F	50,000
B	40,000
D	35,000
I	25,000
E	20,000
J	20,000
G	15,000

BUILDING A PARETO DIAGRAM

1. List all sources of a phenomenon. For each source list the contribution to the phenomenon in the relevant measure (financial, frequency, contribution to response time, downtime, etc.). See Table 3.1.
2. Rank all sources in descending order from the source whose contribution is the largest to the source with the smallest contribution (see Table 3.2).

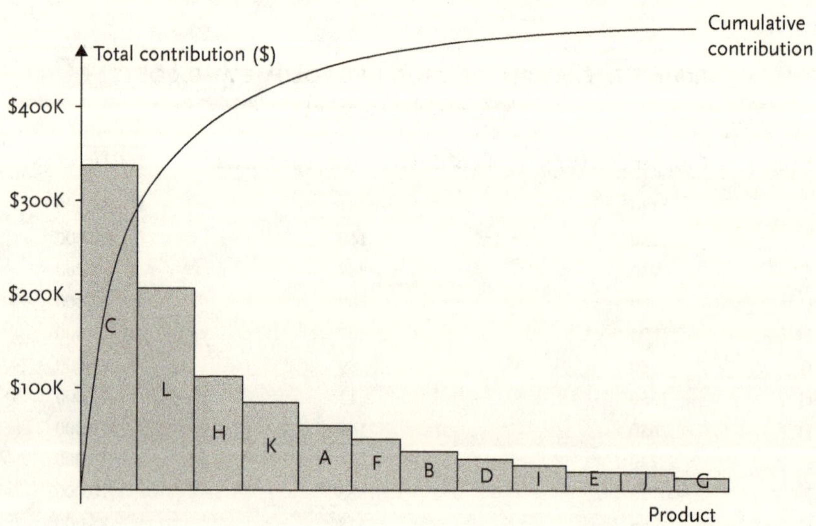

Figure 3.2:
Pareto diagram—Analysis of drug costs

3. Draw a histogram of the sources where the Y axis depicts the contribution such that the height of the bar for each source is proportional to the contribution of that source. See Figure 3.2.

THE PARETO-BASED FOCUSING METHODOLOGY

Managers use the Pareto rule in all areas of life, some intuitively, and some rather more methodically. The Pareto rule is effective and efficient in the presence of resource constraints (also known as "a scarce resource" or "bottleneck") as will be discussed in chapter 4. As we shall see there, managers are frequently the bottlenecks of their system, and the Pareto rule can sort things out. This is also true for sales and marketing personnel, purchasers, and any other scarce resource entity. The Pareto rule leads to focusing on areas with resource shortages (bottlenecks). Without it, one must devote full attention to all areas.

To effectively apply the Pareto rule, one must use the focusing methodology:

1. **Classification**—classify the sources of the phenomenon into classes A, B, and C (based on the Pareto analysis).
2. **Differentiation**—apply a differential policy to members of each class.
3. **Resource allocation**—assign resources appropriately.

Example: In a large health maintenance organization (HMO), the purchasing personnel in the purchasing department are a system bottleneck. They do not have the time to negotiate successfully with all suppliers, and must, therefore, use focusing methodology as follows.

Classification

Purchasers must classify suppliers by the A, B, and C classification previously described:

- Group A suppliers—the big suppliers are 20% of all suppliers and account for 80% of the dollar value of all purchases.
- Group B suppliers—the 30% medium suppliers that account for 10% of total value of purchases.
- Group C suppliers—the small suppliers constitute 50% of all suppliers but account for only 10% of purchase value.

Differentiation

A differential policy must be set for each supplier group:

- For group A suppliers, comprehensive negotiations should be carried out at the beginning of the year while detailed case by case negotiations on the largest purchasing orders should be carried out throughout the year.
- For group B suppliers, a group of selected suppliers will be chosen and periodic comparative price follow-up will be done for items purchased from them.
- For group C suppliers, annual negotiations on price discounts will be carried out.

Resource Allocation

- Most purchasers' resources should be devoted to negotiations with group A suppliers.
- Few resources should be invested in dealing with group B suppliers.
- Group C suppliers will occasionally be evaluated by a purchasing officer.

Note: The previous examples related to classification of suppliers or parts by monetary contribution and emphasized that using the methodology is essential for effective management. It may not always be sufficient to focus on monetary contribution. Occasionally one should adopt other criteria to classify the criticality of items such as response time from order of item until delivery; whether the delayed item halts the operation or puts patients at risk; whether the item is produced by a single manufacturer; or whether there is a major risk of future shortages in the item. The purchasing department should, therefore, along with other technical departments, classify items using another Pareto classification that relates to item criticality (see Livne and Ronen, 1990).

Example: A large HMO wished to examine and control the drug consumption of its patients.

Classification

Patients were classified according to the monetary value of the drugs they consumed:

- Group A patients are 15% of patients who were responsible for 75% of the dollar cost of drug consumption.
- Group B patients are the 25% of patients with moderate drug consumption that accounts for 15% of total drug costs.
- Group C are the remaining 60% of patients who consume only 10% of the drugs.

Differentiation

A different policy is applied to each group.

- Group A patients will be regularly valuated by the medical director of the HMO and the chief pharmacist. Every prescription must be approved by the medical director.
- Random sampling of prescriptions for Group B patients will be initiated to verify reasonable and cost-effective practice. The sample will cover about 10% of prescriptions.
- Only 5% of patients in Group C will be randomly evaluated.

Resource Allocation

- Most cost-containment resources for managing drug consumption will be devoted to group A. Only limited resources will be targeted to groups B and C.

THE FOCUSING TABLE AND THE FOCUSING MATRIX

The focusing table and the focusing matrix are methods that expand the Pareto analysis, and include the effort or cost involved in dealing with each factor as well as the benefit.

The analysis has two stages:

1. Building the focusing table (also known as the easy–important table).
2. Building the focusing matrix.

The Focusing Table

The following example will demonstrate the building of the focusing table.

Table 3.3. EMERGENCY DEPARTMENT FOCUSING TABLE

Number	Suggestion	Importance	Ease of implementing
1	Separate emergency department into surgical and internal wards	4	2
2	Change strategy regarding amount of testing	5	2
3	Open additional imaging room using same personnel	4	5
4	Increase frequency of visits by specialists	4	4
5	Increase frequency of lab workup	5	5
6	Measure average waiting times	4	4
7	Shorten discharge procedure	5	4
8	Redesign admission process	3	3

Example: The emergency department (ED) of a large hospital was considering improving its mode of operation. It convened all people involved in the routine operation of the ED as well as some top-level executives of the hospital. After many discussions and feedback, they were left with eight suggestions for change and improvement. Every suggestion was assessed its importance in terms of being able to bring improvement, and each suggestion was also assessed the ease in terms of time and money for implementing it. Each suggestion was given an importance score ranging from 1 (unimportant) to 5 (very important) and a score for ease of implementation ranging from 1 (very difficult to implement due to many bottlenecks and resources) to 5 (very easy to implement).

Note: The focusing table approximates "specific contribution" ranking, which will be discussed in chapter 5. If the relevant performance measures can be adequately quantified, it is better to rank by specific contribution.

The focusing table for the ED example is given in Table 3.3.

Generating the Focusing Matrix

Once the focusing table is complete, the focusing matrix is generated as shown in Figure 3.3. The preferred suggestions are those near the upper right corner of the matrix. Suggestion 5 is dominant over all others as it is the most important and the easiest to implement. Between suggestions 3 and 7 there is no dominance relationship and the decision makers can exercise priorities. The decision makers must choose a set of suggestions

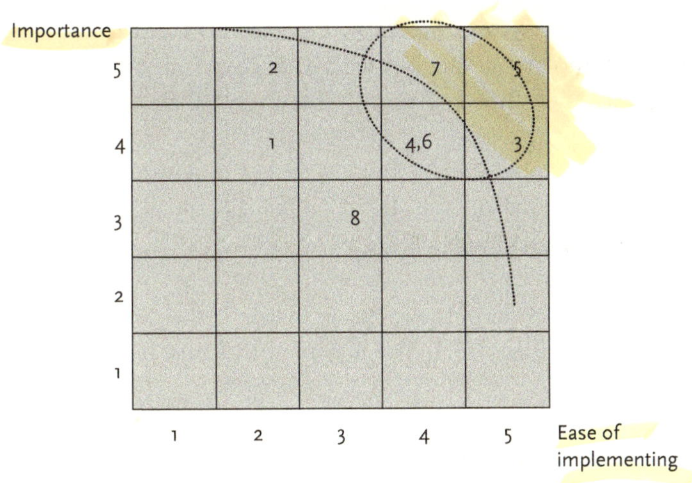

Figure 3.3:
Focusing matrix for emergency room example

to implement and the focusing matrix is an effective tool for making this selection.

The focusing matrix can be very useful for the following situations, some of which will be discussed in the sequel:

- Choice among patient case studies to be discussed in morning rounds.
- Choice among projects to be budgeted using the hospital's development fund.
- Choice among activities in the process of organizational improvement.

Guidelines for Using the Focusing Table and Focusing Matrix

1. Make a list of subjects to deal with (8–12 subjects) and arrange them in a focusing table like the example of Table 3.3—number, subject, importance and ease of implementing.
2. Arrange the subjects in a focusing matrix by importance and ease of implementing, as in Figure 3.3.
3. Choose the subjects for immediate attention. Preference is for subjects in the upper right-hand corner of the matrix, which are both important and are easy to implement.

Occasionally it may be wise to even choose subjects that are difficult to implement, but their value is very big and can achieve the long-term improvement of the system. Similarly, it may be also wise to consider steps that are easily implementable but with little contribution, just to demonstrate quick achievements and results. The eventual choice of subjects is a portfolio choice problem.

The Conceptual Focusing Matrix

An even simpler version of the focusing matrix is the conceptual focusing matrix depicted in Figure 3.4. The matrix in this case is divided into four quadrants:

In the upper-right quadrant one inserts the "pearls"—suggestions that are of highest importance and are easy to implement. The upper-left quadrant accommodates suggestions that are highly important but difficult to implement—"oysters." The importance of the suggestions placed in the lower-right quadrant are not very high, however their implementation is rather easy—"low-hanging fruits." Suggestions that are not important and at the same time their implementation is challenging are considered "white elephants" and are placed in the lower-left quadrant and are rarely implemented.

CHAPTER SUMMARY

Pareto analysis is a highly useful tool for managers in every area of management. A manager who does not intensively employ the Pareto rule, does not fully exploit his own potential. The focusing methodology is an effective tool in today's complex management world. The methodology **focuses** managers on what is important and essential, simplifying and clarifying decision-making.

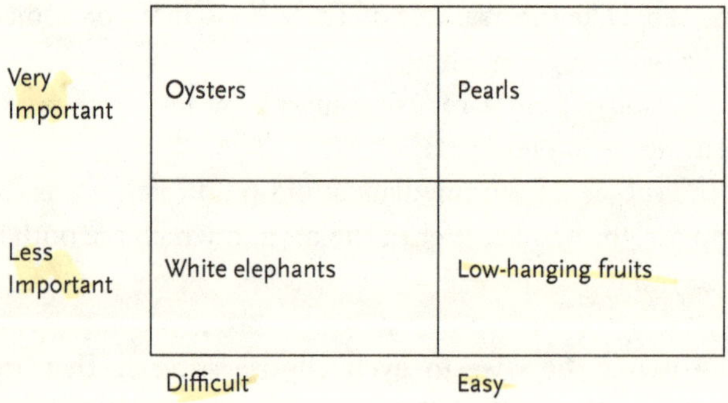

Figure 3.4:
The conceptual focusing matrix

Use of the focusing methodology requires a high level of management, especially during the **differentiation** stage. This stage requires making a variety of simultaneous policy decisions on various levels, and the ability to classify various situations for each policy.

Using the Pareto rule and focusing methodology can greatly assist in managerial decision-making processes. It is a tool that differentiates between the "important" and "more important" and allows focusing on the most important issues. A Pareto analysis using the focusing methodology will focus decision makers on a small number of areas that will require most of their attention. Focusing on group A items or the upper right-hand corner of the focusing matrix allows for an effective use of management time and effort.

This chapter presented some of the simplest, nicest, and easiest to implement tools that allow focusing, exploiting scarce resources, and employing good communication within an organization.

CHAPTER 4

The Seven Focusing Steps of the Theory of Constraints

OBJECTIVES
• How to achieve more with existing resources using the theory of constraints approach. • Identify the various constraints.

Management by constraints is an innovative and very effective approach to management, developed by Goldratt (Goldratt and Cox, 1992). This has been a managerial breakthrough and since then has brought significant improvements in thousands of organizations worldwide. The seven focusing steps of the theory of constraints (TOC) are based on the conceptual foundation of such methods as linear programming (Ronen and Starr, 1990). The methodology of management by constraints is typical for the satisficer approach (chapter 2). It provides satisfactory solutions that bring about significant and rather rapid improvements in organizational performance.

Management by constraints is based on a seven-step process:

1. Determine the system's goal.
2. Establish global performance measures.
3. Identify the system constraint.
4. Decide how to exploit the constraint; "break" dummy and policy constraints.
5. Subordinate the rest of the system to the constraint.
6. Elevate and break the constraint.
7. If the constraint is broken, return to step 3. Do not let inertia become the system constraint.

STEP 1—DETERMINE THE SYSTEM'S GOAL

The goal of the organization is of utmost importance as it should guide every decision and action in the organization. Once the goal has been determined, every person in the organization must evaluate every decision or action as to its congruence with this goal. Unfortunately, not enough attention is devoted to this important point.

The goal is something to which we aspire but can never achieve. For example: achieving maximal value, having zero accidents, or zero hospital-based infections.

The goal of a **business organization** is to **increase its shareholders' value.** As a first approximation to the real goal of a business organization, one can talk about maximal cash flow or maximum profit along time: simply stated, "making more money now as well as in the future" (Goldratt and Cox, 1992). Such a goal can sustain itself over time only if the interests of workers, suppliers, customers, and the community will be taken into consideration.

In nonprofit organizations, the goal will be determined by the mission of the organization. In such organizations, the goal is usually determined as achieving the maximum of some measure under resource constraints (e.g., budget). For example, the goal of a public healthcare organization is to maximize quality medical services provided to its customers, subject to budgetary constraints. Such organizations may have several goals or complex goals. For example, the goals of highway patrol are to prevent accidents and improve traffic flow. **The process of defining the goal(s) of nonprofit organizations is extremely important even if it may take a long time.**

Example: Consider the **goals** of an emergency department (ED) of a hospital. There could be two approaches to patient management: (i) make a quick decision on admission or discharge or (ii) provide a comprehensive diagnostic workup. These two goals are conflicting ones.

While determining the goal of any suborganization, it is important to ensure congruence of this goal with that of the whole organization. The absence of such congruence can easily lead to suboptimization (see chapter 2 examples).

Example: The medical division of a large health maintenance organization (HMO) set an objective of providing high-quality medical care. One goal of the HMO was to minimize the life-cycle cost of treating its patients. The goal of the medical division was changed to providing adequate preventive services that will improve overall health and will lead to long-term cost reduction.

Example: The head of a surgical ward in a large hospital decided to introduce a rare and complicated surgical procedure to enhance the hospital's prestige since the main competitor was already performing such procedures. The new venture resulted in increased waits and longer queues for the more standard procedures. These procedures actually had a proven record of higher clinical quality to patients and higher profits to the hospital.

STEP 2—ESTABLISH GLOBAL PERFORMANCE MEASURES

To be able to evaluate the activity of an organization and determine if it assists achieving the goal, we must determine global performance measures that are compatible with the goal of the organization. Performance measures of an organization are a guiding compass that points toward the goal. Relevant measure for a business organization is the **value of the company** (defined as the present value of the cash flow). Sometimes it is difficult to see the relation between mid-level managerial decisions and measures of cash flow or value enhancement. Thus, there is a need for additional measures.

There is no single perfect performance measure that after being improved will achieve the organizational goal. However, we suggest an array of six basic performance measures where each one measures a different dimension of organizational performance. They are:

1. Throughput (T).
2. Operating expenses (OE).
3. Inventory (I).
4. Response time (RT).
5. Quality (Q).
6. Due-date performance (DDP).

These measures are used for managerial control, for defining quantitative objectives, for rewarding executives and workers, and for supporting decision-making processes. Chapter 13 expands on this topic.

Performance measures can be the basis for quantitative objectives for the organization a whole, and for managers and employees, with minor adaptations. As opposed to the **goal**, the **objectives** should be defined in a manner that makes them **achievable**.

STEP 3—IDENTIFY THE SYSTEM CONSTRAINT

The philosophy of management by constraints is based on identifying and dealing with the causes that **halt** the system and **prevent** it from achieving its goal.

Constraint—any important factor that prevents an organization from reaching its goal.

The concept behind this approach is unique: there is no search for factors that can assist in improving system performance but rather a search for factors that **restrict** system performance. The relevant question is "What stops the system?" or "What prevents the system from achieving its goal?"

Every system has a constraint. There is always something that prevents it from achieving its goal. If there were no constraints, the system would achieve unbounded outcomes.

Experience shows that systems have a **small number of constraints**—a few factors that prevent them from achieving the goal.

There are four types of constraints in a managerial system:

- Resource constraint.
- Market constraint.
- Policy constraint.
- Dummy constraint.

Resource Constraint

Whenever the the system has a **resource constraint** (bottleneck), the system cannot perform all its tasks. If the capacity of the constraining resource would be bigger, it would be possible to increase system throughput and improve achievement of the goal.

A **resource constraint** (or bottleneck)—the most heavily utilized resource such that it cannot perform all its assigned tasks. This is the resource that constrains the performance of the entire system.

Figure 4.1 presents generic examples for various healthcare systems. The simplified framework of a 1–2–3 process represents a variety of work processes.

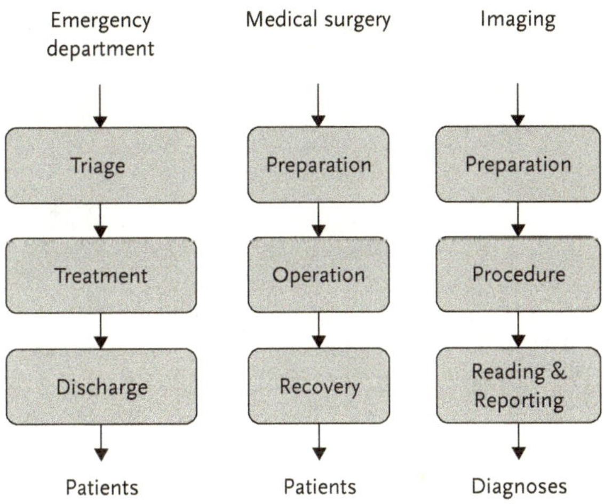

Figure 4.1:
Examples for system processes

In the process depicted in Figure 4.2, every patient must be processed at each of the three departments, beginning in department 1 and ending in department 3. Department 2 is the resource that is the **system constraint** as it can process only 50 patients per day while market demand is for 300 patients per day. Department 2 is the resource that dictates the throughput of the whole system to be at most 50 patients per day. Departments 1 and 3, even though they cannot provide for the full daily demand, are **not factors that constrain** system throughput and will thus not be treated as system constraints.

In the example of Figure 4.2 we see that:

- The system has a **resource constraint**.
- Department 2 is the system **bottleneck**.

It should be noted that if we increase the daily capacity of departments 1 and 3, the throughput (capacity) of the whole system will not change. On the other hand, increasing the capacity of department 2 will increase system throughput. The bottleneck, department 2, dictates the throughput for the whole system and should be treated as the organizational "goose that lays golden eggs." A lost hour in the bottleneck is a lost hour for the entire system (Goldratt and Cox, 1992). We should consider the bottleneck as the "money printing machine" of the organization: the higher its utilization, the higher the throughput of the whole system.

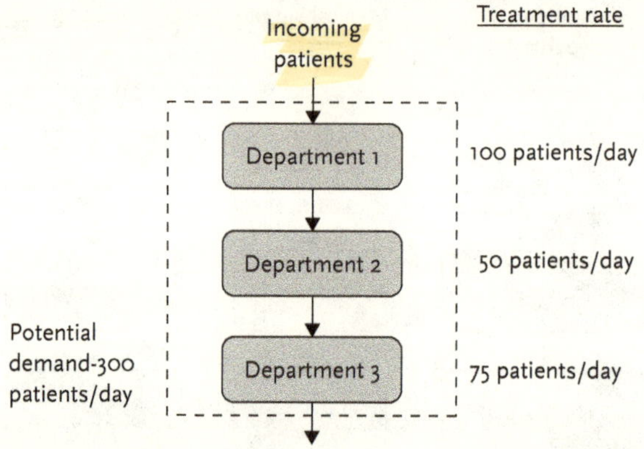

Figure 4.2:
A system with a resource constraint

Bottlenecks exist in all areas of life:

- In an operating department of one hospital, the bottleneck was the surgeons; in another hospital, it was the anesthetists; and in a third hospital the bottleneck was the operating rooms (ORs).
- In the ED of a hospital, the bottleneck was the emergency physicians.
- In a specialty clinic, a very expensive scanner (PET scanner) was the bottleneck.
- In a highway system, the intersection is a bottleneck.
- In a supermarket, a bottleneck could be a cashier or shelf space.
- In an office of health insurance claims, the bottleneck was the lawyers who had to approve every settlement.
- In an airport, during peak times, the bottleneck is the runway.
- In a large HMO outpatient clinic, the bottleneck was the physicians.
- In a hospital obstetrics ED, the bottleneck was the imaging services department; in another hospital, the bottleneck was the attending surgeon.

There are several types of organizational bottlenecks.

Shortage of a Critical Resource

This happens when a resource constraint (also referred to as a bottleneck or internal constraint) is a specific employee, a group of employees, or equipment shortage that makes it a system constraint—for example, highly skilled surgeons in a hospital, anesthetists in an OR, or an MRI machine in a hospital.

It is difficult to open a bottleneck simply by adding resources because it may require extensive capital or long training periods if the bottleneck is a highly skilled professional.

Permanent Bottlenecks

There are situations where a permanent resource constraint and a **permanent bottleneck** exist.

1. An **expensive resource** is always in a state of a permanent bottleneck. Some physicians have rare and unique expertise and knowledge. They very quickly become bottlenecks due to the demand targeted at them—likewise for senior partners in law firms or accounting firms.
2. **Anesthetists** are a permanent bottleneck in many practices due to their short supply.
3. **Sales and marketing personnel** are bottlenecks in their systems. The potential demand for sales people derives from leads reaching their desks, from potential customers, from meetings in trade shows, and from customer lists. The effective demand is virtually infinite relative to the available sales force and as such they are permanent bottlenecks (Pass and Ronen, 2003).
4. **Research and development (R&D) personnel** have an infinite demand for their abilities, talent, and services. The demand stems from customer requests, from ideas of R&D personnel themselves, from ideas of the sales force, and from continual initiatives for changes and improvements. This turns them into permanent bottlenecks.
5. **IT developers in large organizations** such as hospitals, HMOs.

Peak Time Resource Constraints

As opposed to a situation where there is a constant shortage of a critical resource over time, resource constraints during peak time are characterized by shortages in specific times. During other times, the critical resources are not system bottlenecks (Ronen et al., 2001). This situation arises, for example, in a hospital ED during mass casualty events; daily peaks in an ED; the tables in a restaurant at peak times; and accountants in a tax-return preparation firm during tax season. In these work environments, there are resources that are at excess capacity most of the time and at shortage during peak times. System managers must exercise two types of policies: one for times of excess capacity and the other for peak demand. Good management of such situations requires, among other things, differential pricing of goods and services at different demand periods. The issue of peak time management will be detailed in chapter 6.

Seasonality

Some examples of peak time management relate to seasonality where different seasons exhibit different demand patterns. This is a special case of peak time management. During the winter season, for example, there is a peak in the flu epidemic requiring special arrangements at hospital EDs and internal medicine wards, as well as providing enough flu vaccines and medications.

Temporary Resource Constraints

Even firms with excess capacities, occasionally face a shortage of a critical resource due to unforeseen circumstance such as natural disasters, breakdown of equipment, mass casualty events or labor disputes.

These situations demonstrate the need to develop a decision-making methodology for an environment with resource constraints, whether constant or temporary.

Insights into Resource Constraints

We should point out that a constraint must be clearly defined. A phrase like "shortage of high quality skilled personnel" does not define a constraint of an OR. The definition must be more **specific**. For example, we should specify whether the bottleneck are the surgeons, the anesthetists, the nurses, surgical kits, or the room itself.

A **control test for the identification of a potential constraint** is a test of "**more or less**." We must answer the questions: "If we could increase the capacity of the resource suspected as the bottleneck, would the throughput of the whole system increase? If we reduce the capacity of this resource, will the system throughput decrease?" If the answer is "yes" for both questions, this resource is indeed a system bottleneck.

Market Constraint

This is a situation of an excess capacity of production or providing a service, a situation where the supply exceeds the demand. This raises the need to increase demand.

Market constraint—arises in a situation where the market demand is less than the output capacity of each resource. Thus, market demand is the constraint that prevents the system of achieving its goal.

Let us examine the example of Figure 4.2 and change the market demand from 300 patients to 25. This is depicted in Figure 4.3. The market constrains the systems and prevents it from achieving its goal. Each one of the three resources has an excess capacity. This situation is referred to as a market constraint, excess capacity, or external constraint. To validate that we have correctly identified the market as the system constraint we must apply the **control test**: "If market demand would increase, can we increase system throughput"? If the answer is "yes" (which it is in this case), then indeed the market is the system constraint.

Most industrial and service organizations today face a situation where the market is the constraint, mainly due to global competition. Only a fraction of organizations can afford to be in a situation where an internal constraint will force it to turn away demand due to lack of resources. This will be further discussed in chapter 18. In the healthcare industry, we face both resource and market constraints. In a hospital, for example, the OR may be a bottleneck while the urology ward is with excess capacity (market constraint). At the same time, the hospital laboratory may have a market constraint after 11 AM due to low demand for tests.

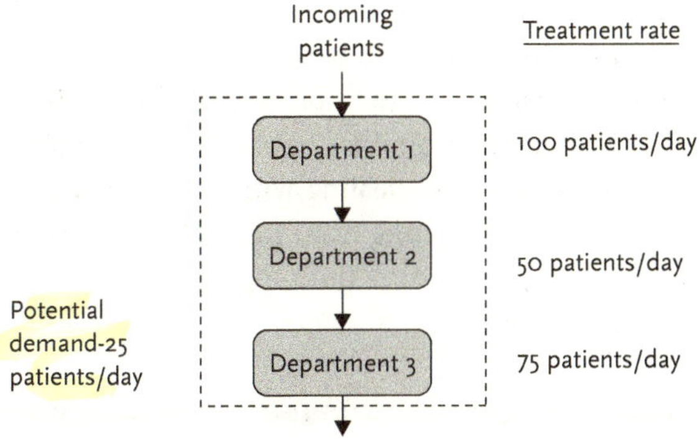

Figure 4.3:
A system with a market constraint

Policy Constraint

A policy constraint prevents the system from achieving its goal. The inappropriate policy is a system constraint. Generally speaking, every organization should set policies in important areas. However, a policy that may have been appropriate in previous years may become a policy constraint when changes occur in the business environment. Likewise, a managerial local view may cause policy constraints that drive the system toward suboptimization.

Policy constraint—adopting an inappropriate policy that limits system performance and achievement of goal that may also push in a direction that is against the organizational goal. This is also known as **policy failure**.

Example: A hospital is reimbursed according to length of stay. This policy leads to a lack of motivation to discharge patients early, leading to longer hospitalization, which increases the incidence of hospital-acquired infections and reduces throughput. This is obviously working against the goal of the hospital, which is to provide the high-quality medical care to a maximum number of patients.

Example: A hospital director, in an effort to contain costs, decided to forbid any overtime work for **all** hospital staff (bottlenecks as well as non-bottlenecks). This constrained the number of patients that could be operated on daily, thus increasing the waiting time for surgery. It also caused some of them to go to another hospital and resulted in adverse effects for some patients. This decision is obviously a policy constraint that worked against the hospital's goals.

Example: The purchasing department of a large HMO gave instructions: "Do not process any purchase orders between the 25th and the end of the month." Such a policy is intended to improve cash flow. This policy may be reasonable in a few cases when purchasing the most expensive items (type A in Pareto). However, if we are dealing with cheap materials, office supplies, and so on, the delays resulting from this policy constraint may harm the organization as it may delay providing appropriate services to patients.

Further examples of policy constraints:

- Incentives that promote only quantities are policy constraints. It can lead to a drive to increase throughput without considering quality and creates an incentive to produce low quality outputs.

- Setting standards that each employee must achieve may lead to "pegging," where there is no incentive to exceed the standard.
- Continued investment in a failing project just because large amounts have already been invested in it is a policy failure (the "sunk cost" effect).
- Uniform (across the board) personnel ("head count") cuts is a policy constraint that may be counterproductive for the organization.
- Measuring OR only by its utilization, disregarding throughput and response time.

Any policy that applies **across the board** throughout an organization is suspect of being a **policy constraint** (e.g., uniform percentage budget cuts). What might be right for one department may not be appropriate for another. There is a need for differential management. A very common policy constraint is the use of local performance measures, or measures that are not congruent with the organizational goal (see chapter 13). Measuring people, units, or processes with inappropriate measures leads to wrong decisions and is a detriment to achieving goals.

To ascertain that we have correctly identified a policy constraint as a system constraint, we apply a **control test**: "If we could 'break' the policy constraint, could we **increase throughput** and improve the firms' value?" If the answer is "yes," then there is a policy constraint that is a system constraint.

Dummy Constraint

A dummy constraint is a situation where system throughput is constrained because of a resource whose cost is marginal.

A **dummy constraint**—a situation where the system bottleneck is a relatively very cheap resource relative to other resources in the system.

Example: A hospital OR used for coronary angiographies failed to keep its schedule of procedures. A careful analysis showed that all the needed resources were available—surgeons, radiologists, nurses, surgical kits, and so on. Even though the OR staff were available, there were times that the OR was not utilized. It turned out that the wasted time resulted from waiting for the cleaning person to clean the OR between procedures. The problem arose from the desire of management to reduce cleaning costs. Initially there were two cleaners during every shift: one was in the OR and the other in the intensive care rooms. A work-flow analysis showed that labor utilization of each cleaner was only 40%. This was very disturbing to management and they laid-off one cleaner, leaving the second responsible for both the OR and the intensive care rooms. When cleaning was needed in the OR, the cleaner was occasionally busy in the intensive care rooms, and vice versa. A very cheap resource, the cleaning person, became a system constraint, resulting in reduced OR productivity and throughput.

Example: In a hospital internal medicine ward, blood specimens were placed in special trays to be transported to the lab. A shortage of trays caused delays in collecting blood from patients, causing delays in receiving results, which in turn caused delays in providing treatment or discharging patients. A very cheap resource, trays, prevented the ward from operating efficiently.

Example: In an ED, there was a shortage of clerical personnel for administering discharges (to the wards or home), resulting in delays of patient discharges and an overcrowding of the ED. A clerk is a rather cheap resource compared to physicians and nurses.

Example: Many hospital EDs and other wards send lab specimens via pneumatic capsules through a tube transport works. There are situations when there is a scarcity of capsules, resulting in waiting to batch several specimens in one capsule. This delays sending the specimens and obviously delays getting results back to waiting patients. The capsules are a very inexpensive item, and there is no justification for a shortage of them.

A shortage in phone lines, fax machines, copying paper, printers, digital thermometers, blood pressure monitors, and so on are all dummy constraints. These are relatively cheap resources compared to the costs of other resources and compared to the potential effect of decreased throughput.

To determine that a dummy constraint is indeed a system constraint, we must apply the **control test**: "If we could 'break' the dummy constraint, could we **increase throughput** and enhance company value?" If the answer is "yes," then the dummy constraint is indeed a system constraint.

Tools for Identifying Constraints in the Healthcare System

A constraint can be identified in several ways:

- **Ask the field people**. The employees in the field know the system, and using their experience and intuition, the manager can usually be able to pinpoint the real bottleneck.

- **Tour the work area.** Touring the work area helps to identify the bottleneck. This is usually the place where patients, materials, or paperwork pile up.

Several methodological ways described later in this chapter include:

- Process flow diagram.
- The gross/net ratio.
- The new position test.
- Time analysis.
- Load analysis.
- Cost-utilization (CUT) diagram.

Process Flow Diagram

A process flow diagram is a basic flow chart describing the work flow in the system. It depicts the steps of the process and the decision nodes. To facilitate bottleneck identification, it is recommended that the process flow diagram (8-12 steps) be simplified to reflect only the **main work process** and ignore marginal ones and unusual ones. An example of a process flow diagram is presented in Figure 4.4.

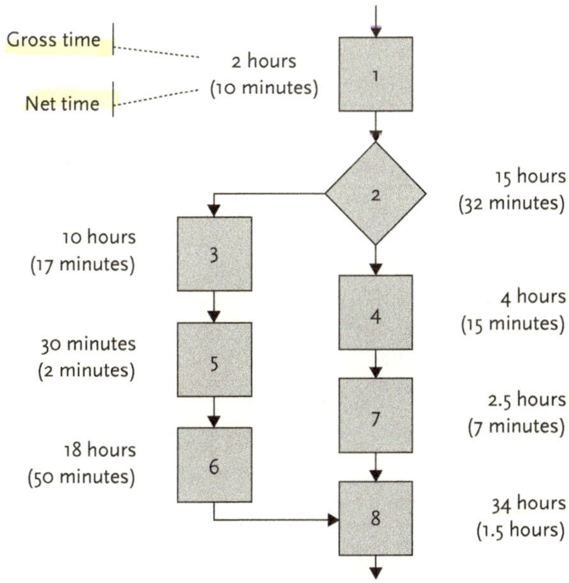

Figure 4.4:
A process flow diagram (net time is in parentheses)

It is recommended that each work step include the two time parameters:

1. Actual processing time of step (**net time**).
2. Total time of step that includes both the actual processing time and the waiting time (**gross time**).

The basic process flow diagram can be expanded into a two-dimensional diagram that presents the various units in the organization that perform the various tasks. Such a diagram is presented in Figure 4.5.

The process flow diagram has an added importance in improving communication within the organization. It is a simple visual aid that helps people understand the work flow. In many cases, the actual drawing of a process flow diagram in itself provides people with new insights of their own process, which might have been a routine for them for many years. It can even happen that during the initial drawing of a process flow diagram, one can identify the system bottleneck.

The New Position Test

Another way to validate the bottleneck identification is the new position test: If the head of the system would grant you another position, no matter its cost, you will probably point out the bottleneck resource.

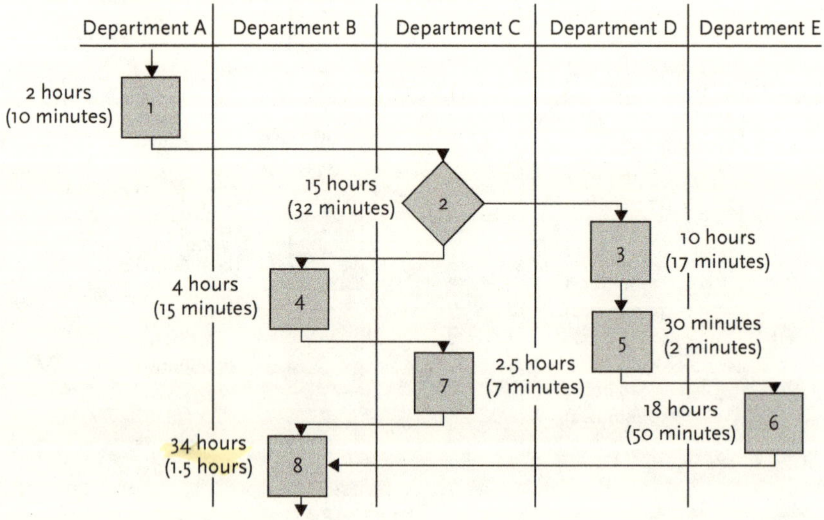

Figure 4.5:
A two-dimensional process flow diagram

Time Analysis

Analyzing the gross time that a typical entity (patient, record, product, customer, batch, etc.) spends in the different stations of the system enables identification of the station where it spent the longest time. This station most probably is a system constraint. The long stay in this station is usually due to waiting in queue before the constraint.

For example, step 8 in Figure 4.5 has the longest (gross) duration of 34 hours and is thus a suspect for a system constraint.

Load Analysis (Capacity Utilization)

Load analysis is a simple and clear tool for identifying the system bottleneck that is the most heavily utilized resource in the system.

To determine the load on resources in the system during the time of analysis, several data must be examined:

1. Total number of processing hours available during the period analyzed.
2. The overall planned work—number of units we plan to work on (provide service, produce, plan, etc.) with a specification of quantities by type of customer, product, development task, or other service.
3. A table describing the effort (in processing hours) that each resource is required to invest in each product, customer, development, and so on.

Example: A manufacturer of surgical equipment received many orders for surgical kits, and the question is whether they can produce the entire order. The manufacturer has 190 monthly processing hours at its disposal. The orders for next month consists of 100 kits of type A, 50 of type B, 25 of type C, and 200 of type D. The company has four production stations. Table 4.1 provides the number of labor hours required for the assembly of each kit type at each station.

Table 4.1. LABOR HOURS PER UNIT PER STATION

Surgical kit	Labor hours per surgical kit			
	Station 1	Station 2	Station 3	Station 4
A	0.6	0.15	0.73	–
B	0.35	0.72	1.18	0.5
C	1.6	–	1.36	2.56
D	0.2	0.06	0.44	0.41

Table 4.2. LOAD ANALYSIS

Surgical kit	Quantity	Station 1	Station 2	Station 3	Station 4
A	100	100*0.6 = 60	100*0.15 = 15	100*0.73 = 73	–
B	50	50*0.35 = 17	50*0.72 = 36	50*1.18 = 59	50*0.5 = 25
C	25	25*1.6 = 40	–	25*1.36 = 34	25*2.56 = 64
D	200	200*0.2 = 40	200*0.06 = 12	200*0.44 = 88	200*0.41 = 82
Total hours		157	63	254	171
Load		83%	33%	134%	90%

In the load analysis table (Table 4.2) we multiply, for each kit and each resource, the planned quantity by the labor hours of the resource for the kit. As a second step, we add all the labor hours invested by the resource in the different kits and divide by the total number of labor hours per month—190.

The load analysis shows that station 3 cannot perform all its tasks to meet market demand. It is the most heavily utilized station and is therefore the system constraint.

Using a Cost-Utilization (CUT) Diagram to Identify the Constraint

A cost-utilization (CUT) diagram of a system is a simple graphic tool for analysis of system constraints (Ronen and Spector, 1992).

A CUT diagram is a bar graph (histogram) where every bar represents a resource. The height of the bar represents the resource utilization (load) between 0% and 100%. The width of each bar represents the relative cost of the resource. The relative costs of the resources can be defined in several ways:

- Based on the marginal cost of each resource—the cost associated with adding one unit of the resource. This could be adding one employee to a work station or adding a machine or component. This is the recommended approach for creating a CUT diagram.
- Based on the total cost of each resource.
- Based on the amortization of each resource.
- Based on a cost ratio derived from subjective cost assessments made by the people preparing the diagram. This represents the subjective view of the relative cost or relative scarcity of the resource.

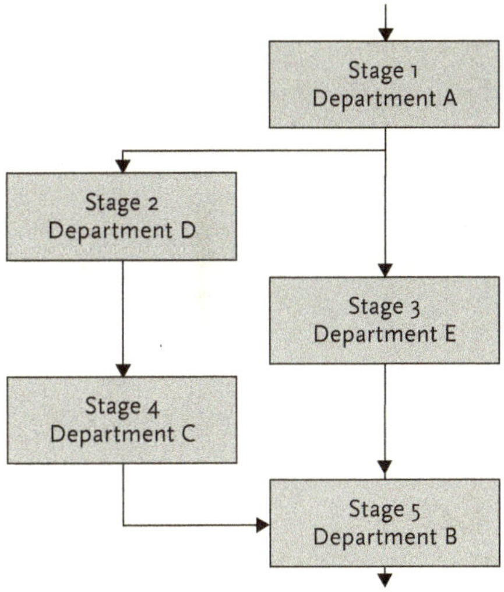

Figure 4.6:
An example of a system and its work process

Note that the order of bars on the horizontal axis is of no importance. In a sequential process, it makes sense to arrange the bars according to the sequence of resources in the process.

To understand the value of the CUT diagram, let us examine the process depicted in Figure 4.6.

Let us consider the load and resource cost of the various departments (Table 4.3).

The CUT diagram of Figure 4.7 is based on the previous data. It shows that the bottleneck is department E, and there are no capacity problems in the other four departments.

Figure 4.7 depicts a situation where the expensive bottleneck is the only resource at full utilization. Such situations arise in operating rooms where the surgeon or the anesthetist is a bottleneck while other resources are only partially utilized, or, for example, in an airline where all the planes are fully

Table 4.3. LOAD ANALYSIS WITH A BOTTLENECK

Resource	Load (%)	Cost of resource (in thous. $)
Department A	55	100
Department B	80	50
Department C	45	40
Department D	65	100
Department E	100	280

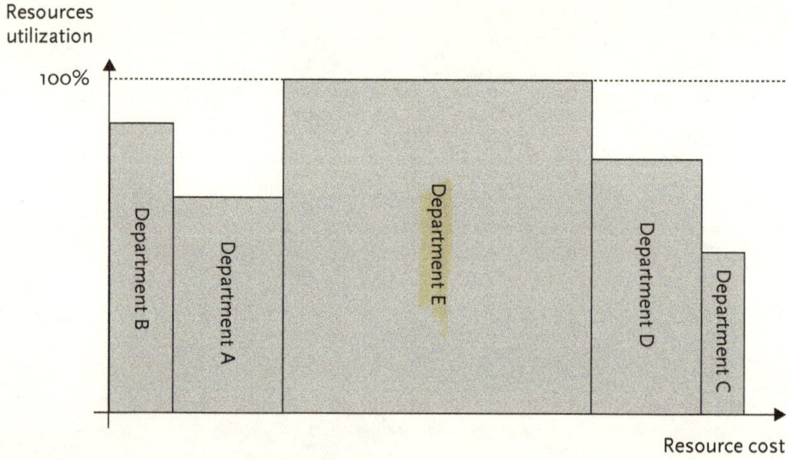

Figure 4.7:
A CUT diagram for a system with a resource constraint

utilized and the crews are only partially utilized or in an imaging department where one piece of equipment is fully utilized and others are not.

In this situation, the following points need attention:

- Management must decide whether it is acceptable that the resource constraining the system is an internal/resource constraint, or perhaps for strategic and economic reasons, it should have excess capacity.
- When a system has excess capacity in non-bottleneck components, management should consider selling or renting out this excess capacity in an external market. For example, if surgeons are the bottleneck in the surgery department of a hospital and as a result the OR is underutilized, it may be worthwhile to rent out the OR time to external surgeons. Alternatively, an effort could be made to elevate this constraint by hiring additional surgeons.
- One must evaluate the selling price of services or products that use the bottleneck resources.

Let us examine a comparable system whose process is also represented by the scheme in Figure 4.6. However, in this case, the load relations of the resources as well as their relative prices are different. Table 4.4 presents the new data.

The CUT diagram for Table 4.4 is presented in Figure 4.8.

The CUT diagram shows that the system has market demands that are lower than the capacity of each of its resources. The system has a market constraint and is at excess capacity. The throughput is 80% of the potential throughput of the component with the highest utilization.

Table 4.4. LOAD ANALYSIS IN A SYSTEM WITH A MARKET CONSTRAINT

Resource	Load (%)	Cost of resource (in thous. $)
Department A	65	10
Department B	80	17
Department C	45	15
Department D	70	15
Department E	55	28

The following points deserve attention:

- The organization must decide whether it prefers that the constraint should be an external (market) constraint. This decision implies that all resources within the system possess excess capacity.
- Management must analyze whether the market constraint is temporary, seasonal, or permanent and identify the reasons for its existence (internal factors such as quality, price, response time, or external factors like competitors, demographic or regulatory changes, and a change in customers' tastes and preferences).
- Management should consider the option of taking on additional work, while making sure this does not create a bottleneck. The planning phase requires reserving a protective capacity to protect the process throughput from variability (see chapter 14).

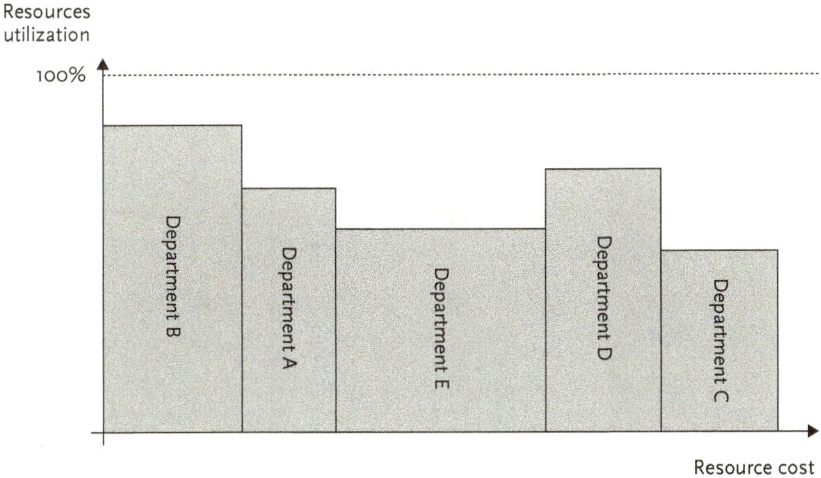

Figure 4.8:
A CUT diagram for a system with a market constraint

Table 4.5. LOAD ANALYSIS FOR A SYSTEM WITH A DUMMY CONSTRAINT

Resource	Load (%)	Cost of resource (in thous. $)
Department A	65	200
Department B	75	350
Department C	40	380
Department D	70	590
Department E	100	10

Let us now consider a third example whose process is also described by Figure 4.6. The load and cost figures are different from the previous examples, as shown in Table 4.5.

The CUT diagram presented in Figure 4.9 illustrates the system's problem. System output is constrained by a very cheap resource. Only a small investment may be needed to increase capacity in department E, leading to increased system output. This is a dummy constraint.

Here are some uses of the CUT diagram for two decision problems:

1. **Investment decisions.** The CUT diagram serves as a tool for investment decisions that relate to one or more components of the process. We should assure that the additional throughput achieved by breaking the constraint is worth the investment. Very frequently, if we, for example, double the resource of the bottleneck, we do not double the system throughput as the bottleneck may have shifted to another resource

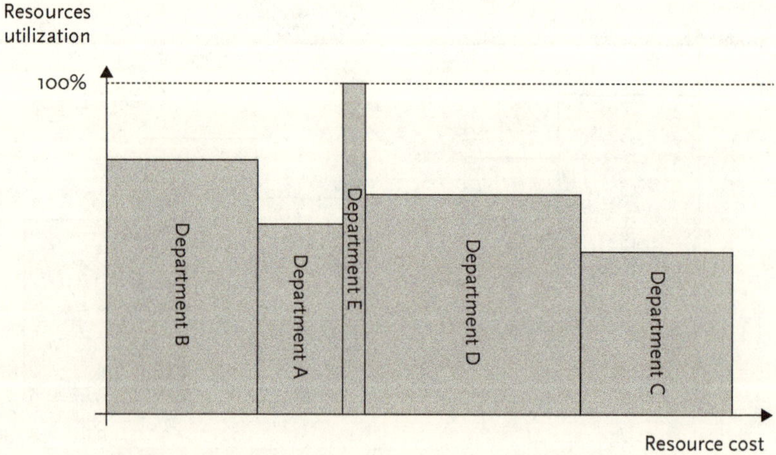

Figure 4.9:
CUT diagram for a system with a dummy constraint

or step and the gains in throughput are only marginal. Before we make the investment, we should analyze the impact of the new capacity on the entire system. This model will assist the decision maker in deciding whether to also invest in another department that may now become the new bottleneck.

2. **Make or buy decisions.** This tool is also useful in assessing the impact of a decision to provide a new service or produce a new product on the overall loads of the system. The new load will form the basis for a make or buy decision. This tool is also useful for choosing the products or services to be delegated to subcontractors.

The CUT diagram also assists in decision-making on stopping a service or production of a certain product and strategic decisions on price policy and its impact on operational loads (see details in chapter 16).

Routine uses of CUT diagrams include:

1. Construct a table that compiles for the various resources the load percentage and the cost of each.
2. Draw a histogram where every resource has a bar whose height represents load and width represents cost. Draw the 100% load line.
3. Identify any problems that emerge in the diagram (dummy constraints, large excess capacity, etc.).
4. Decide how to rectify the problem.

CHAPTER SUMMARY

Management by constraints is a management theory that focuses on the system's constraints, which are the factors that limit and constrain system performance.

Constraints can be categorized into four types: resource constraints (bottlenecks), market constraints (excess capacity), policy constraints, and dummy constraints.

The most common constraints in the competitive business environment are market constraints. However, there are many instances where resource constraints and bottlenecks are the causes that prevent the system from achieving its goal. There are always bottlenecks in area of R&D, sales, and marketing. Expensive resources or temporary loads during peak times bring resource constraints upon the system. Dummy constraints are very cheap bottlenecks and must be quickly eliminated. Policy constraints result from policy and rules set by the organization (usually out-of-date ones) that hinder performance.

Bottlenecks identification can be achieved by visiting the work areas, interviewing people, or by using process flow diagrams, load analysis, and CUT diagrams.

CHAPTER 5

Constraint Management in a Bottleneck Environment

OBJECTIVES

- How to manage bottlenecks.
- How to exploit constraints using Pareto analysis and strategic gating.
- Why is it difficult to subordinate the system to the constraint.
- Appreciate the value of the offloading mechanism.

This chapter focuses on situations where system throughput is limited because of a resource constraint (bottleneck). In these situations, one must focus on the constraining resource and manage it efficiently and effectively. Any improvement that adds effective capacity to the constraint will add throughput to the whole organization.

STEP 4—DECIDE HOW TO EXPLOIT AND UTILIZE THE CONSTRAINT: BREAKING POLICY AND DUMMY CONSTRAINTS

In situations of resource shortage (human or material), the inclination is to solve the resource shortage by seeking additional personnel for service, sales, development, or production or by acquiring additional equipment.

The step of exploiting and utilizing the constraint means we "can **do much more** with what we already have"—that is, extract significant additional output by applying focused management to the bottleneck resources.

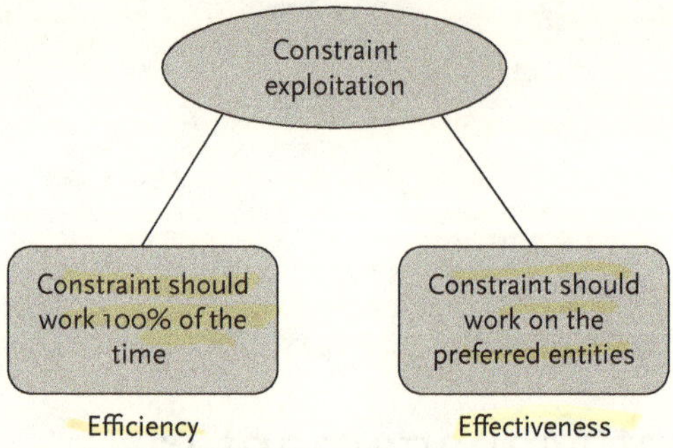

Figure 5.1:
Exploiting and utilizing the resource

The decision on whether to increase resources should be postponed until after full exploitation of the improvement potential of the current bottleneck.

Improvement through exploitation can be achieved relatively fast and is, therefore, the most realistic improvement for the short term. Experience has shown that in **every** system it is possible to extract more by better system management and focus on existing constraints. Exploitation is performed on two dimensions: efficiency and effectiveness (see Figure 5.1). In parallel, we must break policy and dummy constraints.

- **Efficiency**—Increasing bottleneck utilization to as close as possible to 100%.
- **Effectiveness**—As the bottleneck cannot supply the entire demand, one must decide on the product or service mix of the bottleneck.

Efficiency—Increasing Constraint Utilization

The bottleneck determines system throughput. Thus, we must make sure that it operates to the maximal possible utilization—as close as possible to 100% of its time. The constraint is the "goose that lays golden eggs" (or the "money printing machine") for the organization. An additional hour of bottleneck utilization is an additional hour of work for the entire system. An hour lost in the bottleneck is an hour lost for the entire system (Goldratt and Cox, 1992).

Experience gained in hundreds of organizations shows that we can **significantly increase bottleneck throughput** in sales, marketing, development, and operations **without adding resources** by better focused management of their resources (Mabin and Balderstone, 2000).

For the bottleneck to work more efficiently one can operate in two modes:

1. Increasing bottleneck capacity utilization to as close as possible to 100%.
2. Reducing bottleneck's ineffective ("garbage") time.

Increasing Bottleneck Utilization

Increasing bottleneck utilization starts with measuring its idle times and analyzing these times using the Pareto focusing methodology.

Example: In a large hospital, a bottleneck in patient processing was an expensive MRI machine. Measurement of idle time revealed that the machine is idle 32% of the time. Handling idle times was done as follows:

- **Problem classification**: Pareto classification of problems revealed that 20% of problems (type A problems) account for 80% of idle time. These type A problems are:
  1. Allocating fixed blocks of time to wards that do not fully utilize their time.
  2. Concurrent lunch breaks of several technicians.
  3. Maintenance problems.
- **Differential policy**: Management decided to focus only on type A problems. Other sources of idle time will be occasionally monitored to verify that they do not cause more idle time than in the past.
- **Allocation of improvement teams' resources**: Most resources will be devoted to type A problems.

Using existing resources, management took the following steps:

- MRI reserved time blocks were eliminated and imaging was scheduled by appointment or by emergent cases.
- Lunch breaks were staggered across three hours so the bottleneck could operate at full capacity during lunch times.
- Maintenance problems were monitored and preventive maintenance was undertaken.
- The maintenance department was instructed to give the MRI top priority.

Example: The operating rooms (ORs) in a public hospital were a bottleneck and yet were idle 42% of the time. The main causes for the idle times were the waiting for the cleaning crew (dummy constraint) and the operations canceled by the anesthetists whenever it was discovered, just before the operation, that the patient did not undergo all prerequired tests (i.e., arrived with incomplete kits; see chapter 12). Idle times of the ORs drastically decreased when another cleaning crew was designated for the OR area, and a preoperative clinic made sure that a complete kit was accomplished about one week before the scheduled surgery.

Reducing Ineffective Time ("Garbage Time")

The **"garbage plant"** is defined more broadly, also including the wasted materials and all other expenses. Ineffective time may exist in different ways.

"Garbage time"—the time when the bottleneck is devoted to activities that do not add value to the customer, the service or the product, or to activities it should not perform. This is the ineffective time of the bottleneck.

Example: In a group practice of dentists, the dentists were frequently occupied with typing reports and scheduling patient appointments, which mostly can be done by a secretary.

Example: The bottleneck in the office of a US state claims department were the attorneys who had to sign off on every claim. This created a very big backlog and delays in claim processing. Once they delegated authority to claims specialists, claims were processed much faster.

Example: The sales personnel of a large multinational pharmaceutical firm estimated that 50% of their time was ineffective. This was similar to assessments in similar sales departments. They applied the focusing methodology as follows.

Classifying "garbage time" causes

The various causes were classified into A, B, and C groups.

Group A consisted of 20% of causes and accounted for 80% of the garbage time and included the following:

- Working with an incomplete kit (see chapter 12). The sales force approached customers without acquiring all the knowledge and information on their needs, thus requiring frequent repeat visits. This information was in most cases already available in the firm, but it did not reach the sales department.

- Inappropriate identification of the decision maker in the customer's organization.
- Solving administrative and logistic problems of the customer (shipments, missing items, inquiries, etc.).

Differential policy

The firm decided to treat only the three previously mentioned causes of garbage time.

Resource allocation

Most of the extra managerial efforts were devoted to decreasing the three problems.

As a result of applying the focusing methodology, the garbage time of the sales force was reduced from 50% to 40%, which is equivalent to increasing the sales force by 20%. The volume of contribution to profit was largely increased as a result.

Example: In a large hospital, the major tasks of the chief nurse are to manage the facility and mentor the junior nurses. It turns out that 30% of her time is wasted on dealing with paperwork of newly admitted patients. This paperwork can be easily handled by other veteran nurses.

Example: In the surgical department of a hospital, the bottleneck was the anesthetist. About 30% of his time may be considered ineffective: 10% due to a lack of synchronization with other OR staff (surgeons, nurses), 10% was due to incomplete kits, and 10% was wasted between the end of one surgery and the beginning of the next one ("suturing to cutting").

Effectiveness

Since the bottleneck cannot supply the entire demand, one must decide on the product or service mix or the projects or customers on whom the bottleneck will operate.

Strategic gating—a process of prioritization that assesses the value of the different tasks, products, services, projects, or customers for the organization and then decides **which will be carried out** and in which priority and **which will not be carried out at all.**

Example: In a large firm that produces medical devices, the research and development (R&D) department was working simultaneously on four innovative products, each being a potential breakthrough in its area. Estimating the load in the development department indicated that the timetables dictated by the market will allow the development of only two products. The strategic gating decision was to halt the development of two of the four products. This decision eventually resulted in a very competitive time-to-market for one of the devices, enhancing thus the value of the firm.

Example: A health maintenance organization (HMO) was planning a campaign to increase membership enrollment. They listed 75 big firms and 20 smaller ones as potential targets for marketing. They had only a small window of time in which workers in these firms could change carriers. The short time frame and the large number of potential organizations made it necessary for them to prioritize the firms in terms of size and ease of attracting their workers. Using an "easy–important" table, they focused on 30 large firms and 10 small ones where they applied aggressive marketing steps, while totally ignoring the other firms. This strategic gating resulted in an astonishing 65% recruiting rate.

Example: In a large downtown supermarket, there were 15,000 stock keeping units (SKUs). The bottleneck of the supermarket was shelf space. The purchaser for this supermarket was swamped with suppliers knocking on her door, representing 150,000 relevant SKUs. They needed strategic prioritization to choose the products that would increase contribution to profit the most. Every product has a potential contribution, but a shortage of shelf space required prioritization that excludes some products altogether.

Prioritization Methods—Strategic Gating

There are several methods for prioritization.

Use of the Pareto Diagram

A Pareto diagram can be drawn for the potential contribution to the system or for any other relevant parameter. This is simple and fast method, but it does not consider the bottleneck time needed for each activity.

Use of a Focusing Table ("Easy–Important") and a Focusing Matrix

The potential tasks or projects are listed in a focusing table. For every task, we list the importance (expected contribution volume, value-enhancing capability, or contribution to achieving company goals) on a scale of 1 to 5. Then we list the ease of achieving each task (use of bottleneck time) on a scale of 1 to 5. The various tasks are mapped on a focusing matrix, which leads to the prioritization of tasks.

It is preferred to measure importance and ease of implementation on objective dimensions such as value enhancement or contributions. Ease of implementation can be measured, for example, by work hours needed by the bottleneck resource.

Example: The information technology (IT) department of a large private hospital was the bottleneck for many activities. Every department and every ward requested the development of numerous IT applications. Management had to prioritize projects for development. The ease of development was assessed by the number of person-hours of the development bottlenecks and the importance was assessed by the extra contribution to hospital profits to be achieved in the next three years due to these applications. As a result of this prioritization, out of 1,500 projects and applications that have been waiting for months in the IT department, 750 were chosen and the waiting time decreased dramatically.

Using "Specific Contribution"

The specific contribution is a tool for ranking the most valuable products, jobs, and customers.

Specific contribution—the contribution per unit of constraint of a product, task, service, or customer; the expected contribution divided by the time investment of the constrained resource.

$$\text{Specific contribution} = \frac{\text{Contribution}}{\text{Time invested by bottleneck}}$$

In a strategic gating process, we calculate the specific contribution for every product, service, task, or customer. We then pick the items with the highest specific contribution, up to filling the constraint capacity.

The specific contribution can assist the sales department in deciding on which customers to focus the scarce sales resources. Similarly, marketing and development departments can use specific contribution in new product development decisions.

Note that prioritization based on specific contribution is the correct and complete process for prioritization (Geri and Ronen, 2005). Using a focusing table ("easy–important") is a good approximation when it is difficult to quantify parameters. In a situation where the focusing table and focusing matrix are constructed by parameters such as contribution on the one hand and work hours on the other, the graphic representation is an important step toward calculating specific contribution. Many organizations prefer to perform strategic gating at the level of a focusing table and focusing matrix because the graphic visualization makes it easier to decide.

Example: An R&D department of a bio-tech firm that specializes in imaging technology was considering four projects that are presented in Table 5.1.

Prioritization, determined by specific contribution, will be as follows:

1. MRI 1.
2. MRI 2.
3. CT Scan 1.
4. CT Scan 2.

Example: In typical large supermarkets, shelf space is the resource constraint. Product prioritization should consider specific contribution per shelf length to maximize overall contribution to profits.

Example: A private hospital specializes in providing surgical services where external surgeons bring in external patients. The ORs are the system bottleneck. For several years, it was believed that gynecological surgical procedures were the most profitable for the hospital. A specific contribution

Table 5.1. IMAGING PROJECTS

Project	Contribution ($)	Development effort (person-years)	Specific contribution (in thous. $ per year)
CT Scan 1	56,000	0.5	112
MRI 1	2,470,000	1	2,470
CT Scan 2	345,000	5	69
MRI 2	1,250,000	2	612.5

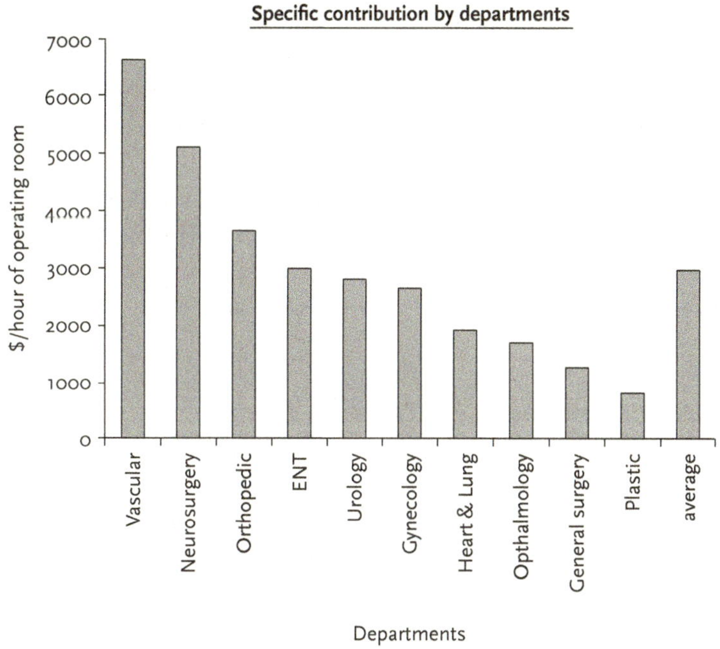

Figure 5.2:
Pareto diagram of specific contribution

analysis was performed, and operations were ranked by descending order of specific contribution per hour of OR in a Pareto diagram. This is presented in Figure 5.2. As the figure shows, the highest specific contribution is from vascular surgery, then neurosurgery; orthopedics; ear, nose, and throat; and urology. Gynecology is only in sixth place. This graph helped the hospital to prioritize the types of operations and identify those they should to focus on. Within 18 months, OR utilization increased by 17%, and hospital profits have almost tripled!

The Mirabilis Effect

Any strategic gating decision can be difficult for decision makers. A decision on **"what to produce and on what to focus"** always carries with it the complimentary decision of **"what to give up."**

As the strategic gating decision is done under conditions of uncertainty, there is always the doubt of correctly assessing the expected contributions and effort needed. There is always the fear that the product rejected through prioritization could have been Mirabilis-like. (Mirabilis was a small Israeli high-tech firm that developed the ICQ software and was sold to AOL for over $400 million.) However, if this was the case, this product should have been assessed a higher expected contribution resulting in a higher specific contribution. The fact that the value assessed for a product is not too high indicates the presence of other products that seem to have higher success probabilities at the time of decision.

Firms need managerial maturity to realize that physical rules cannot be bent, and there is no system that can perform **all the tasks** that one would want. If management will not engage in prioritization, wrong decisions will be made and business opportunities will be missed.

The Global Decision-Making (GDM) Methodology

As we shall see in chapter 16, the specific contribution ranking is only one step of tactical and strategic prioritization and screening process of tasks, services or products. In chapter 16, we will see the full decision-making process using global decision-making (GDM):

1. **Make a global economic decision from the CEO's perspective.** In this process, we evaluate the decision from a global perspective by looking at the whole system. The process may utilize specific contribution.
2. **Add strategic considerations.** We must consider long-term and other strategic considerations only after we are able to assess the financial implications of any changes from the set of priorities accomplished in the first step. When one or more of the alternatives in the prioritization process has indirect marketing implications or broader strategic implications, we must expand the analysis of their expected contributions and prepare a mini business plan for each alternative.
3. **Change, if needed, local performance measures.** Local performance measures may occasionally distort the prioritization process and should therefore be changed. For example, prioritizing customers by a local performance measure of "sales volume" requires a change for prioritizing them according to their "specific contribution."

Breaking Policy and Dummy Constraints

Whereas bottlenecks must be exploited efficiently and effectively, dummy and policy constraints must be broken. The dummy constraint of the cleaning person in the OR can be immediately remedied by hiring additional inexpensive personnel. One does not need an economist to perform a cost–benefit analysis to justify this solution.

Policy constraints are a bit more difficult to deal with. For example, elimination of overtime work (which usually occurs at peak times) can be solved by a policy that differentiates between departments or wards that are bottlenecks and others. This allows managers to manage a petty cash account of the overtime budget for the bottlenecks.

STEP 5—SUBORDINATE THE SYSTEM TO THE CONSTRAINT

Once we focus on the constraint (the bottleneck) and improve its management, we need to create a policy for managing and operating the noncritical resources. The remaining resources should **serve and assist the bottleneck.** Thus, the noncritical resources should be organized to assist the bottleneck when needed. For example, in a group dental practice, the dentists are the system constraint. The other workers (hygienists, assistants, secretary) should all assist the dentists.

The noncritical resources must be coordinated and available to assist system constraints, especially in peak times. For example, in peak tourist seasons, the runways of an airport are the bottleneck. All other workers and managers must contribute their share to efficiently exploit the runway times for fast and safe takeoffs and landings.

Example: Henry Ford offered customers the Model T Ford "in any color the customer wants, as long as it is black." Henry Ford's policy resulted from subordination to the assembly line constraint that could not keep up with market demand. For many years, the constraint was a resource constraint. To maximize throughput, it was important for Ford not to change models during production. This policy assured achieving the goal of maximizing the profit and value for the Ford Company by subordinating the whole system to production.

Henry Ford's failure was that he stuck to his policy even when new competitors entered the market and the constraint became a market constraint. This resulted in a steep drop in sales and market share. The right step would have been to realize there was now a market constraint and subordinate the system to this constraint. Ford should have switched to producing a variety of cars—different styles, colors, or amenities—as it was demanded by customers and was offered by his competitors.

Example: In the development of a new drug, a pharmaceutical firm should be driven by the market rather than by pure innovation (e.g., for the sake of prestige).

Example: In an OR in a hospital, the bottleneck could be the anesthetists, nurses, or the OR capacity itself. Management must identify the bottleneck and subordinate all others to serve and assist the bottleneck to ensure it achieves its potential throughput.

From the authors' experience with the last example, implementing the subordination phase may be difficult in certain cases. If the bottleneck is the senior surgeon, the authors did not experience any subordination problems. However, in cases where the anesthetist was the bottleneck, it was very difficult to subordinate the surgeons to the constrained timetable of the anesthetist.

Additional examples:

- Imaging technicians' working in shifts should be scheduled according to the timetables of the senior radiologist if she is the system bottleneck.
- In maintenance, priority should be given to the bottleneck resource. When the bottleneck fails, the relevant maintenance people should drop all other tasks and assist in fixing the bottleneck as it stops all system output.
- Releasing tasks for service or development should be scheduled according to the bottleneck pace.
- If efficient use of a hospital lab calls for batches of 100 specimens at a time, then all wards and logistics should subordinate to this constraint even if they prefer preparing larger batches.

Subordination Mechanisms

Subordinating noncritical resources to an organizational constraint can be achieved using the following mechanisms:

1. Tactical gating.
2. Drum–buffer–rope (DBR).

Tactical Gating

To help the system perform to its utmost, the constraint must work efficiently and effectively. Subordinating the rest of the system to the constraint is achieved via a mechanism of releasing tasks into the system. This is the tactical gating mechanism. Tactical gating means the controlled release of tasks (jobs) to the system. To assure efficient operation of the bottleneck, the tactical gating mechanism will employ the following policy:

1. Only tasks screened by the strategic gating process will be released for workup.
2. All tasks will be released only through the body or person in charge of the gating (the "gater"). A task that was not screened and released by the gater will not be processed.

3. All tasks will enter the system with a **complete kit** (see chapter 13).
4. All tasks will enter according to an appropriate **scheduling mechanism**, example, the DBR.
5. From time to time release entities according to shortest processing time (SPT) priority rule (see chapter 11).

Drum–Buffer–Rope (DBR)

The drum-buffer-rope (DBR) mechanism presented in Figure 5.3 is a scheduling mechanism for entering tasks into the system (Goldratt and Cox, 1992; Schragenheim and Ronen, 1990). It is appropriate for health-care systems, service industries, production, and R&D).

Drum

The drum provides the rhythm for the flow of tasks through the system. The system constraint determines the rate at which tasks should enter the system and flow through it. In the presence of a resource constraint, the drum will be the **processing rate of the bottleneck.** In the case of a market constraint, the **rate of market demand** will dictate the pace for the whole system. Thus, the rate of releasing tasks into the system will be governed by the constraint and not by noncritical resources (see chapter 10).

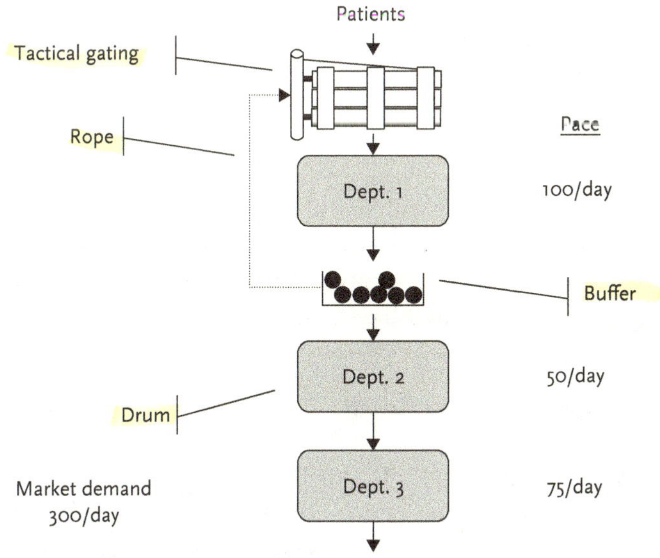

Figure 5.3:
The drum–buffer–rope mechanism

Buffer

The buffer is a controlled quantity of tasks that is accumulated before the bottleneck to assure it is fully utilized. The buffer serves to protect the system against fluctuations that can arise from malfunctions and delays in the chain feeding the bottleneck. Such fluctuations can be caused by:

- Absenteeism.
- Technical problems and human error in the service or treatment process.
- Low quality of information or materials.
- No-shows of patients to the clinic or hospital.

The buffer protects the bottleneck output from various variations by assuring continuity of its operation (see chapter 15 for a discussion on variation).

The size of the buffer is measured in terms of the bottleneck utilization time (e.g., a four-hour buffer) or by number patients waiting. To decide on buffer size, we must examine the various variations and time to correct them. For example, if 95% of variation is handled within four hours, this time will determine the buffer size.

Note that there should also exist an overflow buffer. Malfunctions may occur in steps that come after the bottleneck. To protect for the bottleneck throughput in such situations, additional capacity must be arranged for the throughput of the bottleneck to provide for a continuity of work. This capacity is the overflow buffer. For example, the recovery room should have enough beds to accommodate the expected output of the ORs. It doesn't make sense if the bottlenecked OR will have to stop because the recovery room is fully occupied.

Rope

This is a "logical rope" feedback mechanism that transfers information on the situation in the buffer to the gater to coordinate release of tasks into the system. When the number of tasks in the buffer becomes smaller, additional tasks are released into the system.

Examples for using the DBR mechanism

DBR in an orthodontics clinic. The orthodontists and clerical staff of the clinic schedule patient appointments so the orthodontists (the bottleneck) will be utilized without idle times. They create a buffer of about a 15-minute wait for each orthodontist (about two patients waiting). If the buffer were larger, patients would complain about the excessive waiting. In this clinic, each orthodontist (the constraint) works in three rooms in parallel. While the orthodontist is seeing a patient on one room, the two other rooms serve as buffers where patients are waiting to be seen. In addition to the two buffer rooms, two additional patients are waiting in the waiting area. All this involves only an average of 15 minutes waiting time for patients but assures a high capacity utilization of the orthodontists.

To reduce potential fluctuations in patient arrivals, the clinic staff call the patients a day before the scheduled appointment to verify their arrival.

DBR in an OR. Since the duration of surgery is uncertain, one should schedule patients using the DBR methodology. The drum is the system bottleneck (e.g., the surgeon's rate of performing surgery). A buffer of patients (e.g., on standby) will be waiting in the preoperative room. When the patient is wheeled into the operating room, the rope will signal the ward to send another patient. In a situation with short duration operations, the buffer should be measured by time (e.g., 30- or 60-minute buffer). The buffer size depends on the fluctuations of the system.

DBR in airports. In airports, the **runways** are a bottleneck. To assure they operate close to 100% capacity, there are buffers for taking off and for landing airplanes. Side runways accommodate the buffer for taking off airplanes. Arriving planes are asked occasionally to circle above the airport and serve as buffers. The buffer size will, of course, depend on safety considerations. When the buffer is full, approaching aircraft are instructed to slow down their approach, fly in wider circles, or, in extreme situations, are diverted to other airports. The control tower is responsible for gating. When a plane lands, it is immediately directed to a side runway to allow for another plane to land and another plane to enter the buffer.

An example of applying DBR in a primary care clinic and the implementation of other TOC concepts is illustrated in Cox et al. (2016).

DBR in sales. In a multinational firm, every sales person oversaw 40 existing customers and 100 new potential customers. The company shifted to DBR scheduling of sales personnel. Today they operate in a focused manner where the buffer is defined by a 10+10 approach: every sales person oversees managing and preserving 10 existing customers and 10 potential new customers.

STEP 6—ELEVATE THE CONSTRAINT

Up to this point, the first five steps of management by constraints dealt with increasing the output of a given constraint, without any changes in the system itself. Now it is time for **structural changes** in the system to **increase the effective capacity** of the bottleneck. Increasing this capacity will increase the throughput of the whole system.

Elevating and breaking the constraint can be achieved in two manners:

- Elevating using capital investment.
- Elevating that does not need investment with the use of the offloading mechanism.

Elevating With Capital Investment

An effective increase in the capacity of the constraint through the acquisition of additional resources can be achieved in one of the following ways:

- Recruiting additional staff.
- Purchasing additional equipment.
- Working additional shifts.
- Working overtime.
- Hiring subcontractors.
- Outsourcing.
- Recruiting distributors and value-added retailers for the sales force.

Example: In an emergency department of a hospital, the consulting surgeons were the bottleneck. Management decided to hire some retired surgeons (who no longer operate but have great diagnostic skills) to elevate the system's constraint.

Example: A large HMO had many litigations concerning malpractice suits. Their own attorneys became a bottleneck so they started using the services of outside law firms.

Offloading

The offload process involves transfer of tasks from the constraint to noncritical resources that have excess capacity. From the system's perspective, it does not matter if these resources perform the task of the bottleneck at a slower pace than the bottleneck. The important fact is that they contribute to the overall output. In some cases, the offload is achieved using structured processes that need lesser expertise.

Offload—relieving the load from the bottleneck by transferring some of the workload to noncritical resources.

Example: In many HMO clinics, physicians and nurse practitioners formed doctor–nurse practitioner teams so that the doctors could offload some of their tasks to the nurses.

Example: In a large HMO, a senior vice-president had to sign every request for surgery in nonaffiliated hospitals. She was the bottleneck that caused delays and resulted in adverse outcomes to patients and law suits. She had the responsibility of verifying need, justifying surgery in a specific hospital, and determining the level of copayment. Her level of expertise was second to none, and she was indeed a scarce resource.

Offloading was achieved by training some clerks and other employees to do some of her tasks. It turned out that about 25% of requests were rather standard, and their approval process was structured and straightforward. Even though each such case required a short processing time by the specialist, offloading these cases to others released 15% of the specialist's time. This resulted in shorter response times to approve requests and increased system output (see Eden and Ronen, 1993).

Additional examples include:

- A dental hygienist relieves the burden from the dentist by performing some of the tasks.
- In a supermarket during peak times, the number of registries is the bottleneck. Adding packers at each registry offloads some of the cashiers' work to a less-expensive resource.
- In university hospitals, teaching assistants and research assistants serve as offloads for the expensive resource of the professors and senior researchers who do both clinical and academic work.
- In many complex surgeries, the beginning of the operations as well as the ending (closing) is performed by junior surgeons.
- Phlebotomists largely offload physicians in most tasks related to blood samples taking. These resources are widely available and inexpensive.
- Scribes offload physicians in recording patient data and information.
- Physician assistants (PAs) and paramedicas offload physicians in many clinical tasks.

STEP 7—IF A CONSTRAINT IS "BROKEN," GO BACK TO STEP 3: DO NOT LET INERTIA BECOME THE SYSTEM CONSTRAINT

If a constraint is broken, we must return to the third step of identifying the emergent system constraint and refrain from letting inertia become the

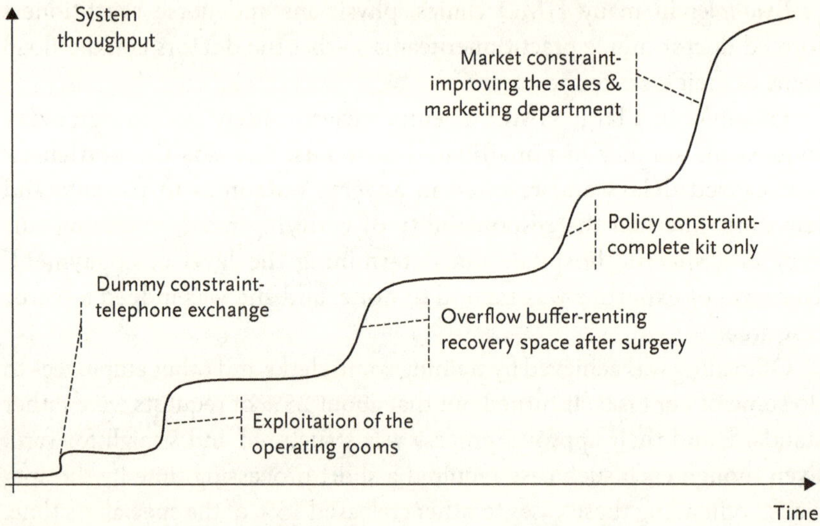

Figure 5.4:
Continuous improvement in a surgical department

system constraint. There is always a constraint (bottleneck) in a system. The task is to identify constraints, manage them, break them, and face a new constraint that may appear elsewhere. By moving from constraint to constraint, system output increases. Figure 5.4 describes the improvement process in the surgical department of a hospital.

In routine processes, constraints do not change frequently and are rather stable. In one-time processes (projects, sales campaigns, etc.), constraints change rapidly, and bottlenecks can move from one place to another.

Managerial inertia can be detriment to organizational performance. An organization accustomed to a constraint being in one place may occasionally behave as if the constraint is still there, even though improvement steps broke this constraint and another constraint was formed elsewhere.

The previously mentioned example of Henry Ford exemplifies this. Even though the resource constraint at the assembly line was broken and the constraint became a market constraint, the management of Ford continued, out of inertia, to focus on efficient use of internal resources and did not view the market as the system constraint.

Example: In an emergency department, the bottleneck was in radiology services. By using existing equipment and breaking some policy constraints, management could operate the two X-ray rooms in the following manner. They divided the patients needing X-rays into two groups: walking patients and lying patients. The patients who could walk on their own, simply walked into one designated X-ray room, not requiring any assistance. The second X-ray room was devoted to lying patients who were wheeled into the room on specially purchased beds that did not require their transfer to a stationary bed in the room. Thus, the radiology constraint was broken. The next constraint was lack of expert surgical consultants. Previously a consultant was called for consultation only when at least two to three patients required a consult (unless, of course, there was an emergency). The hospital assigned a special surgeon who was continuously present in the emergency department. Once the surgical consultant constraint was broken, the system faced a policy constraint in the discharge process. A team of nurses, physicians, and administrators solved the problem by redesigning the discharge process. All these actions have gradually reduced the average waiting time by 40%.

The "Curse of the Blessing"

Use of the techniques described in this book, such as management by constraints, frequently result in rapid increase in throughput and a significant decrease in response times to customers as well as improvement in quality.

As a result of these improvements, the organization usually becomes more attractive to its customers or patients, and the demand for its services or products increases. Managements that are not cautious may take on commitments beyond the new effective capacity. This may lead to delays in treating patients, operational difficulties, and a severe blow to the recently enhanced reputation. This phenomenon is called the "curse of the blessing." When the organization achieves significant improvement, it must be careful with dealing with the increased demand and always proceed gradually while being proactive.

CHAPTER SUMMARY

Management by constraints is one of the most advanced management methods today. It includes focusing steps that significantly increase system throughput within a short time by focusing on bottlenecks and other constraints. The methodology allows to significantly improve performance of healthcare, sales, marketing, service, R&D, and production systems in a relatively short time frame while using existing resources. The next chapter will demonstrate how to use the theory of constraints when the market is the system constraint.

CHAPTER 6

Constraint Management under a Market Constraint

OBJECTIVES

- How to sell more using the same resources in a market-constrained environment.
- Understand how to cope with peaks in demand using the peak management approach.
- How answering the three questions on organizational resources can affect strategy.

A system always has a constraint. In the previous chapter, we discussed situations involving scarce resources where the constraints were these resources. There are many organizations with excess operational capacity and then the market becomes the system constraint. Proper use of TOC methodology in these situations yields improvements in throughput, quality, profits, and value of the firm.

Even private or budgeted hospitals and health maintenance organizations (HMOs) must realize that they may have excess capacity and need a strong marketing function. They should resist the temptation to lay off people during slow times. Perhaps they should consider bringing in outside tasks to exploit this excess capacity.

Example: A hospital buys an expensive imaging machine. The decision is a correct one as the machine is essential for some diagnoses. However, there is not enough demand for its use. Rather than refer more patients that do not need this expensive imaging, the hospital can sell imaging services to outside bodies such as HMOs and private physicians.

Example: A technological change may cause excess capacity at bottlenecks. The development of cardiac angiography with the introduction of stents has brought many cardiologists to engage in this practice and refer more patients to these techniques. As a result, cardiac surgeons who used to be a system bottleneck in the past find themselves with excess capacity because the market for their operations such as coronary bypass surgery has shrunk dramatically.

The steps of management by constraints in a system where the market is the constraint are the same steps as with resource constraints (Pass and Ronen, 2003):

1. Determine the system's goal.
2. Establish global performance measures.
3. Identify the system constraint.
4. Decide how to exploit the constraint; break dummy and policy constraints.
5. Subordinate the rest of the system to the constraint.
6. Elevate and break the constraint.
7. If the constraint is broken, go back to step 3. Do not let inertia become the system constraint.

Steps 1 to 3, where the goal and performance measures are defined and the system bottleneck is identified, are common to both resource and market constraints. The essence of steps 5 and 6 in both situations is similar, but the methods and tools for dealing with a market constraint are different from the ones appropriate for a resource constraint. Here, too, step 4 (exploiting the constraint) can be implemented immediately. Step 5 is implemented in the intermediate term. Step 6 requires introducing more substantial changes in the system and is therefore a step aimed at the medium to long term.

Treating a market constraint is more difficult than treating a resource constraint. Managing an internal bottleneck offers management more control of what is happening in the "inner circles" of the organization, while some of the factors involved in dealing with a market constraint are beyond management's control.

Most non-healthcare organizations are faced with a market constraint. In today's global fierce competition, it is wise to have excess capacity (or protective capacity) in the production and service resources. Firms cannot usually afford a situation where the marketing and sales force managed to obtain orders, while the operational factor is the constraint that prevents or delays orders fulfillment.

Managing the market constraint is a key for the success of many firms and businesses, and the approaches presented in this chapter should be a valuable tool for this.

STEP 4—DECIDE HOW TO EXPLOIT AND UTILIZE THE CONSTRAINT: BREAK POLICY AND DUMMY CONSTRAINTS

Exploiting a market constraint means exploiting the **existing** market and the **existing** sales ability more efficiently and effectively—in other words, doing more with the same resources. This exploitation will be achieved through efficient operation of marketing and sales and effective strategic marketing, while breaking policy and dummy constraints. Figure 6.1 presents this situation. This implies the need to "strike" the existing market and exploit the full volume of potential contribution from existing and potential customers and products using existing personnel.

Marketing and Sales Efficiency

Exploiting Marketing and Sales Personnel

The marketing and sales personnel are usually a permanent bottleneck. As such, we must exploit them and utilize their time.

- The garbage time of the sales force must be reduced. Sales personnel are frequently busy with logistical problems, with time-consuming efforts to follow-up on orders, and so on. All these must be reduced.
- The sales and marketing operation should be **structured** and with stable and simple processes. There are many cases where marketing and sales processes are not congruent with the organizational needs and the market. For instance, the introduction of a new service or product often suffers from

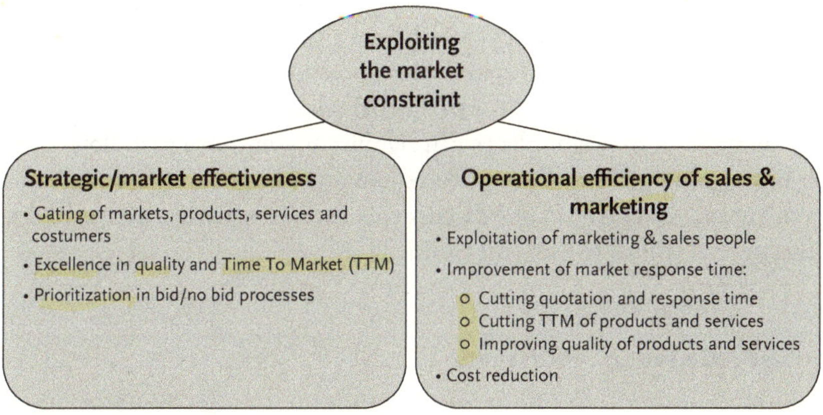

Figure 6.1:
Exploiting a market constraint

incomplete and disorderly marketing and from the fact that information does not reach all relevant parties. In retail, there are many examples that customers are the ones who update the cashiers about various promotions.

Improving Response to Market Needs

- **Reducing response times in price bids, sales and marketing.** The contribution of sales to profits can be improved by shortening response times of preparing tenders, marketing and sales processes. Despite the common claims that "every customer is different" or "every product is unique," there is room for improving work processes to be uniform for every class of customers with similar features. The process of request for quotations for customers, especially in response to bids, must be structured, simple, and clear.
- **Shortening the time to market of services and products.** A shorter time to market of new products and services enables reaching customers faster than the competition and realizing better prices. As such, operational efficiency will enhance sales. Submitting bids with fast quoted lead times for a product or service frequently makes the organization more attractive to customers and increases contribution from sales.
- **Improving service or product quality.** Improvement in the service or operations processes will increase the perceived value of the firm's products or services and will increase contribution of sales.
- **Reducing costs.** Operational efficiency, by the sales and marketing personnel as well as the operational bodies, can improve response times, quality, and system output.

The objective is to achieve, with existing resources and current costs, higher output, higher income, improved cash flow, and value enhancement for the organization. However, this is not always possible, and one must also evaluate the reduction of costs. A careful cost analysis and decisions on cost containment in the right places can significantly improve cash flow. Cost savings can sometime allow price reduction, which may improve competitiveness. Chapter 17 will discuss this further when we compare the "throughput world" to the "cost world."

Strategic-Marketing Effectiveness

The previous chapter introduced the concept of strategic gating, which screens and prioritizes customers or products based on their specific contribution or their positioning of the focusing matrix ("easy–important"). Even when an organization is at excess capacity and is facing a market constraint, the sales and marketing personnel are a permanent bottleneck. The potential demand for their services always exceeds their resources. There are always more potential customers, marketing initiatives, sales to existing customers, and offerings of new services or products than available time of sales and marketing personnel. This screening procedure is, therefore, extremely important and enables focusing on the highest specific contribution products, services, or customers that can contribute most to increase organizational performance and value.

As a result, we can state:

1. One should not abandon sales of services and products to customers and markets where the sales personnel are **minimally** involved, even if the **contribution volume is small**. For example, repeat sales to existing customers should not be rejected even if the throughput may not be too high, because in these sales, most of the marketing and sales efforts have already been done in the past. These sales can actually be considered sales with a high specific contribution, due to the short time invested in them by the sales or marketing people.
2. For sales of services or products or customers that require substantial investments of time, we need to perform a prioritization process of the strategic gating. The prioritization will be carried out relative to the time that the sales and marketing personnel (the bottleneck) need to invest to achieve the contribution volume of the expected sales of these services or products.

Table 6.1 presents the calculation of the specific contribution of the various customers relative to the sales effort involved.

A salesman should first approach the customer with the highest specific contribution relative to her time. The top choice is HMO2. She will then

Table 6.1. THE SPECIFIC CONTRIBUTION OF CUSTOMERS RELATIVE TO THE SALES EFFORT

Customer	Contribution to profit ($)	Sales effort (days)	Specific contribution ($/day)
HMO1	2,345,000	120	19,500
HMO2	5,600,000	30	186,700
Group practice	575,000	80	7,200
Hospital	12,650,000	500	25,300

focus on HMO1, and so on, until she fills up 100% of her time. This analysis must also consider strategic considerations (see the global decision-making model in chapter 17).

Strategic gating will also be performed on the portfolio of services and products that the organization is offering: experience shows that by **focusing** on a **smaller number** of services and products, it is possible to achieve a **higher** overall volume of contributions. Occasionally it is advisable to cease the sale of services and products whose total contribution volume is **negligible**. Cessation of sales can be done in two ways:

1. Discontinue offering them to the market.
2. If there is concern that the market will not react positively to cessation of sales, it is possible to **raise** the price of the product. If there will be no demand at the new price, the product will fade away. However, if demand persists, then the higher price will increase contribution. This situation will reveal that the previous price was too low. There are many cases where raising the price did not diminish demand but rather increased it.

Note that it is common to think that stopping the sale of certain products of a product line may decrease sales of the entire line. Every situation must be examined specifically. With proper planning, it is usually possible to increase contributions.

Making Excellence in Response Times and Quality into a Strategic Leverage

Years ago, Japanese firms captured the world market in cars and home electronics through the quality of the products. Their operational excellence, which enabled achieving high quality while incurring low production costs, fast response times, and low inventories, established a strategic advantage in the eye of customers who were willing to pay a premium for "Made in Japan."

Superb operational ability must not stop at achieving low costs and competitive operating expenses. The challenge is to translate the excellence in quality and operations into a strategic advantage for the organization. See the following examples:

- The Mayo Clinic in Rochester Minnesota established a name for itself even though it is located in a remote town. It attracts patients from all over the world who are willing to pay a premium for the perceived superior quality of care.

- The computer manufacturer Dell achieved fast response times and low inventory costs through efficient operations and logistics management. As a result, it captured a large market share of personal computers and servers segment.

Prioritizing in Bid/No-Bid Processes

In companies where most of sales are done through participation in bids, there must be an important step of deciding whether to respond with a bid. This process is known as "bid/no-bid" (or "go/no-go"). The bids should be evaluated on their compatibility with the company strategy, the chances of winning, and the potential contribution to profits. Tenders that do not meet the criteria should be answered with a no-bid, thus preventing unnecessary effort by the permanent bottlenecks of the system (marketing and sales personnel, technical experts). A policy where an organization responds positively (bid) to every request becomes a policy constraint.

Breaking Policy and Dummy Constraints

To increase the contribution volume of sales, we must identify policy and dummy constraints that interfere with the organization's efforts to cope with the market:

- **Avoid blind use of traditional cost-accounting.** As we will see in chapter 16, the blind use of classical pricing can harm the organization. There are organizations where the selling price is built on "cost+." The desire to **always** have the selling price above the costs (including indirect costs) may lead to erroneous decisions and loss of business opportunities.
- **Avoid giving up small customer orders.** There is no reason to reject small customers or small orders that do not take up much time of the sales and marketing bottlenecks.
- **Avoid selling only complete sets or service bundles.** Certain industries (e.g., shoes and clothing) tend to sell to stores in complete sets only. These sets have a predetermined assortment of styles and sizes. However, preparing a specified, nonstandard, assortment according to the needs of a specific store does not take up too much bottleneck time so there is no reason not to sell what the customer wants. For example, a hospital lab may be willing to sell excess capacity to outside customers. They should not insist on selling predetermined bundles of services (blood, urine,

etc.) and can afford to sell what customers actually need. It is wise to follow the demand patterns so even if a firm offers only complete bundles, they should be designed according to actual demand trends.

- **Avoid selling a complete product line or nothing.** There are companies with a policy of selling customers an entire basket of services or products or nothing at all. In many cases, selling a partial basket can yield nice profits.
- **Avoid rewarding sales personnel by sales volume.** This is one of the most common forms of incentives and rewards, but this encourages the sales force to maximize sales volume and not necessarily the total contribution to profits. There is a need to shift to a reward and measurement system where profit or contribution plays the important role.
- **Avoid rewarding sales personnel on sales regardless of returns and cancellations.** This policy constraint encourages sales persons to sign as many contracts as possible with many customers without checking the real need of the customers and their ability to pay. This policy constraint can be easily rectified by rewarding the sales force by **actual** contribution volume (subtracting returns and cancellations) and only after payment has been received.
- **Avoid dummy constraints.** For example, lack of a fax machine or other communication mode for sales personnel.

Breaking such policy and dummy constraints illustrated in the previous points is an important factor in increasing the volume of contribution to the organization.

STEP 5—SUBORDINATE THE SYSTEM TO THE CONSTRAINT

There is an obvious advantage for an organization that satisfies its customers' needs better than the competition. Organizations with a market constraint must **subordinate the whole system to the market**, meaning that every member of the organization must subordinate himself to the market and its needs.

Subordinating the organization to the market will be done in the following dimensions:

- **Customization to customer demands and needs.** In a competitive market, there is a need to customize services and products to the various needs of customers. Customization is important and especially worthwhile when the customization does not require development or marketing resources but only efforts from operational entities that are not bottlenecks. When customization does require some development, strategic gating will help decide how to best utilize the constrained development resources.

- **Fast response to customer needs.** To beat the competition, one must adjust to the due date required by the customer and subordinate the whole system to the market-dictated timetables.
- **Direct link to the end customer.** Establishing a direct link with the end customer is especially important in those cases where the organization uses external distributors to sell its services and products to the end customers. The organization must then establish a permanent communications process to determine the needs of the distributors and end customers. It is worthwhile to make an effort to establish a connection with the end customers by bypassing the hurdles of the distribution channels and agents. For example, if a hospital or clinic has referrals from HMOs or other insurance companies, the hospital should establish a direct link with the insured to fully understand their needs.
- **Adjusting the organizational structure to customer types or customer needs.** To better serve the market, one must assure that the organizational structure is compatible with customers' needs. Occasionally, the organizational structure is based on a geographical segmentation or is geared toward achieving operational efficiency. It may be better to redesign the structure to reflect different customer types and needs. For example, rather than designing a large HMO to be geographically based, where every region is assigned proportionate resources, the resource allocation should be targeted to different patient groups, such as young versus old, chronically ill versus acutely ill, and men versus women.
- **Subordinating technology to market needs.** High-tech cutting-edge medical organizations have a constant conflict between marketing and development departments. Many technological organizations were built on their technological know-how and development breakthrough. In such situations, development may occasionally dictate the organizational road map. Development and technology must be subordinated to the market via the marketing department and its personnel. Defining the services and products should be done in harmony between marketing and development, but the subordination should always be to the market.
- **Market segmentation and product differentiation.** In the case of excess capacity, an organization can meet specific demands of various market segments by product and price differentiation. This allows the organization to channel the excess operational capacity toward generating additional contributions. It is essential to assure the cooperation and good will of the operations people, as this segmentation involves additional operational complexity (see chapter 18).

Example: In the past, obstetrical services in a hospital had internal resource constraints, usually the obstetricians/gynecologists. The providers could dictate the level of service and quality to the customers. In today's highly competitive market of hospitals, HMOs, private practices, and so on, the market has become the constraint. Hospitals have completely subordinated their operation to the market. Everything is targeted to please the potential patient: Support services for the delivering mother and her family were established, hotels were built to accommodate relatives, shopping malls targeted at the baby market have been built, and so on.

STEP 6—ELEVATE AND BREAK THE CONSTRAINT

In this step, we need to examine how to increase the contribution from sales or services by creating added value to existing customers, introducing new products or services, approaching new markets, identifying new customers, combining marketing with new sales channels, and strategic cooperation.

This step requires establishing a **focused strategy**. Occasionally, in situations with a market constraint, organizations are tempted to "shoot in all directions" or cast a **wide** net and wait "until the fish are caught." Such a policy can put the bottleneck resource of sales and marketing to waste. In contrast, a focused policy targeting the main objectives and focusing the efforts on these targets usually yields better outcomes.

To elevate and break the market constraint, the following steps are recommended:

1. **Establishing a focused strategy:** A focused strategy is a necessary condition for increasing profit. For details, see chapter 18.
2. **Entering a new product/market:** Mergers and acquisitions of organizations that have an appropriate product or market.
3. **Adding marketing and sales channels:** Adding marketing and sales channels such as a new distributor or entering the world of e-Business.
4. **Market segmentation and product differentiation:** Every market segment has different needs and requirements. Products and services must be adapted according to the targeted segments.
5. **"Stretching the brand name:"** "Stretching the brand name" implies taking advantage of the success of one brand name to create a family of related or similar services or products that will be sold under the same brand name.
6. **Creating added value for the customer:** In this category, we can include product features that add perceived value to the customer:

- Creating a package of services and products that complement each other.
- Managing the customer's facilities, shift to outsourcing of customer activities.
- Managing inventory for the customer.
- Building customer loyalty (customer clubs).
- Customer relationships management.
- Outpatient clinics.
- Establishing rehabilitation facilities.
- Alternative medicine.

7. **Cooperation and strategic alliances**

STEP 7—IF A CONSTRAINT IS BROKEN, GO BACK TO STEP 3: DO NOT LET INERTIA BECOME THE SYSTEM CONSTRAINT

If the constraint is broken, we must look for the next constraint and manage the system accordingly. There are situations where a constrained system loses some demand and becomes a system with excess capacity, and vice versa.

Managing Marketing and Sales

Focusing on Most Valuable Customers as a Value Enhancer

Investing in marketing and sales efforts in existing customers and potential ones enables to increase contribution. To make the best use of the scarce time of the marketing and sales personnel, they should focus on existing and potential customers with a high specific contribution. For potential customers, specific contribution calculations are based on estimates.

These customers with high specific contributions are called **most valuable customers (MVCs)**. The MVCs are type A customers in the Pareto analysis of the organization—about 20% of customers (existing and potential) contribute 80% of contribution volume.

Such focusing enables better response to the needs of the MVCs:

- Establishing tight personal contacts with influential people in the customer organization.
- Collecting and analyzing data on the customer, competitors, and the relevant markets.

- Providing special service level to the MVCs in all units of the organization (the red carpet or VIP treatment).
- Analysis of MVCs' needs and identifying channels for providing more **value to the customer** both to the MVCs and to all other customers.
- Determining policy vis-à-vis the customer.
- Risk and opportunity management vis-à-vis the customer.
- Structured management of meetings with the customer.
- Structured management of contracts with the customer.

It is nearly impossible to give VIP treatment to all customers, but attention should focus on MVCs, thus enabling to increase the contribution of sales.

Peak Management

An important area derived from management by constraints is reducing the effect of peak time loads. Appropriate management of such systems requires sometimes differential pricing of products or services during different times. The reduction of temporary loads during peak times can be achieved using the following steps (Ronen et al., 2001):

- **Stretching peak times.** Stretching peak times allows spreading work over a longer period. For example, to overcome the load on a clinic during peak hours, a clinic can move back the start time of employees in certain departments and move up the opening time of the clinic (see also chapter 11). Another example is a private hospital where the ORs moved to a 6:00 AM–11:00 PM schedule of performing surgery.
- **Capacity planning.** It is common to plan capacity for an average load. This results in excess capacity during slow periods and to resource constraints with lost sales during peak periods. Good planning should provide for adequate service and performance at all times. Hence a strategic decision of capacity planning to provide for peak times can reduce or even prevent the peak time loads. Examples can be found in walk-in clinics, fast-food restaurants, planning the number of tellers in a bank, or the number of pharmacists in a busy pharmacy. Planning should be such that it provides the infrastructure for peak times and a mechanism for adjusting the level of the labor force to vary by load.
- **Transferring load to low load periods.** An appropriate pricing or reward policy can divert some of the demand to low load periods. Examples include the pricing policies of airlines and phone companies.
- **Using temporary help.** Peak times are characterized by lack of production or service resources in certain distinct periods. Using temporary

help can remedy these situations. For example, tax firms hire temporary help during tax season and restaurants hire temporary help during lunch breaks.

In a work environment with obvious peak times, some resources are at excess capacity most of the time and in shortage during the peak times. As a result, management must handle two types of policy: one for times of excess capacity and one for shortage of resources. In emergency departments (EDs) of hospitals, there is a big variation in arrival times between day and night. These departments are managed with excess capacity during the day and as operating under resource constraints during the night. Also, EDs and other healthcare systems must instill procedures for the extra-high load resulting from mass terror attacks or wars.

Where Should the Constraint Be Located?

An important strategic issue is determining where the system constraint should be located. Until now, we considered situations with a given system, and the goal was to improve it. To strategically plan the best place for the constraint, we must consider three strategic questions about the resources of the organization:

1. Where should the constraint be?
2. Where is the constraint now?
3. How can we transfer the constraint to the proper place?

The first question of where the constraint should be can be broken down into two parts:

- Does the constraint have to be an internal one (resource constraint) or external (market constraint)?
- If the constraint is a resource constraint, which resource should be the constraint?

The advantages of placing the constraint inside the system as an internal bottleneck are obvious: savings in resources and control over demand and over the system. This translates into the ability to sort and screen orders, customers, services, and products and to better control the planning and implementation. In this case, the cost of the system and the cost of operating it are relatively low. On the other hand, the firm misses out on business opportunities due to lack of capacity and allows competitors to enter the market. A situation of choosing a resource constraint is appropriate for firms that have a critical or highly expensive resource whose capacity is difficult to increase. Namely, it creates a strategic advantage for the organization and is one of its core competencies.

If indeed the decision is to have a resource constraint, the constraint should be in the most critical or most expensive resource in the system.

Example: in a large public hospital, management has decided that the constraint of the ED will be the ED specialists. This resulted in analyzing the ED specialists and offloading them by nurses, physician assistants, and so on.

The question of where the constraint should be leads to an equally important question: Where should the constraint **not** be?

In today's competitive market, the constraint should nearly always not be in operations. Moreover, we should not reach the point where operations are the system constraint. Operations are a function that can usually be expanded or have some of its tasks given to subcontractors. When production is based on standard processes, operations should not be a system constraint. The role of the head of operations in a business firm is to make operations transparent to decision makers; that is, operations will see to it that the needed quantities will be produced at the predetermined timetables, and at the required quality. Operations will thus contribute its share to strategy and the business success of the firm. Good and effective operations are a complex and complicated issue; hence, transparency for decision makers is difficult. To achieve this, operations should have protective capacity and may occasionally be at excess capacity. Production plants in Japan realized this from accumulated experience, and they are designing their production lines with an excess capacity of about 30%. Protective capacity is just one way to create transparent operations. The appropriate implementation of the managerial approaches described in earlier chapters is a necessary condition for achieving a situation where operations are not a system constraint.

The advantages of having a market constraint (excess capacity) are the disadvantage of being in a state of resource constraints: an organization with excess capacity does not give up on orders and on opportunities for increasing output. This has strategic importance: giving up market share because of a resource constraint allows competitors to enter the market, which poses a threat to the organization in the long run. Excess capacity can also help the firm to deal with occasional demands and large contracts and to exploit market opportunities.

Having a market constraint, however, carries a higher price tag as the investment in resources costs more. A market constraint is more appropriate for organizations where resource costs are not big.

An organization must also examine whether research and development, marketing, and sales are indeed permanent bottlenecks. In situations where these departments are not bottlenecks, the causes should be examined at the strategic and tactical levels.

CHAPTER SUMMARY

Sales and marketing personnel are a permanent bottleneck in an organization. To increase their output, we must deal with their efficiency and effectiveness. Efficiency of the sales force can be achieved by reducing their noneffective time. Effectiveness will be achieved by focusing on existing and potential high-value customers through strategic gating. The seven steps of management by constraints, in addition to product differentiation and market segmentation, can increase the contribution of sales and enhance the value of the organization.

CHAPTER 7

Focused Current Reality Tree

OBJECTIVES

- Appreciate how many undesirable effects are caused by a very few core problems.
- How to identify the root problems of the organization.

A current reality tree is a novel focusing tool based on logical thinking (Dettmer, 1998; Goldratt, 1994). The tool is used to identify the **core problems** in the organization. The underlying assumption is that the organization has a few core problems, and most of the other problems are symptoms of the core problems. If we solve the core problems, then many of the other problems will be solved as well.

The objectives of the tool are:

- Identifying the core problems of the organization, the system, or subsystem.
- Deepening the understanding that every system has a **small** number of core problems and that they are the cause of **most** problems.
- Improving communication channels among managers in the organization.

When a patient goes to her doctor for a check-up and complains about various symptoms (headaches, perspiration, high fever), a good doctor will try to find the patient's core problems and treat them.

A graph of a focused current reality tree (fCRT) is a graph depicted as a logical tree describing cause–outcome relations among the problems of the organization (Ronen & Pass, 2008). A template for a fCRT is given in Figure 7.1.

Focused current reality tree (fCRT)—a graphic tool for identification of the core problems of the system or organization.

USING A fCRT

Principles of Constructing a fCRT

Constructing a fCRT can be done by a single manager or by a team. As the use of the tool is subjective and organizational problems look differently from different perspectives, it is better to construct the fCRT by a team of managers and employees.

The fCRT is usually constructed by managers and employees of the organization and occasionally by an outside consulting group called in to diagnose the organization's problems.

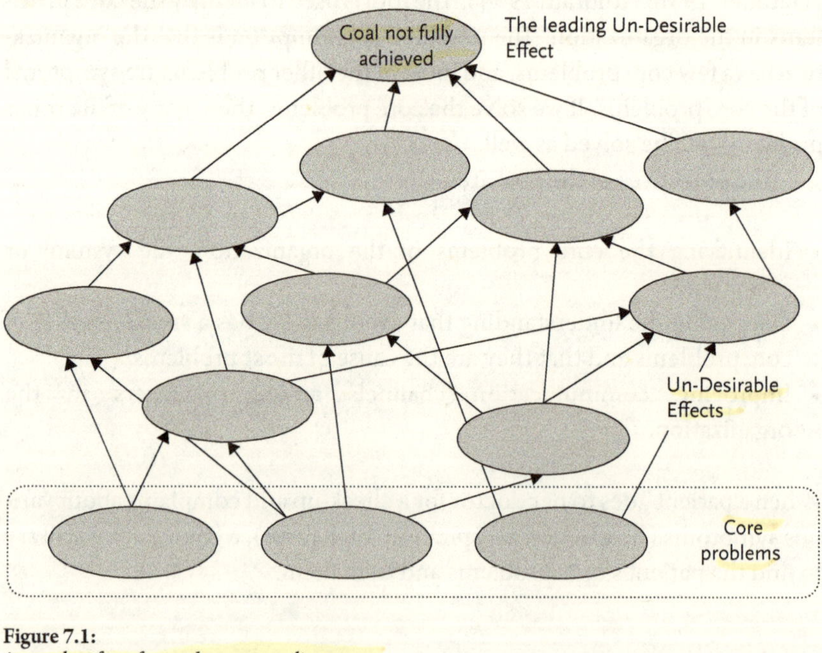

Figure 7.1:
A template for a focused current reality tree

Information Sources

The information sources for constructing a fCRT are:

- Personal knowledge of managers and employees.
- Interviews with managers and employees.
- Visits to the firm's or organization's sites.
- Balance sheets, marketing reports, operations reports, and other reports in the organization.
- Interviews with customers and suppliers.

Listing of Undesirable Effects

For a phenomenon to be considered an undesirable effect (UDE) and to be included in the fCRT, three conditions must be satisfied.

UDE—an **undesirable effect**

---

1. The phenomenon must **exist.**
2. The phenomenon must be **undesirable.**
3. The phenomenon must be **under our control or influence**.

The third condition is especially important. A statement like "Winters are too cold" (and therefore more patients are expected in the emergency department) will not enter the analysis as a UDE—we have no control over the weather and cannot influence it.

On the other hand, there are phenomena beyond our control, but we do influence them. For example, "Many customers leave our health maintenance organization" is a legitimate UDE. Competition is a predominantly affecting abandonment, but we also have a strong **influence** on customer abandonment.

UDEs will always be written as **negative** statements.

The Leading UDE

The list of UDEs will always include the leading UDE, which expresses the fact that we are not achieving the goal. In business organizations, the leading UDE will be expressed as "The value of the firm is not sufficiently enhanced." In other organizations, the leading UDE could simply be stated in the form of "Goal not fully achieved." For example, the chief medical director of a hospital can list the leading UDE as "The number of hospital deaths is too high."

All UDEs in a fCRT will relate, directly or indirectly, to the leading UDE. When an issue is categorized as an UDE, it means that this issue contributes to the leading UDE of not achieving the goal.

Focusing on the Important UDEs

For an analysis using the fCRT to be simple and fast, we should limit our focus to 8 to 14 UDEs. Brainstorming, interviews, and examination of documents and reports usually result in too many UDEs. The reduction of the number of UDEs can be done in one of two ways:

- Aggregation of similar UDEs under one UDE.
- Deletion of UDEs that are less important relative to others on the list.

Finding Logical Relations among UDEs

Cause–Effect Relation

A cause–effect relation between UDEs will be depicted as an arrow leading from the UDE that is the cause up to the UDE that is the outcome. Figure 7.2 describes graphically a causal relation between two UDEs.

An example of a cause–effect relation is presented in Figure 7.3.

An **extensive "or" relation** is presented in Figure 7.4.

When an extensive "or" relationship exists, then when **both** UDE A **and** UDE B exist, UDE C is realized much more severely. An example is presented in Figure 7.5.

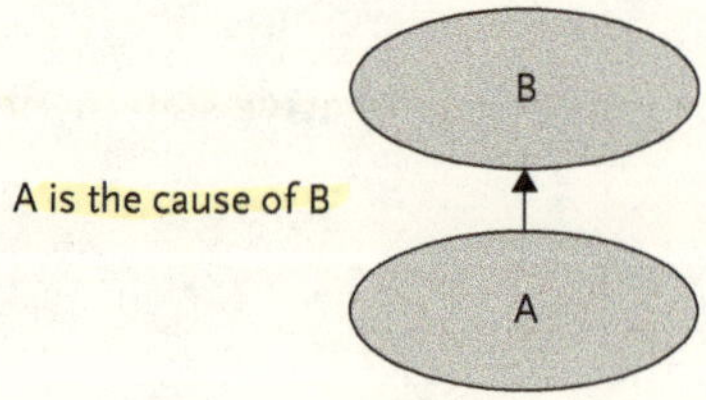

Figure 7.2:
Cause–outcome relation between undesirable effects

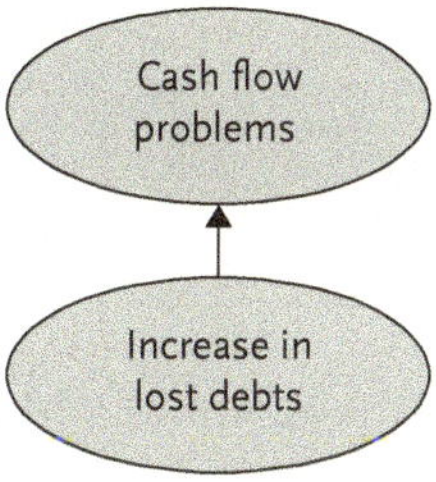

Figure 7.3:
Example for cause–outcome relation between undesirable effects

When the price is higher than competitors' prices, customers abandon. When the performance of the product is inferior, customers abandon. If both UDEs happen (high price **and** poor performance), more customers abandon the system.

An **"and" relation** is depicted in Figure 7.6.

The advantage of identifying such an "and" logical relation is that it is enough to solve either problem A or problem B to avoid problem C. There is no need to deal with both A and B. An example is presented in Figure 7.7.

The contribution volume in the example dropped greatly because of the coexistence of the two UDEs: the contribution per unit dropped and the number of units sold did not increase. It is enough to deal with one of these UDEs to solve the problem of decreasing contribution volume.

Loop Relation

UDE A is the cause for B, UDE B is the cause for C, and UDE C is the cause for A. This is depicted in Figure 7.8.

An example of a loop relation is presented in Figure 7.9.

Inferences

Inferences are explanations or conclusions and insights that were not included in the UDEs. These are usually logical relations that explain

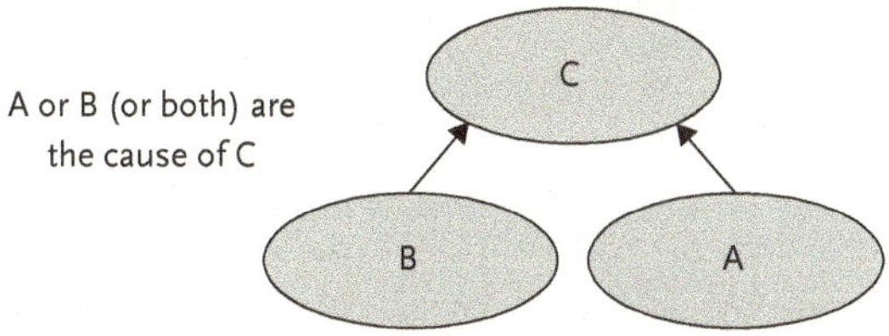

Figure 7.4:
Logical relation of "extensive or"

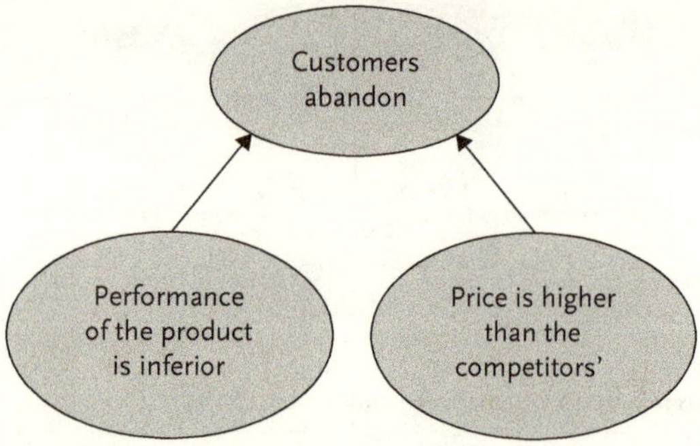

Figure 7.5:
An example of an "extensive or" logical relation

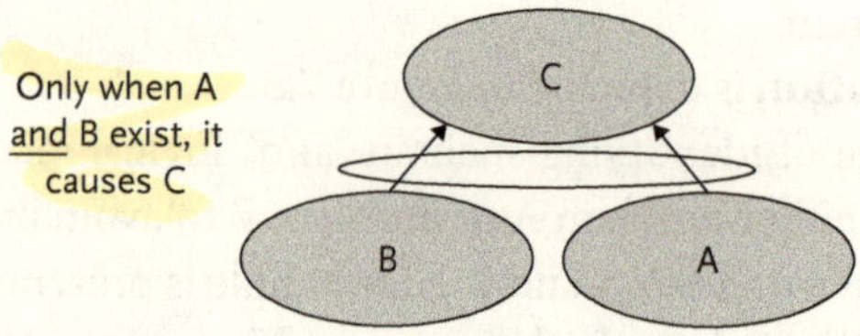

Figure 7.6:
Logical "and" relation

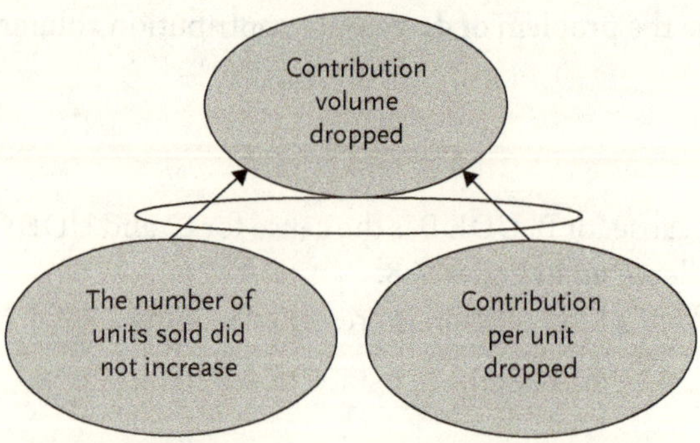

Figure 7.7:
An example of an "and" logical relation

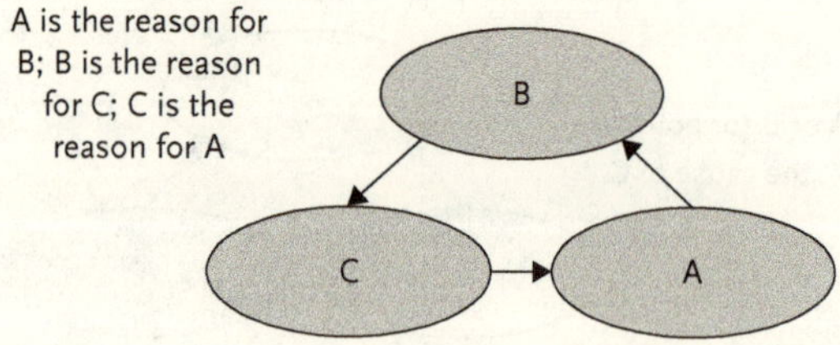

Figure 7.8:
Logical loop relation

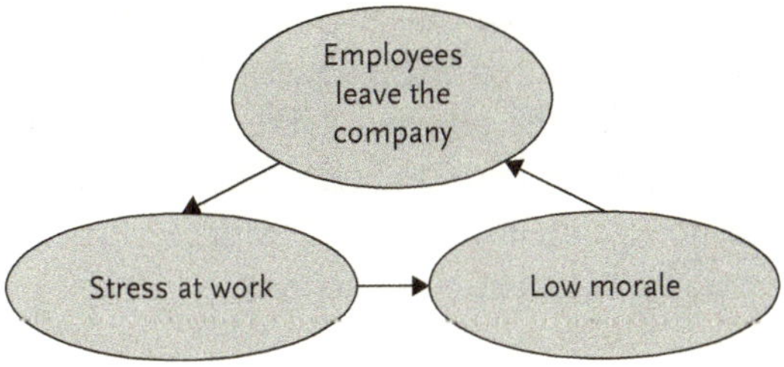

Figure 7.9:
Example of a loop relation

nontrivial relations among UDEs. Relations will be drawn as rectangles (see Figure 7.10).

Constructing a fCRT

Construction of the fCRT begins with the leading UDE. Under the leading UDE, we will position all the UDEs that were identified as direct causes for the leading UDE, and they will be linked by cause–effect arrows. We will add, layer by layer, the UDEs that are causes for the previously included UDEs. As needed, we will add inferences that explain nontrivial relations among UDEs and insights learned during the tree construction. At the end of the process, we will have at the bottom of the tree a small number of UDEs that have no other UDEs that are causing them. These are the **core problems**.

Identifying Core Problems

At the end of constructing the fCRT, we are left with a small number of core problems. Core problems could be UDEs or inferences that we infer to be core problems. The number of core problems is small, usually one to

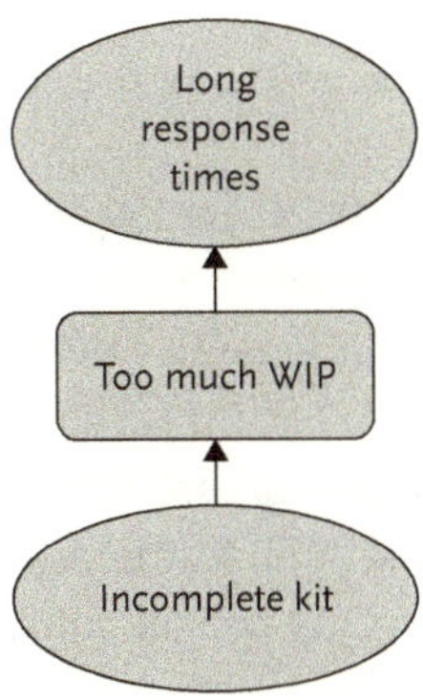

Figure 7.10:
Example for inference

three. If we end up with many UDEs at the bottom of the tree, we can try to think of a factor or issue that can be the cause for most them. This inferred UDE will be listed under the previous UDEs, linked to them by causal links, and it will be the real core problem. Core problems can therefore be UDEs or inferences (conclusions of the team constructing the fCRT).

Examples of core problems in organizations:

- A manager/management that is too centralized.
- Lack of a clear strategy.
- Unstructured processes.
- Inappropriate performance measures.
- Lack of focus.
- The company is driven by technological thinking rather than by business thinking.
- Gap between professional and managerial abilities.

Exercising Orthogonal Control

Orthogonal control is an independent validation of core problems. After the core problems have been identified, we must ask the question: "If we solve the core problems, will the leading UDE significantly change?"

For example, a core problem in a fCRT was identified as "lack of focus." Will solving this problem significantly enhance the value of the firm? If the answer is "yes," this is indeed a core problem, and it must be dealt with. If not, the tree should be reexamined.

Example of a fCRT

Figure 7.11 presents a typical fCRT.

Advantages and Disadvantages of Using the fCRT

The advantages of using the fCRT are the simplicity of the tool and the ability to focus on the core problems. The tool enables better communication within the organization and enables distinction between a symptom (UDE) and a core problem.

The disadvantage of the fCRT is that it is a subjective tool. This disadvantage can be reduced by having a team construct the fCRT, especially if the team is interdisciplinary. Orthogonal control also helps diminish this disadvantage.

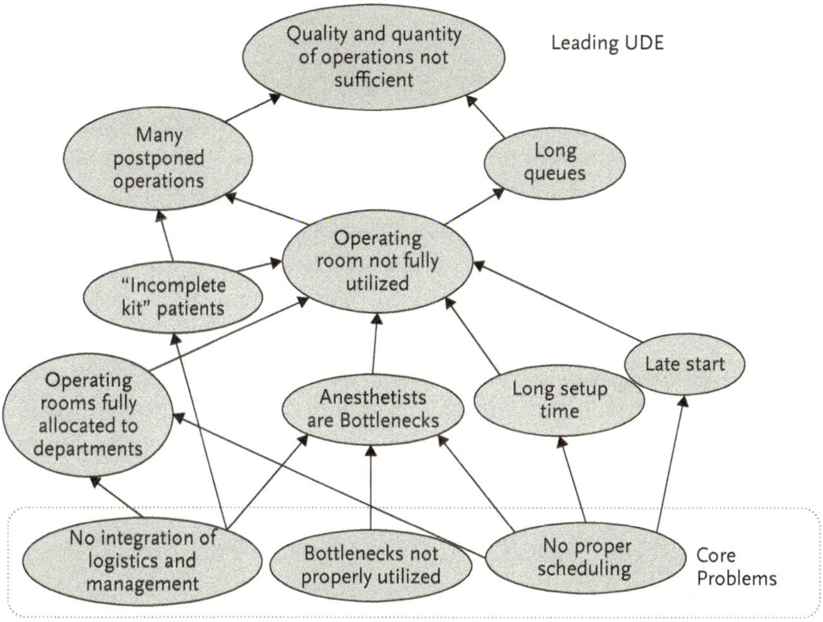

Figure 7.11:
An example of a typical focused current reality tree

The Routine Use of a fCRT

1. Collect information about the problems in the organization (personal knowledge of managers, interviews with managers and workers, site visits, analyzing reports and documents, interviews with customers and suppliers).
2. Articulate the **leading UDE** of the organization. In a business organization, the leading UDE is "Value enhancement of the organization is insufficient." In other organizations, one must determine the organizational goal and accordingly state the leading UDE.
3. List the main UDEs (8–14 UDEs).
4. Arrange the UDEs in cause–effect relations where the leading UDE is at the top.
5. Identify the **core problems** of the organization or unit (not more than three).
6. Apply orthogonal control. Ask yourself: "Will solving each of the identified core problems significantly improve the **leading UDE**?"
7. Make a list of action items that will deal with the core problems. Use a focusing table and a focusing matrix.

THE CORE COMPETENCES TREE

The core competences tree (CCT) is a logical tree that shows the interrelationships among the various competences of an organization and is aimed at identifying the core competences. The process of building a CCT as demonstrated in this chapter's case study is similar to the process of building an fCRT (as previously described in this chapter).

Take 8 to 12 very desirable effects, which are the competences that enhance the value of the organization. Links among the very desirable effects reflect managerial insights and logic. The leading very desirable effects of the organization is "The organization has achieved much of its goal" or, in for-profit organizations, "Shareholders' value increased." At the bottom of the CCT, identify one to three core competences that are the strategic competences of the organization. These core competences are considered strategic because they represent those strengths that should be continuously augmented and supported by the whole organization. See an example in Figure 7.12.

Following the CCT analysis, define the **conservation strategy** for the core competences of the organization. The most effective action items should be selected with the aid of the focusing table and the focusing matrix.

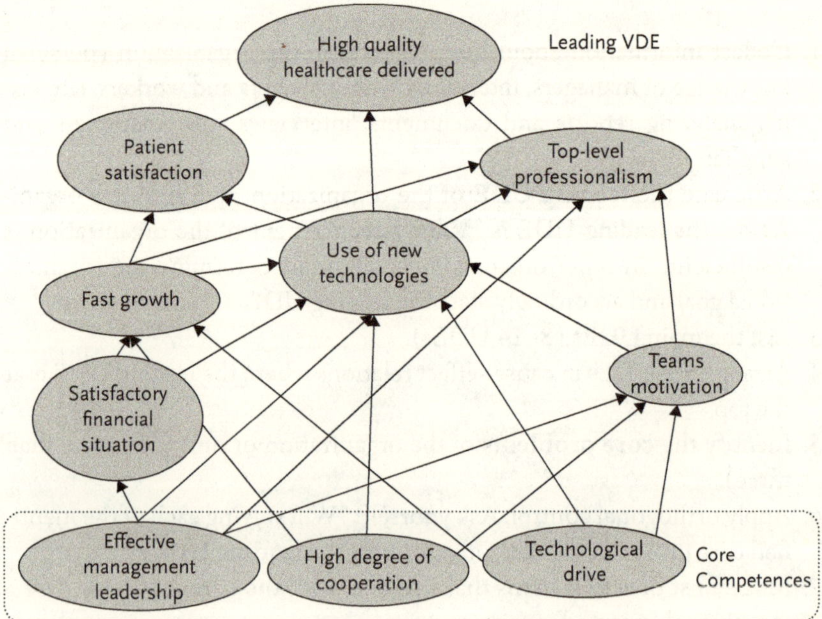

Figure 7.12:
An example of a core competences tree

CHAPTER SUMMARY

An fCRT is a simple tool for detecting the core problems of the organization. This tool provides the insight that the organization only has a small number of core problems, and solving them will enhance the value of the organization. The fCRT also serves as a communication tool within the organization. As this is a subjective tool, it is recommended that it be constructed by interdisciplinary teams.

A CCT is the complementary tool for identification and focusing of the strengths of the organization.

CHAPTER 8

Resolving Managerial Conflicts

OBJECTIVE

- Understand the nature of managerial conflicts and how to resolve them in win–win ways.

The Webster dictionary defines conflict as "a prolonged struggle; a trial of strength; strong disagreement". We will focus on those managerial conflicts where the opposing alternatives have a **common goal**.

Conflict—a clash between two alternative actions that have a common goal.

For example:

- Decentralization versus centralization. *Example:* centralization of management within a health maintenance organization (HMO) versus decentralization of management to individual clinics.
- A large variety of services or products versus a limited variety. For example, center for women's health may offer comprehensive health care services vs. only gynecological ones.
- Developing a generic future product versus developing a specific product requested by a customer.
- Opposing policies—for example, in the emergency department of a hospital, a policy of comprehensive medical examination versus a policy of quick decisions on either admission or discharge.

We will use the following three-step methodology to deal with managerial conflicts:

1. Describe the conflict with a conflict resolution diagram (CRD) (Goldratt, 1994).
2. Solve the conflict by challenging the assumptions on the CRD with the following approaches:
   - Differentiation
   - Globalization
   - Breaking assumptions
3. Create actions for implementation based on ideas resulting from the attempted challenging mechanisms.

Let us consider, for example, a situation involving a basket of services. An HMO is considering offering a large basket of services, procedures, and medications versus offering a limited variety. Every alternative has its own advantages. Offering a large variety can improve contribution and enhance the value of the HMO. Offering only a limited variety allows for focusing, specialization, and cost reduction. Both alternative actions create value for the HMO. The common goal, of course, is value enhancement.

A conflict is sometimes dealt with erroneously by searching for a compromise using various optimization techniques. In the previous example, an optimization tool may suggest an exact optimal solution of offering—for example, exactly 17 services and procedures. Using such compromise solution will cause us to lose the advantage of diversification with a large variety as well the advantages of focusing and quality achieved with a small variety.

The suggested methodology solves conflicts in one of two ways:

1. Generating a solution that will preserve most of the advantages of each alternative and will reduce the disadvantages of each. This is a win–win approach. It can be achieved through differentiation, globalization, and breaking of assumptions. Identifying win–win solutions is not assured, but experience shows that it is frequently possible.
2. Presenting one alternative as irrelevant as it is based on wrong assumptions. Hence, there is no real conflict.

Figure 8.1 summarizes the approaches to deal with conflicts.

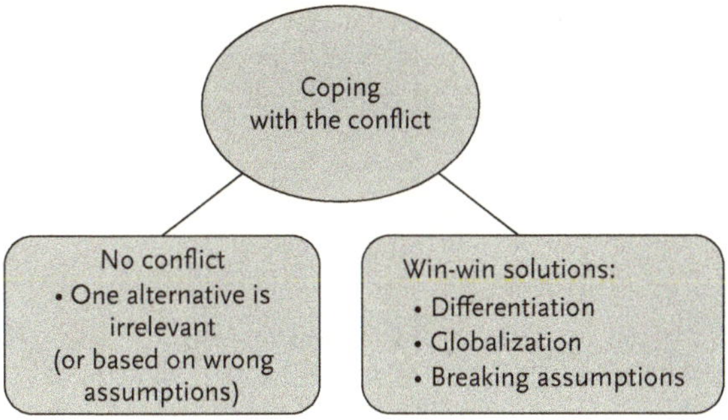

Figure 8.1:
Dealing with conflicts

STEPS IN DEALING WITH MANAGERIAL CONFLICTS

Drawing the Conflict Resolution Diagram

The conflict resolution diagram (CRD) is an important communication tool to present conflicts and try to solve them. The following elements appear in the CRD:

- The goal of the system or subsystem.
- The two alternatives that create the conflict.
- The advantages of each alternative, or the need for each, based on the system's goal.
- The various elements are logically linked: Arrows 1, 2, 3, and 4 represent conditional relations, and arrow 5 depicts the alleged impossibility of simultaneously satisfying both alternatives.

The basic structure of a CRD is presented in Figure 8.2.

The assumptions in the CRD are:

- Assumption 1—The advantages of alternative A contribute to achieving the goal.
- Assumption 2—The advantages of alternative B contribute to achieving the goal.
- Assumption 3—Action based on alternative A brings the advantages for achieving the goal.
- Assumption 4—Action based on alternative B brings the advantages for achieving the goal.
- Assumption 5—Alternatives A and B **cannot** be realized simultaneously.

The CRD of the HMO services variety example is presented in Figure 8.3.

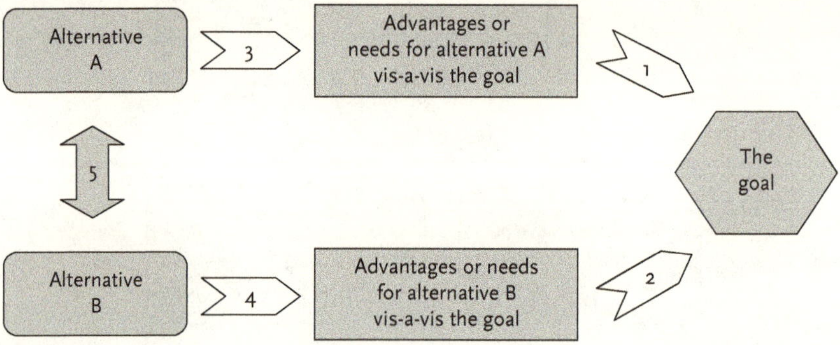

Figure 8.2:
The generic conflict resolution diagram

Conflict Resolution

We will now demonstrate conflict resolution using:

- Differentiation.
- Globalization.
- Breaking of assumptions.

Differentiation

We will illustrate the conflict resolution via the differentiation mechanism using the previous service (or product) variety conflict example.

A Pareto analysis of the various services shows that 20% of services account for 80% of the HMO's profits. The inclination is to offer the entire variety of services to the HMO members. However, the services of group A in the Pareto analysis will be provided by the HMO **itself**, while group B and C services will be provided through **subcontractors.**

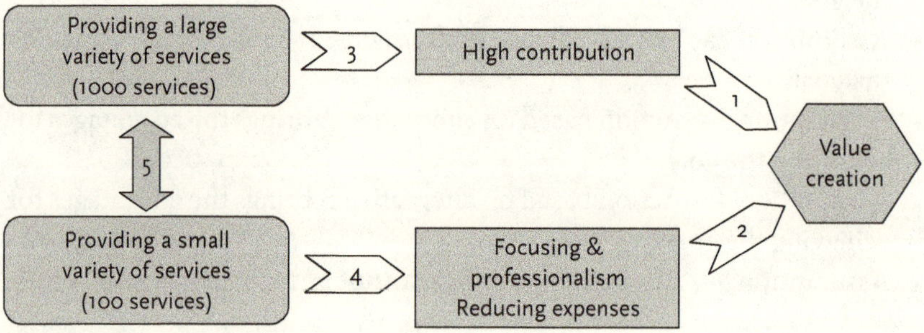

Figure 8.3:
A conflict resolution diagram for services variety

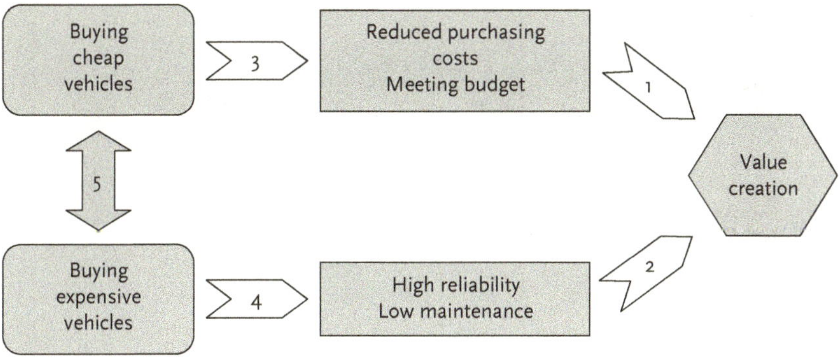

Figure 8.4:
A conflict resolution diagram for the car fleet example

Globalization

Globalization is demonstrated by the following example. A large public organization had to renew its fleet of cars. The conflict was whether to buy low-price cars or more expensive yet reliable ones.

The CRD is presented in Figure 8.4.

Considering at the car purchases from a global perspective, we should assess the life cycle cost (LCC) of the fleet. This is an expansion (or globalization) of the time horizon. Analysis shows that from the LCC perspective, buying the expensive cars is actually cheaper. The maintenance and fuel costs, given the high mileage that these cars are expected to drive, make the purchase price only a small part of the LCC. The budget constraint problem was also resolved by agreeing to spread the purchase price over a period of several years.

In this example, the alternative of buying the low-price cars is irrelevant, and thus there is no conflict.

Breaking Assumptions

- The mechanism for **breaking assumptions** checks the assumptions that exist in every CRD.

We will demonstrate this mechanism using the following example.

The development department of a medical software firm is developing a **special version** of a computerized patient records system for a specific HMO. The conflict that brought on a heated discussion in the weekly management meeting was answering the question: "Should we start development immediately, or should we first spend time to define the project in an orderly and structured manner?" This conflict is presented in Figure 8.5.

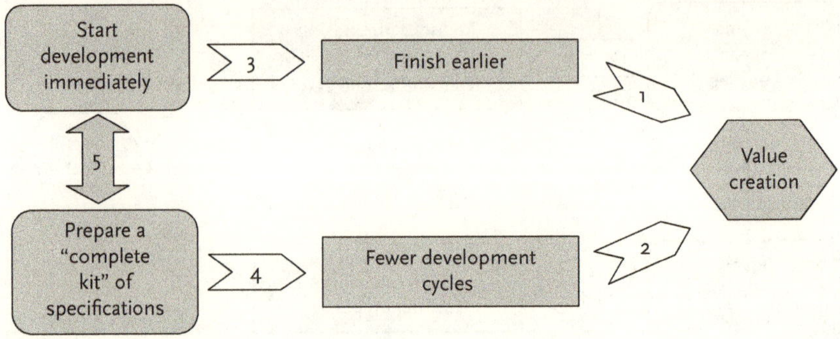

Figure 8.5:
A conflict resolution diagram for software development example

The assumptions at the basis of this conflict are:

- Assumption 1—An early completion of the project enhances the value of the firm.
- Assumption 2—Development in fewer cycles enhances the value of the firm.
- Assumption 3—If we start the project earlier, we will finish it earlier.
- Assumption 4—If we provide orderly definitions for requested changes and all the requirements of the customer, development can be done in fewer development cycles.
- Assumption 5—It is not possible to start development immediately and obtain the complete and structured requirements definition.

To demonstrate that one of the alternatives is not relevant, we will try to break the weakest assumption, which is assumption 3. It is clear that an earlier start of the project doesn't necessarily translate to an earlier completion. If this is the case, the top alternative ("start immediately") is actually irrelevant, and the bottom one should be chosen.

Resolving a conflict by breaking an assumption is called **injection**. The injection is added to the CRD in Figure 8.6.

EXAMPLES OF MANAGERIAL CONFLICTS

Figures 8.7 through 8.14 present some common conflicts in healthcare organizations.

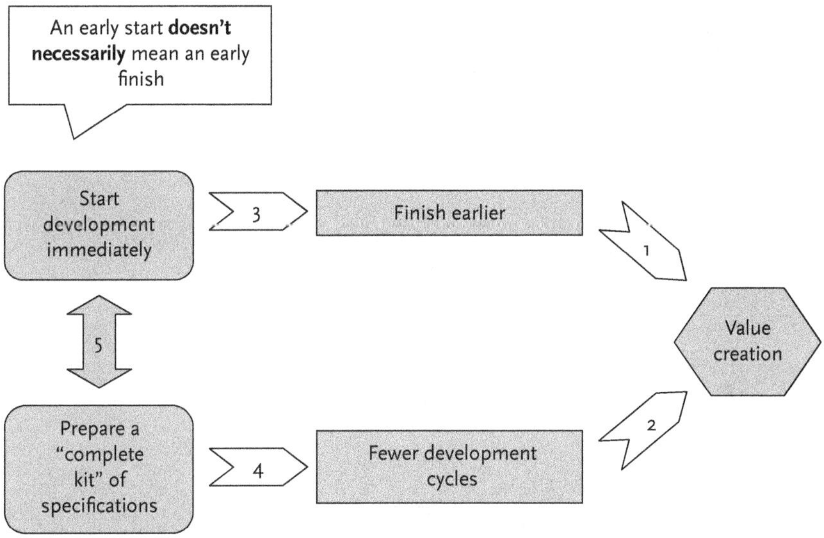

Figure 8.6:
Example of an injection in a conflict resolution diagram

ROUTINE USE OF THE CONFLICT RESOLUTION APPROACH

1. Define the goal of the system or subsystem.
2. Display the conflict in a CRD.
3. Try to resolve the conflict by differentiation, globalization, or breaking of assumptions.
4. When breaking assumptions, add the injection(s) to the CRD.
5. Make a list of action items that will resolve the conflict using a focusing table and focusing matrix.

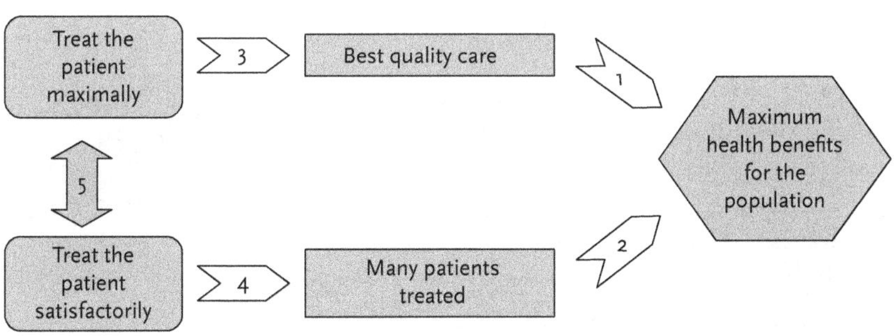

Figure 8.7:
Public hospital outpatient clinic (treating many vs. treating well)

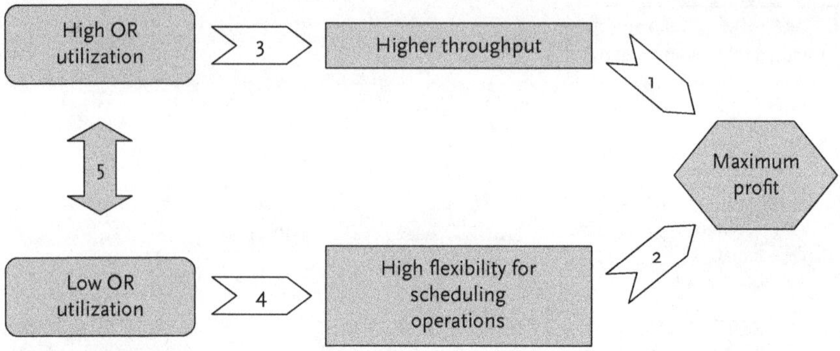

Figure 8.8:
Private hospital operating room scheduling (volume vs. flexibility)

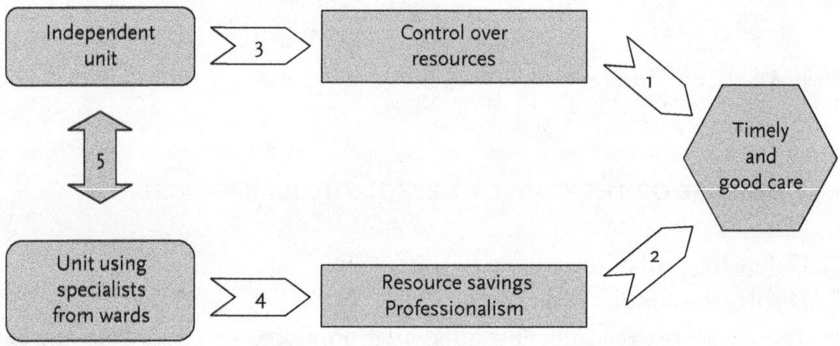

Figure 8.9:
An emergency department conflict (1)

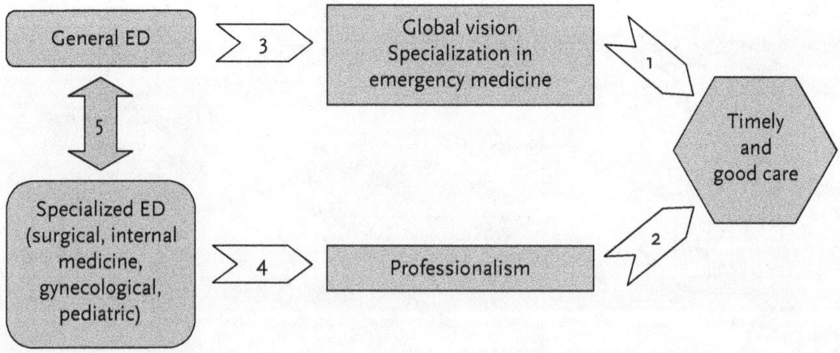

Figure 8.10:
An emergency department conflict (2)

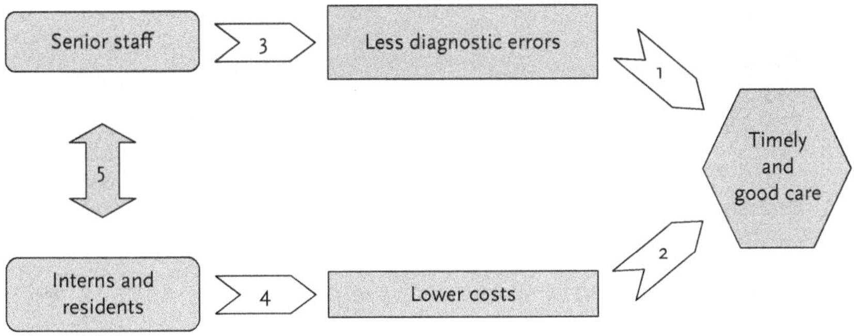

Figure 8.11:
An emergency department conflict (3) (errors vs. cost)

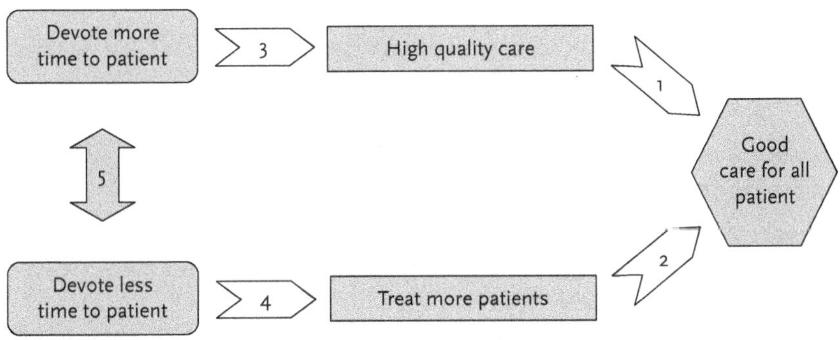

Figure 8.12:
Clinical conflict in diagnosis

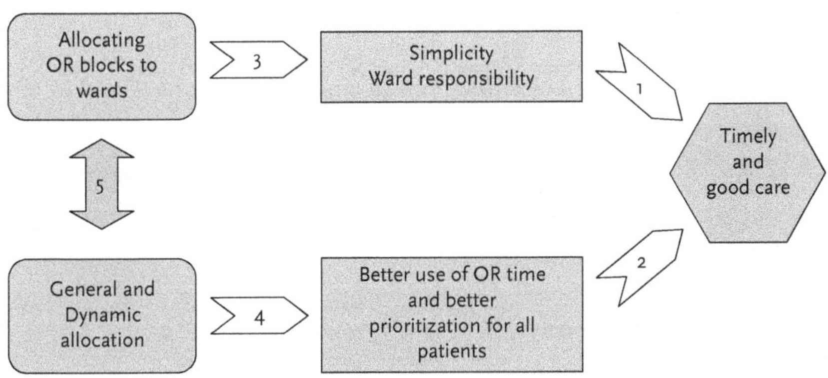

Figure 8.13:
An operating room conflict

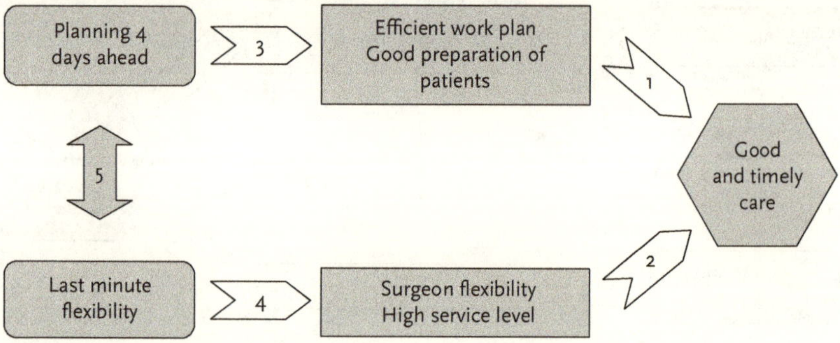

Figure 8.14:
Flexibility conflict in operating room scheduling

THE CAREGIVER CONFLICT

Every caregiver in a healthcare system experiences the conflict as described in Figure 8.15.

STEPS IN CONFLICT RESOLUTION

- Apply differentiation: Use different care policies for different patient segments based on severity of their health condition.
  - Invest about 80% of the resources in population A—20% of patients with a severe condition.
  - Invest about 20% of the resources in populations B and C: the healthier 80% of the population using alternative methods of treatment:

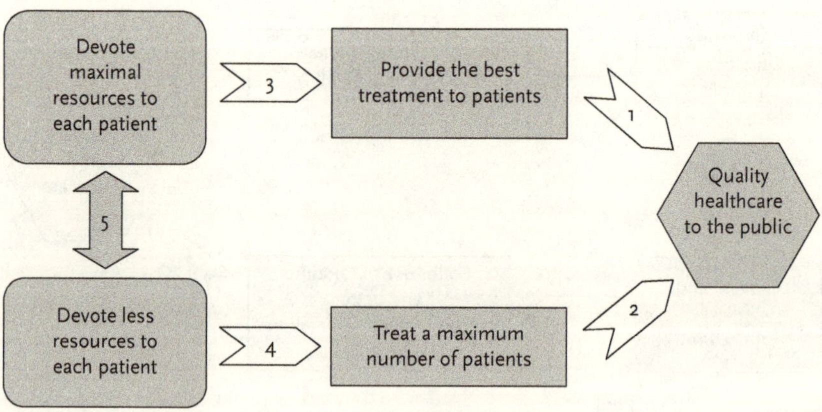

Figure 8.15:
The caregiver conflict

    - Offload the busy physician, giving the required medical treatment by physician assistants, nurses, and so on.
    - Rely on standard treatment procedures.
    - Provide treatment at home.
    - Use community facilities rather than hospital facilities.
- Break assumption 3: Investing more resources does not necessarily lead to better treatment. For example, relying on excessive tests or medical procedures does not necessarily improve the outcome.
- Go to a different dimension: For example, provide treatment through Web communication with patients, telemedicine, artificial intelligence for image interpretation, and so on.

CHAPTER SUMMARY

Managerial conflicts are seemingly contradicting alternatives with a common objective function. Many conflicts can be resolved either through win–win solutions or by showing that one alternative is irrelevant.

Conflict resolution is achieved by displaying the conflict on a CRD and analysis of the CRD using differentiation, globalization, and breaking of assumptions.

CHAPTER 9

The Efficiencies Syndrome

OBJECTIVE

- What are the human aspects of the efficiencies syndrome, its negative effects, and how to avoid it.

In previous chapters, we have seen that the bottlenecks, the critical resources of the organization, must be exploited. The other resources must be subordinated to the constraint.

Experience has shown that management of noncritical resources of an organization is usually associated with a painful policy failure (policy constraint) known as the "efficiencies syndrome" (Goldratt and Cox, 1992). This failure is common among managers and workers of all types of organizations (service, manufacturing, healthcare, development, and nonprofit organizations).

This phenomenon is illustrated by the 1–2–3 process in Figure 9.1.

Efficiencies syndrome—a situation in which there is a desire to operate the noncritical resources **more** than is needed, while emphasizing utilization of inputs rather than focusing on outputs.

Under current conditions, the output of this 1–2–3 process is 50 units per day, and the (capacity) utilization of the resources of the three departments is 50%, 100%, and 67%, respectively.

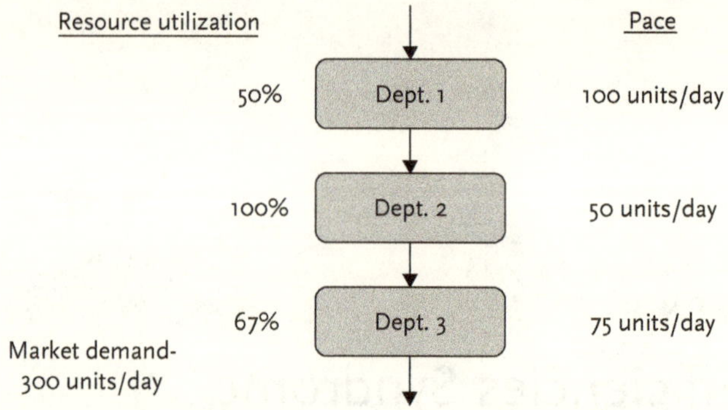

Figure 9.1:
A 1–2–3 process and department utilization

What will happen if the system is measured by the average resource utilization? The average utilization is 72%. To increase the average utilization, workers in department 1 will try to achieve a maximal resource utilization of 100%. As a result, the average utilization will increase to 90%. In department 3, they will also try to increase utilization to 100%, but they are limited by what department 2 (the bottleneck) supplies them.

Even though the average resource utilization increases (from 72% to 90%), the system output has not been improved. On the other hand, overexploiting the other resources may result in undesirable effects on the system, such as:

- People work harder without increasing effective output.
- Deterioration of the control of what is important.
- Decrease in the quality of decisions.
- Increase in the amount of work in process inventory.
- Resource wastage (personnel and equipment).
- Increase in expenditures.
- Decrease in output.
- A feeling of working harder with declining output, leading to loss of confidence in management.

The efficiencies syndrome results from behavior of managers and workers:

1. Fear of looking lazy. Western culture views an idle person as being lazy. Thus, one must work or at least look like he is working.
2. Fear of being transferred or laid off.
3. Lack of a global vision and a belief that fully utilizing resources contributes to achieving the goal.

4. Lack of distinction between critical resources (bottlenecks) and non-critical resources (having excess capacity).
5. Feeling that purchasing of equipment or hiring of personnel must be justified.
6. Measuring systems by inputs (as is reflected in local-view premiums, norms, and incentives).
7. Measuring systems by resource utilization.
8. Desire to look important and busy.

Example: In a large public hospital OR utilization was the primary measure for the ORs. As a result, many activities that should have been performed before the patient entered the OR where performed in the OR, resulting in increased utilization. For example, verifying that all test results are available.

Example: In the customer service department of a hospital, there was a need for an additional sophisticated computer for a newly hired data entry operator. Management declined the request on grounds that the utilization of the other computers was low, and several operators could share a computer. The result was that one of the operators spent time writing an application that is busy duplicating files, just to increase the capacity utilization of the computers in hope of justifying the need for another one.

Example: A worker in a firm told the following story: "In the morning we throw out the garbage from the garbage cans onto the floor, and we start sweeping the floor. When the boss arrives, he is reassured that we are busy."

Example: A large organization experienced the "neon effect." All the workers were eager to show that they work late. The neon lights were left on until the late hours of the evening (even when the workers were not there). The hours of lighted offices were perceived as a measure of workers' diligence and their importance to the system. In this organization, it was known that some of the managers call their subordinates' offices at very late hours, without any necessity, just so they know that the boss may be looking for them late.

Example: In a nonprofit organization, all meetings begin at 10:00 PM because before that everybody seems busy.

Example: In a high-tech organization, management decided to evaluate the capacity utilization of newly purchased equipment. They generated comparative data on utilization on similar machines in various departments. As a result, workers kept the engines of the machines running even during calibration, eventually resulting in serious damage to some machines.

Example: In a newly created start-up firm, everybody works from early morning to late night, as this is the customary culture in similar companies.

The efficiencies syndrome is responsible for "stretching time" and the "drawer effect" where the worker makes sure she has some work to do at "times of trouble" (when she must justify her existence).

Example: In the repair shop of instruments in a hospital, technicians always leave aside a few defective instruments before trying to diagnose their problems. They use these as an "alibi" for keeping busy during days when they don't have other repairs.

DEALING WITH THE EFFICIENCIES SYNDROME

The failure of the efficiencies syndrome is rather clear and is an example of "system chaos." This phenomenon does not exist with individuals as private people: nobody judges their car use by its utilization but rather by its effectiveness. People do not expect their computers to work all the time.

We must shift our orientation to measuring throughput and learn to live with the fact that noncritical resources should be idle some of the time, especially if they want to be able to achieve fast response times.

What should a worker do during idle times?

- Flexible training and self-learning.
- Activities for process improvement and quality management.
- Shift departments to help at bottlenecks.
- Shift work from the bottleneck departments to less busy departments.
- Preventive maintenance.

From a global perspective, a product or service line does not have to be balanced in terms of its capacity. The line contains different resources, some cheap, some expensive. It is not expected that the capacity utilization of the clerical or cleaning staff in a clinic will be the same as the capacity utilization of the expensive resources like physicians and nurses. It is inconceivable that a cheap worker will be a bottleneck and will bring the whole system to a halt. Hence, line balancing does not stand the test of reality. Because of fluctuations, there is an extra motivation to create some **excess capacity** in some resources, as we will discuss further in chapter 14.

However, the existence of excess capacity in the system, which is important for the system and its throughput, could be suddenly removed, thus hurting the system if people somehow contract the efficiencies syndrome. This could lead to non-bottleneck resources becoming system constraints. A good manager should be able to deal with the efficiencies syndrome and find appropriate solutions. It is not easy to deal with this syndrome, and it requires a common language and a common managerial approach for managers and employees.

Example: In many hospitals, the common measure for operating room (OR) performance is capacity utilization, measured in percentage. This is their measure of efficiency, and they promote actions to increase utilization. The correct measure should be throughput, and it should be measured directly. This is usually difficult to measure so they resort to measuring utilization.

If utilization is the goal, it is easy to reach 100%. In some ORs, the system encourages bringing patients into the OR and only then verifying that they are entering with a complete kit. This keeps the OR "busy" and contributes to "efficiency." There are cases where at the end of surgery, the senior surgeon instructs the junior surgeons to "take their time with suturing."

An extreme example to achieve 100% utilization is to have a very slow surgeon start operating in the morning and telling him to finish late in the afternoon.

The correct measure should be throughput. If the case mix of surgeries is rather stable, then the number of operations is the appropriate measure. In other cases, one should weight the number of surgeries by their complexity to achieve weighted throughput.

It should be mentioned, however, that measuring the efficiencies/loads of resources is very important as long as it is used for long-term resources planning and not used for motivating employees and managers to strive for high efficiencies or for justifying layoffs.

CHAPTER SUMMARY

The efficiencies syndrome causes human resources and equipment to work **more** than necessary. This syndrome is fueled by managerial and cultural factors. The desire to show that one is busy, taking a local perspective, and inappropriate measurement, all lead to enhancing this syndrome.

Resolving the syndrome requires a change in organizational thinking, which is not easy to implement.

CHAPTER 10

The "Evils" of Long Response Times

OBJECTIVE

- Understand the many negative effects of long response times and high levels of work in process (WIP).

Long response times for service, production, and development processes are a major concern in today's management world. To find ways to shorten these response times, we will examine in this chapter the relation between response time and the amount of WIP inventory.

TYPES OF INVENTORIES

The management of physical inventories (hardware, components, materials, documents, files, etc.) and nonphysical and human inventories (software applications in development, business information in processing, patients hospitalized or waiting for tests, customers waiting in a bank, etc.) plays an important role in the management of business systems, operational systems, healthcare systems and nonprofit systems.

There are three types of inventories as shown in Figure 10.1.

Raw materials—materials, components, information, tasks, and so on before they enter the system for processing. Tasks that have not yet been handled.

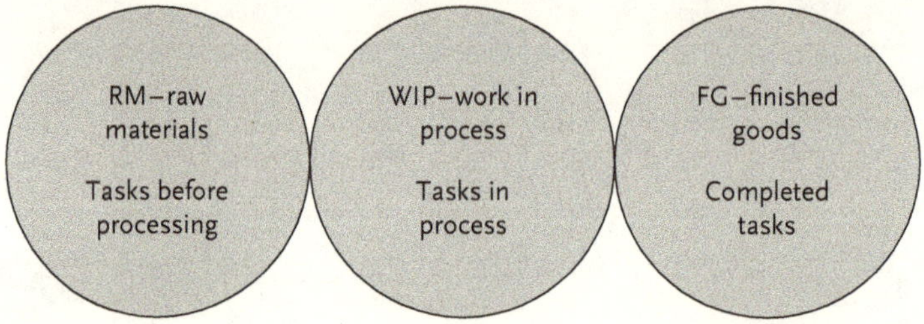

Figure 10.1:
Types of inventories

Work in process (WIP)—intermediate products or tasks that their handling has started but not yet completed. Tasks in process.

Examples of WIP:

- Patients being treated in the emergency department.
- Software applications in development.
- Purchase orders in the negotiating process or in stages of approval.
- Receipts handled in the accounting department.
- Patients waiting for treatment in an oncology outpatient clinic.
- Equipment and instruments being repaired in the maintenance department.

Note: This chapter will focus only on WIP. Methods for managing WIP are different from those for managing raw materials or finished goods. Applying the concepts and considerations for WIP management to other inventory types can harm the organization.

Finished goods—Products, information and tasks whose processing has been completed. Completed missions.

THE "EVILS" OF WIP

Figure 10.2 presents two imaging/testing centers of two competing health maintenance organizations. The clinics are similar and perform identical functions. This example is relevant for many types of organizations.

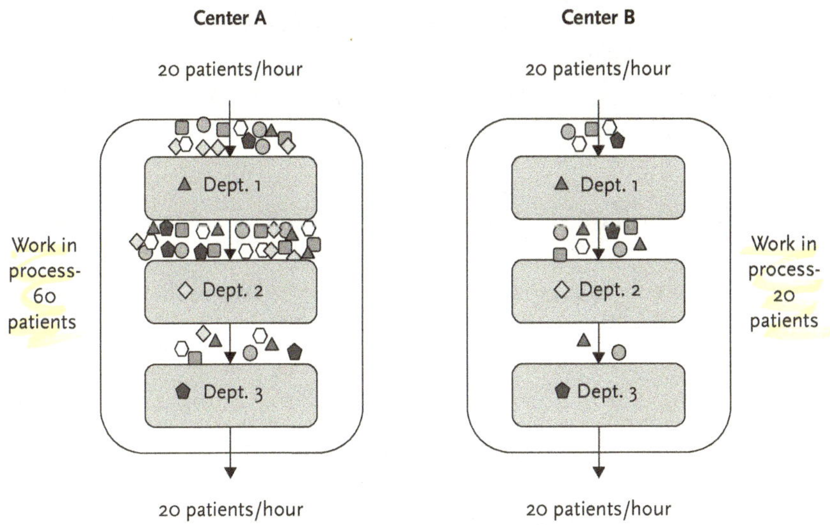

Figure 10.2:
The high work in progress center versus the low work in progress center

Both imaging centers operate in the same market and have similar resources and capabilities. The arrival rate of patients in each center is 20 patients per hour, and the departure rate is also about 20 per hour. The difference between the two centers is the amount of WIP: Center A has 60 patients present in the system, and Center B has 20 patients. These numbers include patients being seen or treated in each department as well as patients waiting before each department. Let us put aside for the moment the reasons causing the difference in the amount of WIP between the two centers and focus on the question, "Does the higher level of WIP in Center A improve or harm this center's performance?"

THE RELATION BETWEEN RESPONSE TIME AND LEVEL OF WIP

High levels of WIP lead to long response times and the average response time of the system is proportional to the WIP level.

The number of patients waiting in Center A is 60 compared to 20 in Center B. On average, the throughput time (time from entry until departure) of a patient arriving in Center A will be three hours (60/20 = 3) while it will be only one hour in Center B (20/20 = 1).

This is calculated according to one of the Little formulas of queuing theory that states that the average response time of the process equals the WIP divided by the system throughput rate. It can be shown that this relation is true for any queue discipline (first in–first out, last in–first out, etc.; see Hillier and Lieberman, 2002).

Let us now examine the gross and net response times of the system.

Gross response time (throughput time) of the process—equals the sum of **processing times (net times)** of the single entity (patient) in the various stations plus the sum of the **waiting times** of the entity (patient) before the various stations.

In most situations, almost all the gross response times originate from waiting times at the various work stations. Treatment/processing times are rather short. Several studies on response times in various service and industry organizations show that the net processing time is only 5% to 10% of the total response time. The experience of the authors shows that in many cases, **work time is no more than 1% of total response time**. Several examples will demonstrate this surprising ratio:

The response time of a process is proportional to the amount of work in process (WIP)—if we reduce the amount of WIP, the response time will be reduced.

"Evils" of work in process (WIP)—the damage to the performance of the organization caused by high levels of WIP. These are the undesirable consequences of high levels of WIP.

"Evils" of a long response time—the damage to the performance of the organization caused by its long response time. These are undesirable consequences resulting from the long response time.

- The average gross time for a patient in a hospital emergency department is about four hours. The total net treatment time is only a few minutes.
- Processing a purchase request for an item, from the request initiation until the order is sent to the supplier, takes several days (gross time). The actual time spent by the purchasing people on the request at the various work stations barely exceeds one hour.
- The process of approving a loan or a mortgage takes several days, while the actual net time spent on the forms and computer screens is no longer than two hours.
- The response time of a subcontractor for fixing a medical instrument is one to two weeks. The net time spent fixing the instrument is in the magnitude of one to two hours.

Because response time is proportional to the amount of WIP, the "evils" of a long response time can be also called the "evils" of WIP.

THE "EVILS" OF A LONG RESPONSE TIME ("EVILS" OF WIP)

Reduction in Throughput

Windows of opportunity for new services or products stay open for only short time periods. An organization with fast response times (for submitting proposals, development, production, arranging business plans, etc.) can realize these opportunities. Furthermore, the faster an organization comes out with new services or products and the shorter the committed response times, the higher are the prices they can get. Innovative products that reach the market fast and ahead of competitors can reap considerable benefits for being first to the market. There are situations where being first to market enables the organization to capture a significant market share, making it difficult for competitors to penetrate the market.

High Operating Expenses

Accumulation of WIP and long response times lead to high operating expenses (inventory carrying costs, maintenance, and control) and additional finance expenses.

Diminished Quality

The longer the response time and the longer the entity stays in WIP status, the more the damage to quality. Two reasons account for this:

1. People and materials with long stays in the process are left unprotected and vulnerable to environmental, physical, mechanical, and other damages. In service units, the quality of decisions and quality of treatment diminish because of the long time that has passed from the beginning of processing until the end. This is especially true if several different employees take part in the processes (e.g., shift changes).
2. In an over-crowded ED, the physicians are under pressure to attend to the many patients, seeing them several times for short durations, thus reducing their effectiveness vis-a-vis each one of them.
3. The longer the response time is, the later the feedback on earlier mistakes arrives to the station responsible for the mistake. The lack of immediate feedback creates a continuous risk of making errors.

Examples:

- The longer a patient spends in the hospital or in a clinic, the more she is exposed to contracting infections.
- Treatment of a claims case is obviously inferior the longer it stays as WIP. This is due to piling up of nonrelevant papers, distraction by other files, and the changing of treating hands.
- The quality of an insurance claim decision or a law court decision diminishes when the claim or the judicial decision was handled by many people or many judges.

Diminished Control

The piling up of WIP allows workers degrees of freedom in selecting preferred tasks to work on. As a result, the control of managers diminishes as well as their ability to dictate priorities. Reducing the amount of WIP allows better and more effective control. Similarly, if there are too many patients crowded in the waiting room, it is impossible for the personnel to notice and response to the deteriorating situation of a patient.

Diminished Cash Flow

A company needs return capital to finance the WIP. Companies with slow response times and large inventories may face a crisis caused by unfavorable cash flow. They are usually required to pay for raw materials within a short time, while payment will be received rather late due to the long response time. A patient discharged earlier results in an increase in cash flow.

Diminished Motivation of Managers and Workers

Managers and workers operating in a high WIP environment with long response times experience frustration resulting from work pressure and frequent shifting from task to task. Facing a continuous situation of not being able to achieve the desired throughput and the temporary frustration from not meeting timetables diminishes motivation of workers and management.

Missed Deadlines

Accumulation of WIP and long response times diminish an organization's ability to meet deadlines and adhere to time-tables.

Lack of Customer Satisfaction

The service, treatment, or products that are delivered late or with inferior quality create customer dissatisfaction. This can lead to loss of customers.

Also, excessively long waiting times create unrest and nervousness among patients and among the accompanying families and friends, which lead to disruptions in the work of the medical stuff and sometimes even to violence.

Diminished Forecasting Capability

Forecasting is important to organizations for planning the human resources, raw materials inventory, developing marketing and sales channels, and cash

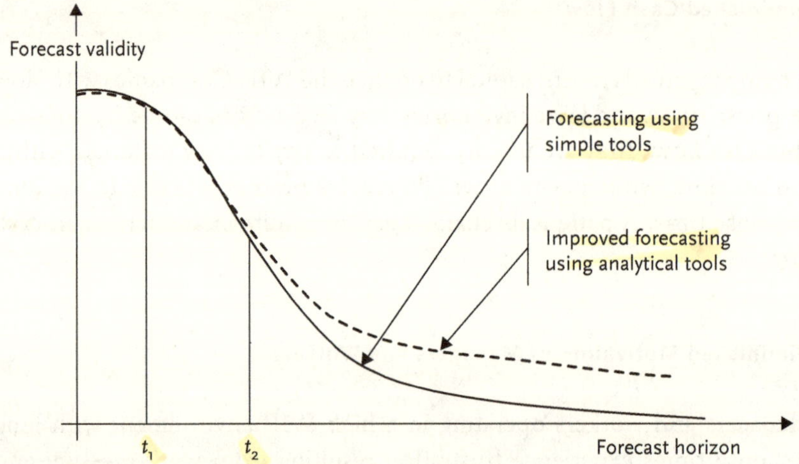

Figure 10.3:
The effect of the forecasting horizon on forecasting validity

flow. Forecasting ability is a function of the forecasting horizon. The relation between the quality of forecasts and the forecasting horizon is presented in Figure 10.3 (Goldratt and Cox, 1992).

Improving forecasting ability through use of analytical and marketing tools can help the organization to some extent. However, reducing system response times will significantly improve forecasting ability. If the system response time is t_2 (weeks or months), then one must forecast the market demand at that time. If the response time is reduced to t_1, the quality for forecasting for market demand will drastically improve. Reducing response time will be achieved by, among other methods, reducing WIP.

Diminished Throughput

High levels of WIP cause system inefficiency, which diminishes throughput. Work that comes in and out of a bottleneck can make the bottleneck ineffective. Jobs that enter the bottleneck not according to schedule, due to lack of control, also diminish system throughput.

Acquired Infections

In hospitals, clinics, and nursing homes, long response times result in high WIP. The longer patients stay in a medical environment and the more patients that are there at any given time, the higher the chances are of acquiring a host of infections, leading to additional morbidity, costs, and mortality along with diminished quality of life.

Example: A firm, specializing in advanced medical testing equipment, won an international contract worth millions of dollars. The firm was characterized by long delays in delivering orders, high production costs, many rejects in quality control and by customers, and problems of management and control. They tried to remedy the situation by introducing technological changes but to no avail. They also considered introducing a sophisticated information systems. A careful analysis of the situation revealed a large amount of WIP, resulting in very long response times. Some components in WIP inventory, when exposed too long to the oxygen and humidity in the air, resulted in excessive oxidation that resulted in component and equipment failure. Once they reduced the WIP inventory and response times, the firm proceeded to produce at high throughput and with near zero failures, to the full satisfaction of customers.

Example: An insurance company offered supplementary health insurance to members of health maintenance organizations. The response time for generating policies was about six weeks from the date the customer signed the request form until the policy took effect. During this long-time period, many potential customers canceled their request. In addition, many files piled up in the office, causing pressure on employees, which resulted in mistakes in writing and approving policies. Some of these mistakes were a result of the file being handled by several different people over the course of several weeks. The reduction of WIP and the resulting reduction in response time yielded higher quality and the number of canceled requests dropped dramatically. This enabled management to focus on the more important issues in the firm—those relating to marketing (see Eden and Ronen, 1993).

Example: In a medical manpower firm, the process of assigning workers to hospitals was very long. As a result, many potential workers simply "disappeared" from the scene as they managed to find assignments on their own or through other agencies. This situation is sometimes referred to "evaporating inventory." Shortening the processing response time greatly improved the situation.

Example: A local community hospital reported a high rate of cross-infections of patients hospitalized in the internal medicine wards. A careful comparative analysis with other local hospitals revealed that this hospital had an average length of stay that was two days longer than others. Some of the causes for the excessive stay were administrative. The discharge policy required too many signatures and the processing of information was also slow. Administrative policies were changed, resulting in an immediate reduction of 1.2 days in the length of stay. The number of cross-infections also dropped.

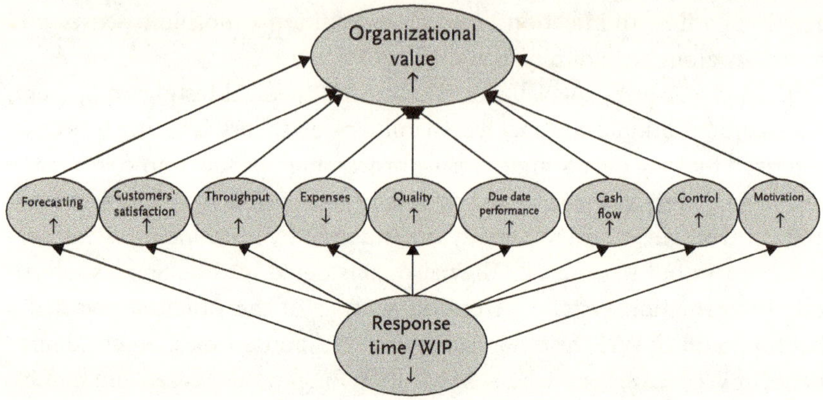

Figure 10.4:
The impact of reducing work in progress on organizational function and value

THE CAUSES OF EXCESS WIP

Several policy constraints are responsible for the accumulation of WIP beyond what is required for efficient operation of the system. These include:

- **The efficiencies syndrome.** Because of this syndrome, which feeds additional (unnecessary) work to noncritical resources, there is an excessive build-up of work in process inventory.
- **Viewing inventory as assets.** Looking at an organization from the narrow perspective of financial accounting can wrongly encourage management to increase inventory to show larger assets on the balance sheet (Geri and Ronen, 2005). The negative effects for the organization resulting from excessive WIP are way beyond the seemingly negative effect of showing less assets in the balance sheets.
- **Unawareness.** Unawareness to the adverse effects of WIP and to the existence of methods and tools for its reduction result in excessive WIP.

CHAPTER SUMMARY

The "evils" of long response times also known as "evils" of WIP are responsible for diminished work quality and customer satisfaction. There is also an effect on diminishing throughput, control, cash flow, and the added expenses resulting from excessive inventories and excessive response times.

Shortening response time and reducing the level of WIP are attainable and serve as a leverage for significant improvements in organizational performance and enhancing its value. Figure 10.4 summarizes this. The methods for reducing the level of WIP and shortening response time are detailed in chapter 11.

CHAPTER 11

Reducing Response Times

OBJECTIVE
• Acquire practical ways to substantially reduce response times.

Short response times have strategic and tactical importance. They serve as a strategic value driver for the organization. At the strategic level, short response times allow the organization flexibility in moving from one product or service to another, from one product or service line to another, and in the ability to better respond to market changes. In a changing market, with its inherent uncertainty, a flexible organization can adapt itself quickly to changes in the environment and increases its chances of survival and success.

At the tactical level, fast response times and working with low levels of WIP reduces costs and increases throughput.

METHODS FOR REDUCING WIP AND RESPONSE TIME

Reducing response times and reducing the amount of WIP can be achieved by various methods. We will first list them and then expand and demonstrate them:

1. Strategic gating.
2. Tactical gating.
3. Working with a complete kit.
4. Managing the bottlenecks.
5. Superzoufing.

6. The Lean/just-in-time (JIT) method and its application in healthcare systems.
    1. Working by Rule 1 of Lean.
    2. Working by Rule 2 of Lean.
        - Working with small and appropriate work batches and work packages.
        - Working with small transfer batches.
    3. Working by Rule 3 of Lean.
7. Measurement and control.
8. Implementing the drum–buffer–rope (DBR) mechanism.
9. Quality improvement and reduction of the "garbage plant" in the process.
10. Avoiding bad multitasking (BMT).
11. Implementing group technology (GT).
12. Working in parallel rather than serially.
13. Implementing the shortest processing time (SPT) prioritization rule.
14. Implementing "traffic lights" systems.

Strategic Gating

Strategic gating is a managerial tool that screens out tasks that should not processed by the system and thus not consume the scarce time of the bottleneck. Organizations that routinely apply strategic gating, especially in areas of development (e.g., pharmaceutical companies), marketing, and sales, reduce workloads by up to 25%, hence reducing the response time for the important tasks. The time to market is also reduced, which, in turn, contributes to competitiveness. There are situations for which strategic gating is not relevant. For example, emergency departments (EDs) of public hospitals do not decide that some patients will not be admitted. However, some strategic gating is exercised through channeling specific patient categories to other departments (e.g., oncological patients). Some hospitals, especially private ones, do exercise strategic gating. A hospital may decide that certain types of surgery will not be performed. Many surgical centers are shying away from gynecological surgery because of the frequent malpractice suites. There are hospitals that specialize in specific procedures, thus screening out others. This is strategic gating.

In cases of military encounters or mass terror attacks, doctors and paramedics, alone in the field, do apply strategic gating. They must make their own priorities when they have to treat numerous severe casualties: whom to treat first and whom later. Strategic gating in these cases is done according to the intuitive prospects of being able to save lives versus the roughly estimated length of treatment.

Tactical Gating

Tactical gating is the controlled release of tasks into the system and is appropriate for all organizations. Tasks that pass the strategic gating screening step must then go through tactical gating (Pass and Ronen, 2003). The roles of tactical gating are:

- Releasing only tasks with a complete kit.
- Assuring that all tasks are released by one person (the "gater") that is responsible for the tactical gating. The timing of task release will be determined by the bottleneck capacity while maintaining an appropriate buffer in front of the bottleneck (see the following section on the DBR mechanism).

The various roles will be further detailed in this chapter.

A good example of tactical gating is a triage nurse. He sets priorities and channels patients to various destinations: surgical emergencies, internal medicine, gynecology, trauma, further treatment in the community, or discharge.

Working with a Complete Kit

Working with a complete kit is one of the important principles in reducing response times. This principle, along with implementation guidelines, are detailed in chapter 12.

Managing Bottlenecks

The application of management by constraints approach for managing bottlenecks yields higher throughput on the one hand and reduction of response time on the other.

The following discussion outlines the contribution of the first two rules of Lean/JIT to reducing response times.

Superzoufing

Superzouf is a managerial method that dramatically cuts response time, increases capacity, and improves quality in high-intensity "paperwork" service organizations.

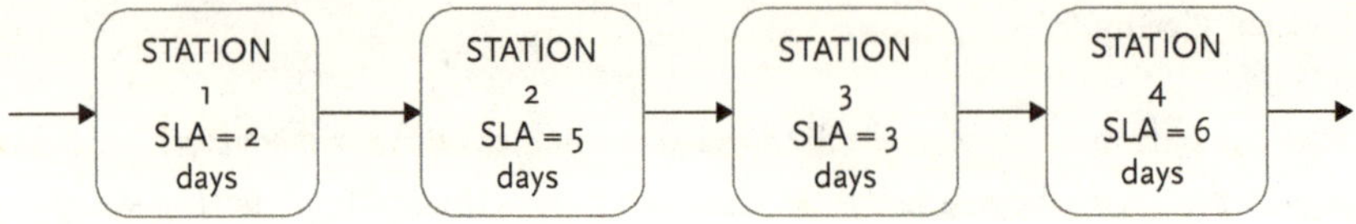

Figure 11.1:
Claims process

Example: Consider a claims office of a large health maintenance organization that handles about 10,000 claims per month. The claims process involves four stations as depicted in Figure 11.1. Each station has a service level agreement (SLA) of two, five, three, and six days, respectively. The average "touch time" for keying in and handling a claim (across all four stations) is 20 minutes.

Question: What is the end-to-end response time?

Answer: Unfortunately, it is the sum of the station SLAs—16 days. Moreover, experience shows that it is at least 16 days and can be longer. The question is why is this so?

There are four reasons for the excessive total time:

1. Parkinson's law: Work will take as long as the time allotted for it. If someone would change the SLA for station 1 to three days, the work will take three days.
2. The student's syndrome: Many students usually wait until the last day to study for an exam. For a given SLA, work will be started near the deadline and will occasionally be finished after the deadline due to unforeseen circumstances.
3. Local view and local measurements: Managers are frequently measured by their conformance to the SLA and hence will try to stretch out the work to fill the allotted time. They probably fear that if work is always completed early, then the SLA will be shortened and hence will put them in strain.
4. Pile up of WIP inventory: Once WIP accumulate, it will be difficult for a station to complete all its tasks within the SLA.

The consequences of excessive response times are:

- Long response times.
- Low quality.
- Excess follow-up on call.
- "Garbage time" (e.g., 30% of employees' time is spent on answering questions about the status of claims).

- High operating expenses.
- Low throughput.

Implementing the Superzouf Method

A necessary condition for applying the Superzouf method is that the throughput rate is greater than the input rate. This is the same requirement as in queueing theory for a queue to reach a steady state. If this condition is not met, the queue will increase without limit. Hence, one objective is to find ways to increase throughput/capacity. This can be achieved by applying the tools of bottleneck management (seven focusing steps of the theory of constraints), tactical gating, strategic gating, complete kits, and elimination of the "garbage time."

We can define four steps in implementing the Superzouf method:

Step 1: Reduce station SLAs.
Step 2: Set a total process SLA.
Step 3: Cleanup desks and assimilate Superzouf culture.
Step 4: Sustain the Superzouf method.

Step 1: Reducing Station SLAs

If we can reduce station SLAs, we will obviously reduce the total response times (usually by the sum of the station SLAs reductions). Very frequently we can identify unnecessary steps/stations. One way to do this is to assign SLA = 0 to such steps and achieve it by having a station handle a task instantly or transferring the task to the next station. In many situations, the first step in a process can operate in a SLA = 0 mode.

Step 2: Set a Total Process SLA

We should aspire to assign a total-process SLA rather than per-station SLAs. This will bypass the current incentives for each step to perform to the local SLA. This approach can be termed "many in a box" or "two in a box." It should be accompanied by assigning responsibility for the process to a single person.

However, even though a total process SLA is very desirable, it fits only about 90% of the entities.

Step 3: Clean Up Desks and Assimilate Superzouf culture

A one-time effort should take place to drastically reduce WIP inventory. We are dealing mainly with paper-handling processes so we don't have customers waiting but rather paper waiting to be processed. This can be achieved by working overtime or additional shifts for a limited time.

In addition to the "desk cleanup" process, we should assimilate the Superzouf culture. This includes working on tasks as soon as possible and handing over the processed entities promptly to the next step. Trivial cases should be completed entirely by the first (gating) station.

Step 4: Sustain the Superzouf Method

Several steps should be taken to sustain the culture and process:

- Introduce appropriate measurements.
- Debrief for exception cases and outliers.
- Introduce a dynamic SLA management.
- Maintain protective capacity to account for variability and unforeseen circumstances.

The example in Table 11.1 demonstrates the results of a typical process in a service company, where Superzoufing has been implemented.

In summary, Superzoufing is applicable to any large service organization that has a service center, a call center, or a telemarketing unit or is paperwork intensive. It is highly relevant for many healthcare organizations and other government agencies (e.g., courts).

A per-station SLAs policy causes longer response times. Superzoufing can reduce total process response times as much as 90%. The more complex the process is, the larger the potential of response time reduction can be.

Table 11.1. A SUPERZOUFING EXAMPLE

	Baseline	After six months	Change (%)
WIP	1,362	476	–65
Input (inquiries per day)	155	110	–29
Throughput (closed inquiries per day)	164	120	–27
Operating expenses (head count)	52	35	–32
End-to-end response time (days)	**8 days**	**4 days**	**–50**
Closing within three hours	19%	50%	+163

The Lean/JIT Concept and Its Application in Healthcare Systems

Just-In-Time (JIT) theory (Schonberger, 1986) is of utmost importance in reducing response times. It emerged from industrial plants in Japan and was also successfully utilized in service organizations, military organizations, and healthcare organizations. Most of the JIT principles are based on universal concepts and techniques and do not relate to the Japanese culture. Hence, JIT has successfully been applied not only in Japan but also worldwide. The small number of the underlying JIT principles are culture-dependent and will not be addressed in this book.

JIT is a theory that stands on its own and can be applied as is. However, experience clearly demonstrates that the application outcomes are better when JIT is combined with other managerial approaches such as management by constraints, managing for quality, the complete kit concept, and others. JIT has been around for several decades and is currently referred to as Lean.

LEAN PRINCIPLES

The Lean (JIT) concept can be summarized by three basic and simple rules:

- Rule 1 of Lean: Work only as needed in terms of time, quantity, and specifications.
- Rule 2 of Lean: Work in small, appropriate, and "smart" batches.
- Rule 3 of Lean: Avoid waste and activities that do not add value to the organization.

Rule 1 of Lean

Rule 1 of Lean—work only as needed in terms of time, quantity, and specifications.

This rule implies that a product or service should not be delivered earlier or later than the target time; one should not produce more than or less than the required quantity; and a product should not be under- or overdesigned with regard to its requirements and specifications. This sounds so simple and obvious that one wonders what is new here.

We can identify two types of managerial deviations.

Shortage Deviation

For example, demand is 10 units and the actual supply is only 8. This is a serious deviation that interferes with supply to customers and cash flow and damages reputation. However, such a deviation can be dealt with by routine control mechanisms of the organization as well as natural mechanisms that will usually close the gap:

- The employee herself, knowing she will not meet demand, will meet the shortage within a short time.
- The employee's superior will monitor the demanded quantities and make sure the deviation is corrected.
- Sales and marketing managers will work to close the gap if others have not done so.
- The financial manager will point out situations with cash flow gaps.
- The customer will approach management with a request to correct the deviation.

In other words, the organizational mechanisms will work toward closing the gap.

Surplus Deviation

For example, demand is 10 units, but 12 units have been provided. This deviation is usually not handled in the short term by the routine mechanisms of the organization and does not naturally generate feedback for employees and managers. Correction mechanisms are not triggered because of the following reasons:

- The employee feels as if she is overachieving.
- Managers sometimes do not care about the surplus as they are busy "putting out fires" elsewhere in the organization.
- Sales and marketing personnel have no knowledge about such a surplus.
- The financial manager will deal with this situation at the end of the year or, at best, at the end of a quarter. At that time, the accountants will become involved in how to write down the inventories.
- The customer may be totally unaware of surpluses.

Surplus deviations are not routinely dealt with even though they create much harm.

- If the resource is a bottleneck, then generating a surplus of two units translates into a harmful waste of the bottleneck resource time and delays for other products/services.
- Generating the surplus required using materials and components beyond those planned for, thus inhibiting their use for other products.
- WIP inventory is increased.
- Creating of unneeded products.

In summary, being too early may be as bad as being too late. Similarly, overproducing may be as bad as underproducing. There is an effect of "double theft" of bottleneck time and materials, causing bad planning and delays in supply. In addition, the increased WIP inventory brings on all the "evils" described in chapter 10. The bottom line of Rule 1 of Lean is that surplus deviations should be prevented.

The implementation of Rule 1 of Lean is very useful and important for maintenance. The implications are that maintenance on equipment should not be done less than needed nor more than needed.

Example: In a large maintenance organization, one third of labor hours were devoted to repairing equipment that was not in demand at the time of repair or equipment that was not used at all (due to introduction of a new generation of equipment or having a surplus of a given equipment). As a result, the organization was late in many of the urgently needed repairs. Working in the spirit of Rule 1 of Lean resulted in a reduction in the number of early repairs and a total prevention of unnecessary repairs. This reduced the backlog and improved the level of meeting deadlines.

Implementing Rule 1 of Lean in Scheduling of Tasks and Meetings

The following simple example demonstrates that the Rule 1 of Lean with respect to timing is very applicable to scheduling: The surgeon wants to start operating at 10:00 AM but tells the operating room (OR) staff he wants everything ready at 9:30 AM. Consequently, the OR staff requests the patient be there at 9:00 AM and the nursing staff on the ward summons an orderly to transport the patient at 8:00 AM.

Violating Rule 1 of Lean

Figure 11.2 demonstrates what happens when Rule 1 of Lean is violated: The model 1–2–3 pharmaceutical production process has a demand of 10 units per month for each of three drugs, A, B, and C.

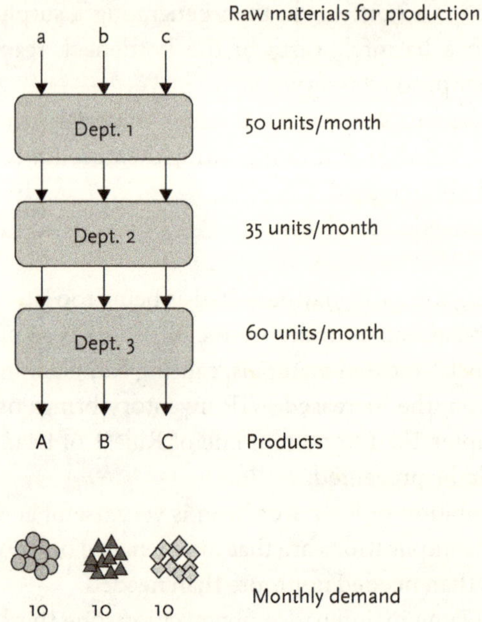

Figure 11.2:
A 1–2–3 production system with three products

The demand can be met with the current resources. Occasionally, the production manager wishes to work on batches of 20 units of every product. His motivation is might be to save set-up times, save paperwork, or just because performance measure for production is quantity processed (a very common policy constraint). The resulting process is presented in Figure 11.3.

- At first, 20 units of product A were put into production. They went through the three-stage process: 10 units were delivered to customers, and 10 units were stacked in finished goods inventory.
- Since the 20-unit batch of product B was "stuck" in department 2, the batch was split: 5 units were left as work in process inventory, and 15 units were transferred forward and finished all three processing stages. 10 of them were delivered to customers, and 5 were left over as surplus finished goods inventory.
- Units of product C were never delivered to customers.

The bottom line result is that the company produced 35 units of products A and B, rather than 30, as ordered. However, product C was not produced at all and hence not supplied to customers. If the firm had worked by Rule 1 of Lean, every product would have been produced in the requested quantity of 10 units and delivery to customers would have been flawless.

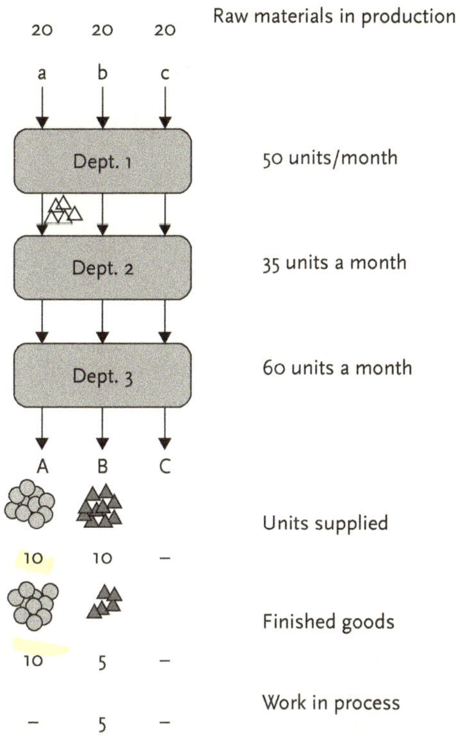

Figure 11.3:
Violation of Rule 1 of Lean

The 40–20–40 Phenomenon

Ignoring Rule 1 of Lean creates the 40–20–40 phenomenon, which is quite prevalent in organizations. This is a situation where:

- 40% of the demand is supplied ahead of time.
- 20% of demand is supplied on time.
- 40% of demand is supplied late.

Observing Rule 1 of Lean "balances the flow" and enables delivering of almost all demands on time. Previously, part of the demand was delivered late while other demands were fulfilled too early.

Example: In an ED, the staff can control whom they treat first, second, and so on. There are patients who are treated earlier than they need to, delaying the treatment of others, thus causing adverse effects. This can be prevented by proper sequencing of attending physicians and consultants done by the nurse in charge. When a consultant is on hand, prioritization should be done according to needs for the consultant.

Rule 2 of Lean—work in small, appropriate, and "smart" batches.

We will distinguish between several batch types.

- Working (production) batch—a group of units that are treated sequentially by an identical process, one after another.
- Transfer batch—a group of units that are transferred together between stations.
- Purchasing batch.
- Shipment batch.

In service or production processes, a working batch reflects several units that are processed at a work center between two set-ups. The determination of batch size is one of the important questions in planning a service or production. In the production of pharmaceuticals, if the work batches are too big relative to the market demand rate, we run the risk of losing products due to expiration dates.

Batch size may vary along the process of material or information flow. For example, in a production process:

- The purchase batch for total production—10,000 units.
- The shipment batch from the materials' supplier—1,000 units.
- Batch size when inspecting a shipment—500 units.
- Production batch—100 units.
- Transfer batch between work-stations—50 units.
- Batch size for delivery to customer—250 units.

Transfer Batches

A transfer batch in healthcare can relate to how **frequently** a consultant-specialist visits the ED or to how **frequently** blood specimens are transferred from the ward to the lab. Transfer batches are a key issue in service organizations.

Transfer batch—number of units transferred between one workstation and another. Sometimes expressed by the related number of processing hours or by the frequency of transfers.

The size of a transfer batch does not necessarily match the work batch (Goldratt and Fox, 1986). The transfer batch can be bigger than, smaller than, or equal to the work batch. The desire is to **make the transfer batches as small as possible**, provided this does not interfere with the process and does not cost more. Figures 11.4 and 11.5 illustrate the effects of transfer batches. Both figures have production batches of 25 units but different transfer batches.

In the work regime described in Figure 11.4, the 25 units of the batch are transferred from station 1 to station 2 once the full batch is processed in station 1. Once fully processed in station 2, the batch is transferred to station 3. After being processed in station 3, the batch is sent to the customer. The system response time under this regime is long, t_1. In addition, there is concern that the bottleneck (e.g., station 2) may have idle time when waiting for the batch at station 1 to be finished.

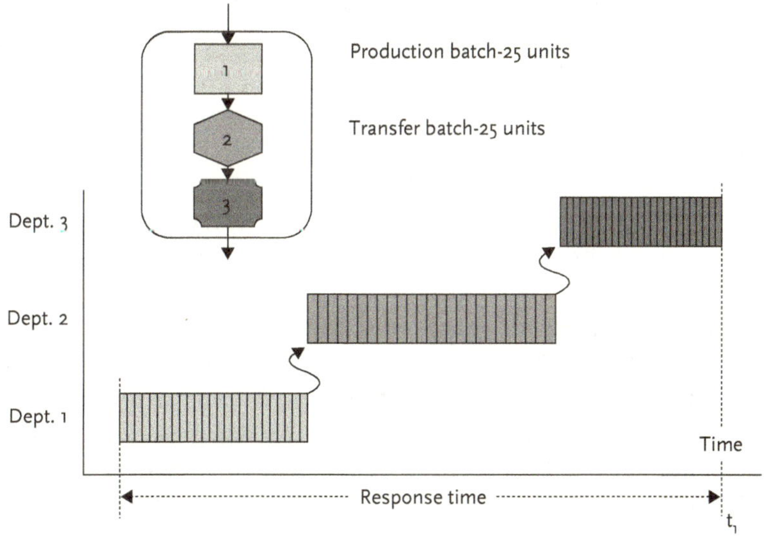

Figure 11.4:
Response time of a 1–2–3 system with a transfer batch of 25 units

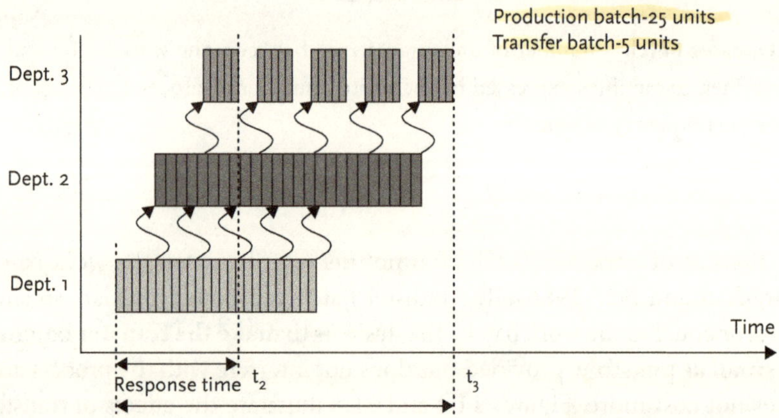

Figure 11.5:
Response time of a 1–2–3 system with a transfer batch of five units

In the work regime of Figure 11.5, they continue to work with a production batch of 25, but the transfer batch has now been cut down to 5 units. Once 5 units have been processed at a given station, they are transferred to the next work station. The obvious result is that the response time has been dramatically reduced from t_1 to the shorter t_3. To fully exploit this improvement, we should create willingness of the customer to accept partial shipments. Thus, the first units can be sent to the customer after a very short time period, t_2. In many situations, customers will be happy to receive some units, with the remainder to follow shortly thereafter.

The ideal transfer batch is one unit. This means that every unit is transferred to the next station once the process at a previous station has finished. The reduction in response time can thus be fully exploited. The inhibitors to implementing a transfer batch of one include the additional conveyance needed and the added efforts in dealing with many transfers of single units from station to station. Most situations in healthcare involve one patient at a time.

Example: In the ED of a large hospital, they were sending the trays containing the blood specimens to the labs every hour. The transfer batch was one hour, causing an average wait of a half an hour for each specimen. Today, each blood sample is immediately transferred to the lab via a pneumatic system. Namely, zero waiting time for blood specimens in the ED. The shorter response times for test results enables quicker diagnosis and treatment and yields a shorter overall patient stay in the ED.

We should stress again that in production and maintenance processes, the transfer batch is usually measured by the number of units. In service organizations, the transfer batch is usually measured in terms of the **frequency of transfer**—for example, a transfer batch of one hour or two days.

Example: In a large logistical organization, the average response time for repairing equipment was several months. Equipment pieces were transferred from station to station once a month. When the transfer batches were cut down to weekly batches, the response time dropped dramatically.

Example: In the wards of a large hospital, the response time of receiving test results from the lab was reduced by a factor of 10 simply by reducing the size of the transfer batch. It turned out that the transfer batch was determined by the size of the transfer trays. Once the large trays were replaced with smaller ones, the frequency of transfers increased and response times were shortened.

Example: The 7-Eleven chain in Tokyo is delivering goods to thousands of its stores every two hours. This enables better use of the limited and expensive shelf space of the stores. The stores' inventory is literally kept on the trucks.

Working (Production) Batches

A new set-up is initiated only when the work on the current batch is completed and we are ready to work on the next batch in a different process or setting.

Working batch (or production batch)—The number of units (or labor hours) that are worked on continuously at a workstation. This is the amount of work between one setup and the next.

Let us now examine the impact of shifting from large working batches to smaller ones. We will see what happens if we take every working batch in Figure 11.6 and split it into four working batches, as seen in Figure 11.7.

Working with small working batches is a major contribution of Japan to the world of management. Reducing batch size brings a miraculous proportional reduction in response time and the amount of work in process. Figures 11.6 and 11.7 show that a shift from monthly batches to weekly ones reduced the amount of WIP from 200 units to 50 units, and the system response time was probably reduced as well. The reduction of the working batch yields two positive outcomes: (i) reduction of WIP and response times, and (ii) working in small batches allows better adherence to timetables, improvement in quality, and service to the customer.

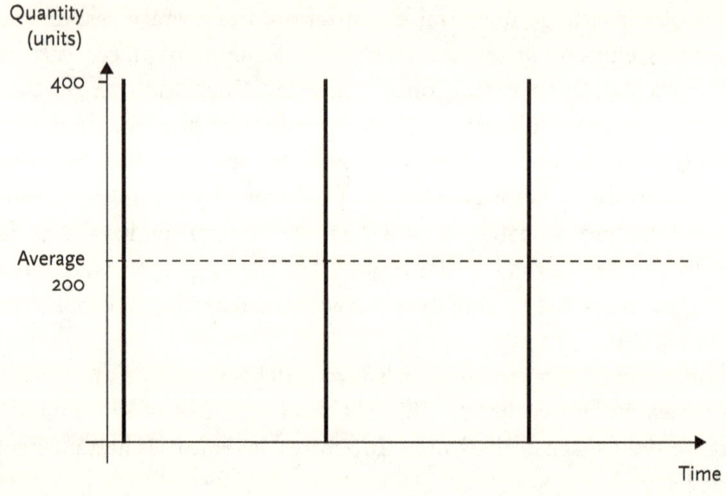

Figure 11.6:
Working with large working batches

Experience shows that the benefits from applying Rule 2 of Lean are immediate.

Example: In a billing department of a large hospital, preparing bills and mailing them was done once a month. At the end of the month there was peak activity and the stress generated problems and mistakes. To overcome this problem, the bills were prepared and sent three times a month. The new work schedule helped overcome most of billing errors and cut down the resources needed to generate and send out the bills. It also allowed better customer service to phone and mail inquiries. It substantially reduced the number of customer calls to the call center during peak hours.

Example: In a hospital lab, the staff used to wait for the tray to fill up fully before starting the auto-analyzer. Cutting down the working batch and operating the analyzer more frequently drastically cut down the response

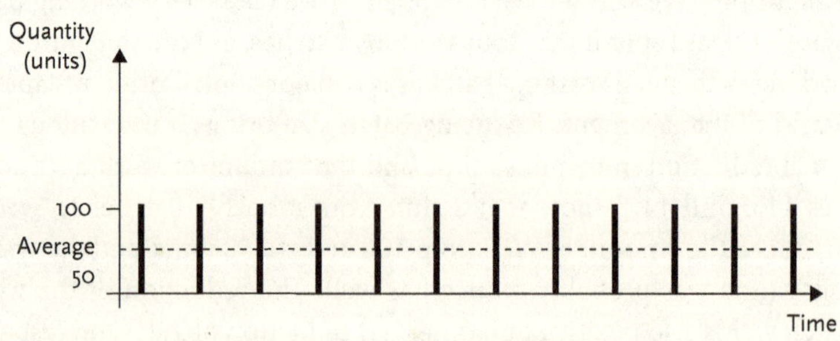

Figure 11.7:
Working with smaller working batches

time for lab results, which in turn resulted in better patient care. The cost of extra reagents and consumables was negligible.

Example: In a medical electronics firm producing expensive imaging equipment, systems were manufactured in batches of six months' supply. While assembling the first units, engineers discovered malfunctions that required changes in the electronic boards. The firm moved to production of small batches with a two-week supply horizon. The cycle time was drastically reduced as well as the number of rejects.

Example: One of the authors (JP) recently experienced the negative results of work batching. A biopsy was sent to the pathology lab, and the patient was told it will take three weeks to receive an answer. It turned out that the results were available after two days. The long wait of three weeks was a result of the batching of the analysis and write-up. If smaller batching would be processed daily as opposed to weekly or biweekly, patients would receive results much faster.

Example: Ambulatory oncology patients are summoned to the clinic at the same time at 8:00 AM. Their treatment times are four to five hours long, but they cannot all start at the same time because of personnel constraints. Thus, some patients end up with much longer and frustrating wait times. Rather than batch process them at registration, they should be scheduled using a DBR approach and staggered throughout the morning.

Rule 2 of Lean recommends working with **small, appropriate, and "smart"** batches:

- **Small batches**—This means usually smaller than those used today. The authors' experience shows that in most situations organizations work with batches that can be made smaller, resulting in shorter response times concurrent with improving other performance measures.
- **Appropriate batches**—This means batch sizes that are congruent with the delivery date expected by the customer.
- **"Smart" batches**—Using common sense in consideration of the special needs of the organization.

Example: In a hospital lab, an overall effort was made to reduce batch sizes, both for collecting samples from wards and for running tests on auto-analyzers. One specific piece of equipment required a rather long set-up and used very expensive reagents. The operator of the machine asked permission to run larger batches as before the change. He was denied on grounds that everybody must adapt to the change. The new batch size was not "smart" for that specific machine: the operator had to keep "smart" by using, in this case, large batches.

"Smart" batches imply that common sense should also enter the considerations in determining batch size.

The effects of reducing batch size (both working batches and transfer batches) are immediate, are relatively easy to implement, and have a major impact on reducing system response times.

The strategic importance of reducing response times and working with small batches

Working with small batches allows firms to produce a **large variety** of products with quick response to evolving market needs. This also enables better compatibility between products and customers and supplying them faster and at higher quality.

Working with big batches implies longer response times. This, in turn, forces organizations to carry larger finished goods inventory, tying down capital, and increasing costs. The higher overall costs result from higher inventory carrying costs and the need to sell occasionally unneeded inventory at low prices.

What prevents us from working with small batches?

- Reluctance to increase the number of set-ups.
- Economies of scale thinking.
- Fear of more complex monitoring and control.
- Fear of increasing cost per unit.

Reluctance to Increase the Number of Set-Ups

The set-up time is a nonproductive time. During set-up, one cannot produce or provide service. Since traditionally the set-up process was long and complex, there was a tendency to avoid set-ups as much as possible, leading to working with larger batches.

The modern approach to set-ups is to refrain from long and disorderly set-ups. Experience demonstrates that set-up times can be reduced significantly without large investments (Shingo, 1996).

Reducing set-up time to some extent (e.g., by 50%) allows a similar reduction in the working batch while maintaining the same ratio between productive time (working on the batch) and nonproductive time (set-up). The result is achieving all the benefits of working with small working batches—short response time, flexible response to different customers, and better quality—without additional costs.

Table 11.2. THE EFFECT OF BATCH SIZE ON THE LOAD OF NONCRITICAL RESOURCES

	Large batch	Small batch (half of the large batch)
Productive work (%)	50	50
Set-up time (%)	10	20
Total capacity utilization (%)	60	70

The framework of management by constraints shows that more set-ups in resources that are not bottlenecks do not cost money. For example, Table 11.2 presents the relation between the capacity utilization and the reduction of 50% in the batch size in a work center with a 60% capacity utilization.

In hospitals and clinics, the setups are usually short and mostly "mental setups", hence there is no justification for large working batches. Most working batches in healthcare should be one (e.g., a single patient or single interpretation of test results).

If the resource is not a bottleneck, working with small batches only moderately affects the capacity utilization of this resource.

Economies of Scale Thinking

People are used to the concept of economies of scale where large quantities imply savings. However, economies of scale may not always be relevant and must be considered in every specific situation.

When batches are processed in a system with excess capacity, economies of scale are not important. On the contrary, working with large batches increases response times and creates many "evils" of WIP. Hence, increasing batch size for the sake of economies of scale might often be a drawback, not a benefit.

This dilemma is remedied by shortening set-up times as much as possible, especially when the workstation is a system bottleneck. In addition, we should check whether a specific situation would benefit by utilizing **larger** batches in the bottleneck station compared to batch sizes used in the other, non-bottleneck stations (Goldratt and Cox, 1992).

Fear of More Complex Monitoring and Control

Working in small batches and splitting a batch into several smaller transfer batches seemingly leads to more complex control as a result of having to monitor and control more batches.

There is no doubt that shifting to smaller working and transfer batches requires handling more batches. However, the shorter times for each batch create a situation where the number of batches in the system at any given time is **smaller** rather than bigger. Hence follow-up and control are easier (Karp and Ronen, 1992). Moreover, working with smaller batches, along with the use of additional tools of strategic and tactical gating, complete kits, and so on "cleans" the system from congestions of work and tasks in process, so control becomes even simpler.

Increasing Cost per Unit

An employee or manager who works in a system that is using the classical costing approach (see details in chapter 16) for control and decision-making may resist working with smaller batches fearing this may negatively affect the "cost per unit" measure.

For example, in a station that is not a bottleneck, set-up time is one hour and the processing time of one unit is 15 minutes (1/4 hour), the cost per unit in a batch of 100 is:

$$T(100) = (1+1/4*100)/100 = 0.26 \text{ hours/unit.}$$

Shifting the batches size to 10 will increase the cost per unit:

$$T(10) = (1+1/4*10)/10 = 0.35 \text{ hours/unit.}$$

This measurement and objectives based on cost per unit represent a local view that causes suboptimization, especially in a station that is not a bottleneck. Global system view requires consideration of the total benefits versus the harms of working in large batches, including the "evils" of WIP.

Rule 3 of Lean

Wastes are activities, processes, or use of capital that do not contribute added value to the organization, the customer, the process, or the product.

Rule 3 of Lean—avoid wastes and activities that do not add value to the organization.

Examples for waste include:

- Overproduction.
- Waiting times.
- Unnecessary conveyance.
- Rejects in processing.
- Surplus stock.
- Poor quality.
- Unnecessary space.
- Capital surplus.
- Overrequirements, overspecification and overdesign of products or services.
- Unnecessary steps and processes.

Rule 3 of Lean is a general principle. Wastes can be dealt with through the Pareto rule, the focusing matrix, or by the principles of management by constraints, as has been demonstrated in earlier chapters.

Measurement and Control of WIP

The mere act of measuring, follow-up, and control of response times and levels of WIP bring rapid improvement in these parameters and the creation of an environment that protects the achievements of improvement efforts. Measurement, even if not supported by other methods, brings real improvement. For more detail, see chapter 13.

Implementing the Drum–Buffer–Rope Mechanism

The DBR mechanism accomplishes the **controlled release** of tasks into the process, thus limiting the amount of WIP. Timing of releases is determined by the capacity of the constraint and by the size of the buffer we wish to build ahead of the bottleneck. Implementing DBR in systems of marketing, sales, production, development, and service leads to a significant reduction of WIP.

Quality Improvement and Reduction of the "Garbage Plant"

Poor quality in processes results in much rework and retreatment, thus increasing response times and the amount of WIP, hence quality assurance is warranted. Approaches for process quality improvement and process control mechanisms will be presented in chapter 17.

Avoiding Bad Multitasking

The phenomenon of BMT is common in all areas of management and is prominent in healthcare processes (Knight, 2014). This is the phenomenon of **jumping among many open tasks** that are waiting to be processed. The results of BMT are:

- Decrease in throughput.
- Longer response times for finishing tasks.
- Late deliveries.
- Reduced work quality.
- Increased WIP, including all its "evils".

To demonstrate the negative effect of BMT, let us analyze a situation where someone develops software modules for three projects that are managed by three different project managers. The development of each module is expected to take two weeks. The first module should be ready in two weeks, the second in four weeks, and the third in six weeks. In reality, things happen somewhat differently as Figure 11.8 shows.

The software engineer starts working on the module for project 1. At first, she has a mental set-up time: she must submerge into the problem, understand it, and then collect the necessary data, ask questions, and arrange the work environment. After finishing this set-up, she begins working on the module for project 1.

After about a week, the software engineer bumps into the manager for project 2 who is surprised to hear that work has not yet begun on the module for her project. Having yielded to the pressure project 2's manager applies on her, the developer **stops** working on project 1 and starts working on project 2.

First, she must start with the mental set-up for project 2 and fully understand the problem well. Then she continues working on the module for

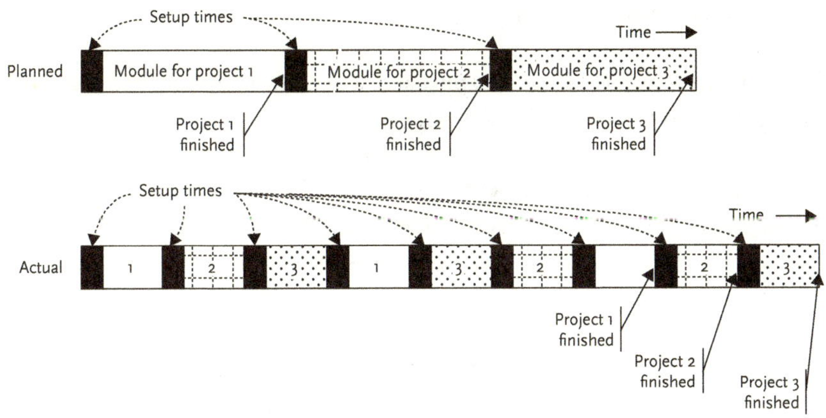

Figure 11.8:
The negative effect of bad multitasking

project 2. The same story repeats itself after several days when she coincidentally meets the project 3 manager in the cafeteria. He too is surprised that his project receives low priority and work on it has not yet begun. After pressure exerted by the manager of project 3, the developer stops working on project 2 and shifts to project 3, again having to go through a mental set-up. Now project 1 manager exerts pressure as he feels his project is already late. So, the developer stops working on project 3 and returns to project 1. However, she must redo the mental set-up (as time passed and she already forgot some things).

At the end, none of the modules was delivered on time. Furthermore, due to the additional mental set-up times while switching among projects, valuable time has been lost at the bottleneck, not to mention the quality of the work.

Reducing BMT can be done using following steps:

- Teaching and explaining.
- Applying strict control using tactical gating.
- Measuring, follow-up, and control of the number of tasks released to each employee.

Field experience shows that development people occasionally work on **too many** tasks concurrently. We are not saying that development people should work only on one task at a time. However, two to four simultaneous open tasks are a reasonable number that will assure that the developer will not be idle when one task is held back—for example, while waiting for data. A significant reduction of BMT will lead to reduced response times and increased throughput and quality.

Implementing Group Technology

Group technology (GT) is an approach where similar tasks are grouped and aggregated under specialized work groups.

For example, a hospital ED may be separated into surgical, internal medicine, walk-in, pediatric, and gynecological. Within each specialized ED, the variance among patients is smaller than there is in a general ED. Each specialized ED can thus offer more professional, structured, and uniform medical diagnosis and treatment as each employs the relevant specialists.

GT also exists in production processes. Work teams are assembled to be responsible for the **entire product** and not just one production function. Insurance companies form work teams that specialize in specific markets and defined clients.

The classical approach for operations management is to create teams that specialize functionally, where the customer or the product moves among the groups. This is demonstrated in Figure 11.9 for an OR situation. Using the GT approach, several integrative teams provide the entire service needed by the corresponding customer groups in one place as Figure 11.10 shows.

Figures 11.9 and 11.10 demonstrate how a complex work flow under the functional structure becomes rather simple under the GT approach.

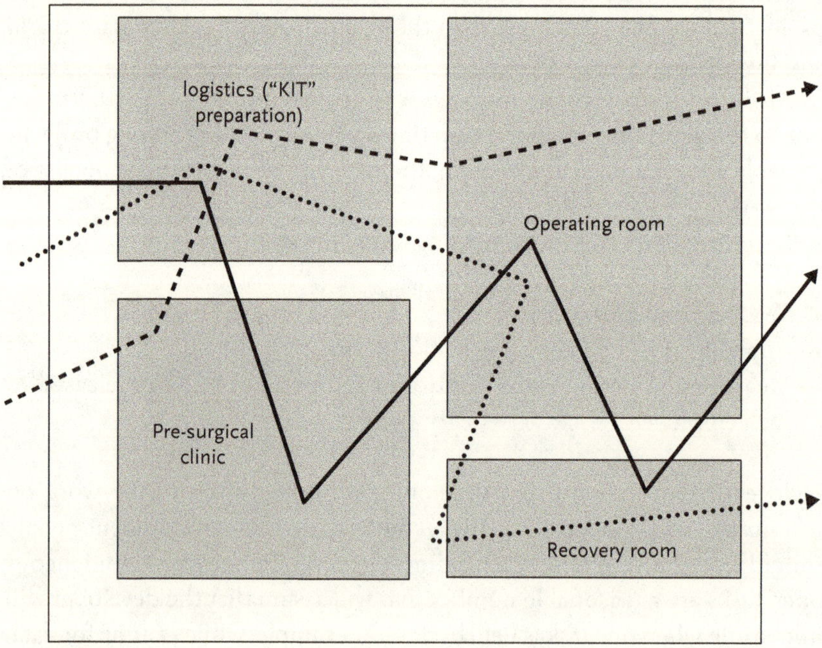

Figure 11.9:
System arrangement with functional structure

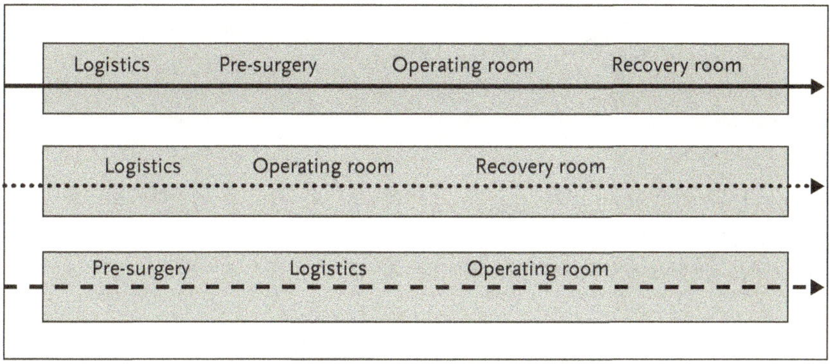

Figure 11.10:
System arrangement using the group technology approach by products or customers

In addition, the GT approach generates a **collective responsibility and accountability of the group** to the customer or the product.

The GT approach yields faster response times, a reduction in WIP, increased output, and enhanced customer satisfaction. Most cases do not require added resources to achieved the improved performance.

Example: In a claims department of a health insurance company, every customer had to go through five steps, as depicted in Figure 11.11. This was a cumbersome and annoying journey. Management decided to form three teams, each handling all five steps, as depicted in Figure 11.12. Each customer was handled by one team that performed all five tasks.

Figure 11.11:
The claims department before group technology

Team 1	Team 2	Team 3
- Receiving - Checking & verifying - Accounting - Approving - Costumer service	- Receiving - Checking & verifying - Accounting - Approving - Costumer service	- Receiving - Checking & verifying - Accounting - Approving - Costumer service

Figure 11.12:
The claims department after applying group technology

Example: In a large governmental hospital, the ED had several subareas such as a casting room, electrocardiography room, and so on. Patients would move from area to area according to their specific needs. Under the GT approach, there are teams that are brought to the patient and provide everything the patient needs in the ED.

A full (100%) GT can only rarely be achieved. We cannot achieve total and full responsibility of the group for every aspect of the service or the product. There are usually some common resources shared by several groups. For example, imaging services can be common for all the specialized EDs in the previous example.

Experience shows that GT succeeds under the following conditions:

- Work volume justifies a specialized group for the long term.
- The resources shared by the various teams are not bottlenecks.
- Creation of motivation and team spirits.

Working in Parallel Rather Than Serially

Performing tasks in parallel rather than serially helps considerably to reduce response times. For example, urine and blood samples are parallely sent and analyzed and not serially.

Implementing the SPT Prioritization Rule

In most healthcare organizations, patients are serviced according to their arrival or appointment time on a first in–first out basis. This provides a sense of fairness and is very common in most queueing situations. However, there are situations when deviations from this

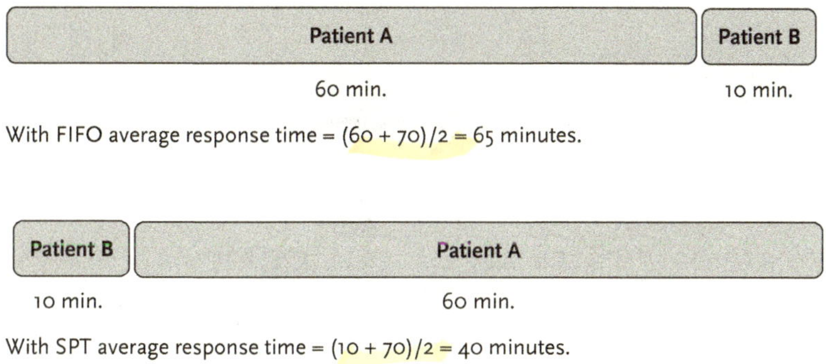

Figure 11.13:
Shortest processing time versus first in–first out

mechanism can provide better overall service by reducing average response time.

One such mechanism is the SPT, where shorter interaction times receive priority over longer ones. The SPT approach can be very useful in healthcare organizations. To see the possible advantage of the SPT regime, consider the following situation.

Two patients, A and B, arrive sequentially at about the same time to the ED, and each requires a procedure. The procedure for patient A is expected to last 60 minutes and for patient B, 10 minutes. If we go by the first in–first out system, patient A will leave after 60 minutes and B after 70 minutes, for an average time spent in the ED of 65 minutes per patient. However, if we employ SPT and treat patient B first, Patient B will leave after 10 minutes and patient A after 70 minutes for an average time of 40 minutes. One can easily see the overall benefit to a group of patients and to the ED. This is depicted in Figure 11.13. The overall time spent by the two patients in the system using first in–first out is 130 minutes and 80 minutes using SPT.

The SPT priority rule can be very relevant for triage where simple cases get treated immediately and for a specialist consulting in the ED where a few "short" cases can be dealt with and discharged, thus relieving the overcrowding in EDs. We see more examples of such priority rules in express lines in pharmacies or supermarkets.

Example: In an ambulatory outpatient oncology ward, most of the patients come in for chemotherapy. Some of them need only a very short treatment (e.g., biological drugs) and are admitted as a special group first thing in the morning, thus saving them long waits and freeing up beds for the longer duration treatments.

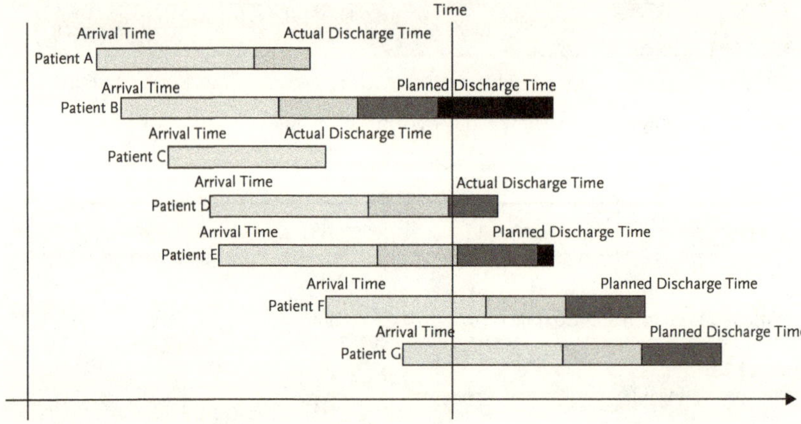

Figure 11.14:
The "traffic lights" emergency department control system

Implementing "Traffic Lights" Systems

The buffer management "traffic lights" system is a twofold mechanism (Knight, 2014):

1. It serves as a tactical tool used by physicians and nurses to prioritize the treatment of patients in the department thus preventing long stay of patients in the system.
2. It is a strategic tool for managers to identify the causes that prevent the department from meeting the agreed-upon completion times.

For example, management of a certain hospital decided that the planned discharge time for patients treated in the ED will be at most four hours. These four hours intervals are divided into three zones, while any overrun is considered "black" (see Figure 11.14).

- The green zone—the first two hours after the arrival of the patient to the ED.
- The yellow zone—the third hour of patient's stay in ED.
- The red zone—the forth hour of patient's stay in ED.
- The black zone—patient's stay in ED exceeding the four-hour planned discharge time.

If a patient currently is in the green zone, then no extramanagerial expediting is needed. If a patient is in the yellow zone, he should be watched carefully. If he is in the red zone, he should be expedited.

Thus, the "traffic lights" system helps physicians and nurses to prioritize the treatment of patients in the department. This control mechanism alerts staff about delayed patient care and helps to prevent long stays for patients in the ED.

CHAPTER SUMMARY

Reducing response times is a strategic and tactical goal for the organization. Using the approaches and techniques presented in this chapter can reduce response time several fold.

The significant contribution of Lean/JIT to management is manifested in focusing on short response times and viewing WIP as a **burden** and not as an **asset.** The Lean/JIT approach turns attention to the "evils" caused by WIP inventory.

Other contributions of Lean/JIT are the techniques of using small working batches and transfer batches and shortening set-up times.

Reducing response time, focusing, management by constraints, changing performance measures, using the complete kit concept, and embracing the global view of enhancing the firm's value all yield significant improvements in the performance of the organization.

CHAPTER 12
The Complete Kit Concept

OBJECTIVES

- Understand the "evils" of working with incomplete kits, and appreciate the value of working with complete kits (CKs).
- Understand why people tend to work with incomplete kits.

The CK concept and its theoretical background are easy to understand and not difficult to implement. This managerial tool has been implemented in various organizations with a high success rate. It is easy to adopt in every environment and situation, providing much benefit in relatively short time spans. We present here the concept of CK and show how it can be implemented in the healthcare system and demonstrate successful accomplishments in numerous medical processes such as emergency departments (EDs) and operating rooms (ORs). Introducing the CK concept leads to fast productivity gains. It is easy to adopt in the healthcare environment and provides much benefit to healthcare organizations in a relatively short period of time, as in other industries today (e.g., see Coman, Koller, and Ronen, 1996; Eden and Ronen, 1993; Grosfeld-Nir and Ronen, 1998; Ronen, 1992). This chapter discusses the CK concept and its implications for better healthcare management (Leshno and Ronen, 2001).

Taking into consideration the CK's simplicity and effectiveness, it is somehow surprising that just-in-time (JIT) adherents like Schonberger (1986) and Suzaki (1987) pay so little attention to it. Proponents of quality management (see chapter 17) such as Deming (1986) relate to it only in general terms by stating "do it right the first time and on time."

WHAT IS A COMPLETE KIT?

Having a CK is confirming the readiness of the kit prior to the start of the procedure.

Complete kit—the set of components, materials, documents, laboratory results and other information needed to complete a given procedure, process or task.

There are two types of kits: the inkit and the outkit.

Inkit—the kit required as an input to the operation or medical procedure.

Outkit—of a given task, the kit expected as an output of the operation or medical procedure.

The outkit of a given operation may be the inkit of the next stage.

THE "EVILS" OF AN INCOMPLETE KIT

To fully understand and value the CK concept, it is important to understand the "evils" of working with an incomplete kit. We will demonstrate the "evils" in three areas of the healthcare environment: the ED, the OR, and pharmaceutical purchase. The following represent some of the adverse consequences in trying to work without a CK.

More Work in Process

Any specific task in a medical environment defines a process. For the ED example, the process includes, among other things, taking the medical history of the patient, nurse and physician physical examinations, medical tests, and a conclusion reached by the physician to either discharge the patient or to hospitalize her. Work in process (WIP) in the ED means, for example, people waiting for completion of the admission process. Using an incomplete kit causes more WIP (i.e., more people waiting in the ED) because the specific task is invariably waiting for one or more components of the kit to arrive. For example, if a specialist consultant is called in for a patient in the ED and he starts the examination without having a CK (i.e., all lab results, imaging results, and electrocardiography), the specialist may need another visit once the results are available. This causes more waiting time for the patient, while the consulting physician is not always available and may be considered a bottleneck. Of course, in cases of extreme emergency and danger to the patient, one can define a shorter mandatory kit of information for the given situation.

Longer Response Time

Response time is the time from the starting point of the process to its end. In the OR, the response time would be the time from when the patient is moved to the OR until she is moved back to the ward or to the intensive care unit. The linear (proportional) relationship between the level WIP and the response time has been widely discussed (Schonberger, 1986); more incomplete kits cause more WIP and hence a longer response time (see also chapter 11). Since response time is a source of tactical and strategic advantage for an organization, it is extremely important to use all possible methods to reduce it to a minimum. Let us examine an all too frequent situation where the patient is brought to the OR without a CK (e.g., he doesn't have the electrolytes lab results). The anesthetist must decide whether to wait until the patient has taken the test and receives the results or to postpone surgery. In either case, this largely extends response times.

High Variance of Planned, Quoted and Actual Response Times

It is very difficult to quote a response time when a major piece of information is missing, and one has to predict when the kit will be completed. If a patient arrives with a CK for a routine procedure or test (e.g., colonoscopy), it is quite easy to predict and commit to the procedure response time; the response time deviation is usually relatively small. However, if a patient arrives with an incomplete kit, the response time variance increases and causes difficulties and distortion of prediction, scheduling, and planning, which eventually result in inefficient performance and poor quality of services.

Poor Quality and More Rework

As was discussed in chapter 10, excessive WIP causes poor quality performance, both in terms of level of service to the patient and in the delivery of clinical quality. Patients arriving with incomplete kits sometimes wait in inadequate facilities for too long. When the missing items or information arrive, the medical documentation is reviewed by the doctors for the second or third time. This undoubtedly leads to waste of scarce resources and poor service quality. The clinical outcome may also be impaired and the fact that a patient coming with an incomplete kit is double- or even triple-handled, in many cases by another physician or another shift team, causes a severe deterioration of clinical quality.

Decline in Throughput

Using an incomplete kit increases both set-up times such as setting the OR for the next patient and the required extra time per patient resulting from duplicate handling. In a paperwork environment, such as that associated with the logistics of purchasing pharmaceuticals for the health organization, the inefficiency factor for using an incomplete kit is assessed to be approximately 80% (Ronen, 1992). This means that in the medical logistics systems, a process that takes 1.0 person hour using a CK, may be increased to 1.8 person hours if part of the required information is missing.

The number of patients being operated on in a specific time interval is the throughput of the OR. Working with an incomplete kit in the OR results in a decline of throughput.

Higher Operating Expenses

High WIP causes higher operating expenses due to more rework, duplicate work and more work put into the task. As noted by Schonberger (1986), any operation that does not add value to the process is a waste. Poor quality costs more money, since more work must be performed (Deming, 1986).

Decline in Staff Motivation

Using an incomplete kit goes against the grain. It diminishes staff motivation and trust in the system when they are forced to put more efforts in apparently unnecessary work. A prime example is that of a physician on duty in the ED needing to see many patients unnecessarily three or more times because an incomplete kit is being used.

Increase in Complexity and Control

If one works using an incomplete kit, controlling the system becomes very complex and sometimes almost impossible.

WHAT STOPS PEOPLE FROM USING A COMPLETE KIT?

If the benefits of using a CK are so obvious, why do people tend to work with incomplete kits? The answer seems to center around certain obstacles on the way to using a CK.

The Efficiencies Syndrome

The efficiencies syndrome is the urge to have resources utilized as much as possible (see chapter 9). Following the fallacious notion that staff should be busy all the time causes managers to have their people working on incomplete kits just so that they should not be idle.

The basic remedy for the efficiencies syndrome is a major change in the state of mind of managers in the organization, such as introducing quality management (Deming, 1986), the theory of constraints (TOC), Lean, and incorporating CK into this overall implementation. Indeed, a CK practice works best as an integral element of a total management philosophy.

The efficiencies syndrome is counterproductive if the operation has either an internal constraint (bottleneck resources) or has excess capacity. In the bottleneck environment, it doesn't make sense to introduce a task when we know that it lacks a CK since there are always other jobs that can turn into immediate throughput. In cases of excess capacity, there is more pressure to use an incomplete kit, just to utilize resources. There is no justification whatsoever for this, since excess capacity means short response times; thus, there is actually no advantage to starting work in an incomplete kit mode.

Pressure for Immediate Response

It is well known that processing time is only a small part of the total response time. Sometimes the physician starts treating a patient with an incomplete kit because of system pressure for immediate results, though she knows she will not be able to finish the procedure without it. Many people believe that if they start earlier (without a CK), they will finish their task earlier. In reality, in most cases, the opposite is true due to excess rework, resulting in delayed completion of the task.

Anxiety to Show Goodwill on the Part of the Staff

As a result of management pressure, laboratory technicians, nurses, and even physicians express their goodwill by releasing incomplete kits to the floor.

The conflict of not using a CK is described in the conflict resolution diagram of Figure 12.1.

MORE EXAMPLES OF THE COMPLETE KIT CONCEPT

Example: Let us demonstrate the use of the CK paradigm for colonoscopy performed in a gastroenterology department. Colonoscopy is one of the most significant diagnostic and therapeutic applications of endoscopy,

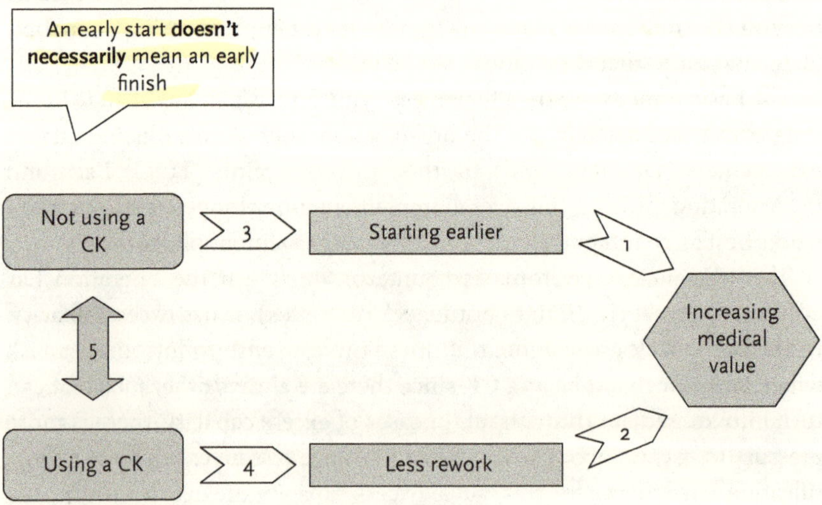

Figure 12.1:
A conflict resolution diagram of using a complete kit

because it can diagnose potentially curable colonic cancers that would be missed by other techniques, and it can also be used for the removal of potentially precancerous adenomatous polyps. Most initial colonoscopies are performed to investigate findings on an abnormal barium enema or to elucidate the cause of gastrointestinal bleeding. The ability to examine the whole colon is also useful in the management of some patients with inflammatory bowel disease and in patients with a family history of colonic polyps or cancer. The CK of a colonoscopy includes various medical devices that are needed for the procedure, such as the endoscope, various medications, and a resuscitation cart ready for any medical life support situation, and completion of all the preparatory procedures. One important procedure before initializing a colonoscopy is the preparation of the patient with laxatives and tap water enemas or by a total gut lavage with a nonabsorbable electrolyte solution. At least 24 hours are needed to achieve good preparation. If a patient now cancels a colonoscopy scheduled for the next day, another patient on the list is invited instead. However, the new patient arrives at the clinic unprepared, and the result in many cases is an incomplete examination and the need for a second colonoscopy. The damage is twofold: there is waste of medical resources and the patient does not receive good healthcare. Moreover, the results of the colonoscopy may be inconclusive and there may be a misdiagnosis. Had the gastroenterology department worked with a CK, situations like these would be rare. Therefore, it is important to instruct the staff not to invite patients for colonoscopy without full preparation. It is preferable to absorb the wasted time and resources due to cancellation rather than to enter a patient without a CK. One can use other methods to improve the operation of the department. For example, if the cancellation rate is 10%, one should overbook for colonoscopy 10% above the capacity of the department, and then three days before the scheduled date call everyone to confirm their arrival. Using the CK methodology will increase the production and the clinical quality of the department by at least 30%.

Example: One of the authors (JSP) was scheduled for hernia surgery. Upon checking into the hospital, he was asked what medications, if any, he is taking. He responded that he is only taking vitamins and low-dose aspirin. The admitting nurse surprisingly asked if the patient was not instructed to stop taking aspirin 10 days prior to surgery. Because the patient was not instructed to do so, the admission was cancelled and surgery postponed. As a result, there was an empty bed in the ward, there was a vacant slot in the OR schedule, and valuable resources were wasted. The incomplete instructions given to the patient are an example of an incomplete kit and its adverse effects.

A proven means for ensuring CKs for most medical procedures and operations is the establishment of a **presurgery clinic** operated by teams of nurses and anesthetists. Patients scheduled for ambulatory procedures are invited to the clinic ahead of the planned date and are requested to bring with them all the relevant documentation and information regarding use of medications that they must furnish according to procedure-related checklists. The nurse checks first the level of kit completion. In case of gaps, patients are instructed to bring the missing components. Whenever there is little chance of completing the kit on time, postponing the procedure is considered. Moreover, the anesthetist describes the forthcoming procedure in great details and eases patients' anxieties. In fact, this contribution of the presurgery clinic was considered before the responsibility of the anesthetists and is also part of the CK for the medical procedure.

Six months after the establishment of the presurgery clinic, one hospital experienced an increase of 20% in the number of operations, with much improved clinical quality. Case mix, before and after, was very similar.

Example: in a paperwork environment such as that characterizing medical logistics, the rule is to start working only if the kit is complete. For example, in the purchasing of pharmaceuticals, the process will not start unless the kit includes all the documents and information needed (i.e., end-user approval, budget number, etc.). In such an environment, a gatekeeper is designated as the only person authorized to release jobs. Since one cannot finish the task if a document or a form is missing, there is no reason to start processing the task until all the documents are at hand.

As demonstrated in the next subsections, implementation of the CK concept in a healthcare environment is well supported by modern management philosophies and techniques such as TOC, quality management (see chapter 18), and Lean.

IMPLEMENTING THE COMPLETE KIT

The following elements are suggested for implementing a CK process.

1. The introduction of a CK process must be part of a major change in the organization. It should be integrated with Lean/JIT, quality management, and TOC implementation.
2. Top management has to be involved in the process. Without the support and commitment of top management, there will be tremendous pressure from second-line managers to start processing despite the incomplete kits, in the belief that this will speed up the work.
3. One person should be appointed in each department to take charge. Usually, it is the gatekeeper (gater)—that is, the person who releases

the jobs or patients to the process. This should be part of the tactical gating mechanism.

4. The process must be monitored: control charts and Pareto charts need to be drawn, classifying incomplete kits by types of treatments, types of patients, or by the missing components. Using cause-and-effect techniques (fishbone diagrams, effect–cause–effect, etc.), causes are sought and appropriate corrective actions applied. The usual quality management way of improving processes may be employed here with good effects.
5. Employees and internal customers need to be informed of the change. Several organizations that have adopted the concept have designed special workshops to cope with this issue. The use of computer simulations and demonstrations using special software has been introduced into the educational process.
6. External customers/partners (such as health maintenance organizations) should be notified that they will get better due-date performance and better quoted response times if they submit a CK. For example, health maintenance organizations should be informed that the laboratories are using the CK methodology and hence will expect that all patients referred to the hospital should arrive with a CK.
7. A checklist defining the CK should be redefined from time to time according to the circumstances (see also Gawande, 2011). A good rule is: work smart and beware of inertia.
8. Components and materials should be ordered in CKs. Instead of ordering batches of the same components, when applicable, the provider should order kits from his suppliers. This applies to both internal and external suppliers.
9. All activities should be synchronized, ensuring that the outkit of a given activity is the inkit of the next one.
10. Components and procedures need to be standardized whenever possible. The more standard items available, the more likely it is that a CK will soon be available.

IMPLICATIONS FOR HEALTHCARE INFORMATION TECHNOLOGY

The information technology (IT) department in a healthcare organization should support activities with certain tools to enable a CK. Thus, applications for CK management tools should be developed. For any activity, the IT department should supply the relevant documents and information to provide compete kits and ensure that activities do not proceed until the kit is complete. The ability to allow for exceptions should be also planned.

Insofar as most of the items in a medical CK are medical information and data, IT plays a major role in reinforcing and implementing the CK paradigm and should be designed accordingly. Using IT technology, the IT department can maintain the CK framework by using an automatic checklist and providing the user the missing items for the CK. CK checklists should be incorporated in every relevant IT system.

Finally, it should be mentioned that the CK approach should be also implemented in the development processes of the IT department of the healthcare organization for the benefit of the organization.

IMPLICATIONS FOR THE MEDICAL PURCHASING AND LOGISTICS DEPARTMENT

The purchasing department would be required to change its procedures according to the CK concept:

1. It would purchase CKs. The orders would be of kits rather than of components.
2. This would force the purchasing department to work with fewer suppliers and purchase more items from each supplier.
3. Suppliers would be evaluated not only by price, response time, and quality but also by the completeness of their kits.

CHAPTER SUMMARY

The CK is a well-established concept, tried and trusted in in many healthcare systems. Strategically, it is a competitive edge because of the faster response times, lower prices, and better quality that it yields.

Our experience shows that the CK concept can be applied with good effects to any healthcare system. Experience in training and educating executives, managers, physicians, nurses, and other paramedical staff shows that, in most cases, practitioners need to have an enforcing formal framework, even though they intuitively appreciate the value of CK. They need the accompanying theoretical background and methodological framework such as those presented in this chapter to better cope with the pressure from bosses to start working with an incomplete kit. Today's medical staff does not have the administration backing to say "no" to an incomplete kit. Management must continuously back employees and departments who point out incomplete kits.

CHAPTER 13

Performance Measures

OBJECTIVES

- Understand the need to evaluate performance and the need to measure it.
- Understand how to use the six global performance measures in practice.

PERFORMANCE MEASURES: LOCAL OR GLOBAL?

Performance measures are a most important managerial tool. They are used to control the activities within the organization toward the achievement of its goal. Performance measures are also used to define quantitative objectives for the whole organization, divisions, and various units. It serves as an effective means for communicating management's policies throughout the organization. Properly defined performance measures motivate managers and employees and can form a suitable infrastructure for an incentives payments system. Lastly, the set of performance measures can assist decision-making. Performance measures are sometimes referred to as key performance indicators.

Global performance measures are tightly connected to the goal of creating more value to the organization. Whenever the set of global performance measures indicates improvement, then the value of the organization is enhanced. However, if the local performance measures are not directly connected to the value of the organization, they can cause damage to the organization. For example, measuring the operating room (OR) by efficiency (e.g., utilization) gets the reverse reaction.

In some situations, local performance measures can be very appropriate. For example, if we want to evaluate programs for curbing hypertension in the community, a possible natural measure can be the percentage of people with hypertension who are balanced with medication. Another possible measure can be the average reduction of diastolic or systolic blood pressures. In treatment and prevention for cancer, acceptable measures include number of cases averted, number of cases in remission and length of remission, among others.

As we have seen in previous chapters, reliance on local performance measures only may distort the decision-making process and lead to suboptimization. A measure such as the number of police traffic tickets will not achieve the goal of reducing the number of traffic accidents and smooth traffic flow. A measure of the number of patients seen in the emergency department (ED) may lead to early discharge and suboptimal treatment. This is the motivation to introduce more global performance measures.

GLOBAL PERFORMANCE MEASURES

We need global performance measures that will yield the following benefits.

Voicing Management Policy regarding the Organization's Goals

People behave according to how they are measured ("Tell me how you behave, and I'll tell you how you are measured"). Clear and simple measures will broadcast management policy in an unambiguous way. Improving these measures should improve the value of the firm in a business environment and advance organizational goals in a nonprofit environment.

Aid Decision-Making

It is expected from top management to consider different alternatives vis-à-vis the organizational goal, so that the chosen alternative will enhance the firm's value for its shareholders. However, middle management will frequently find it difficult to directly see the link between "action in the field" and enhancing the firm's value. Thus, we need performance measures that translate the organizational goal into operative language.

The performance measures are, thus, an intermediary between the decision makers and the organizational goals. For example, in managing the introduction of a new drug, time to market is an important measure for value enhancement. Hence, the project manager will seek to reduce time to market.

Control

Performance measures can be used as a tool for routine control for top and middle management. When measurement reveals problems, it enables correcting them. When it reveals improved performance, it enables learning from successes and replicating them elsewhere in the organization. Performance measure enable an organization to monitor if it is moving toward achieving its goals in the short and long term and what corrective actions are needed to improve performance.

Evaluation and Reward

Good performance measures can serve as part of a system of evaluation and reward in the organization to improve worker motivation and advance organizational goals.

Ability to Decentralize

A CEO, talented as can be, cannot centralize all decisions within the organization. Appropriate performance measures by which the CEO and her subordinates are measured allow decentralized decision-making processes.

Appropriate performance measures should have the following characteristics:

- **Global and effective.** Effective measures are such that their improvement in business organizations will significantly advance the achievement of the organizational goal and will enhance the firm's value; in nonprofit organizations will advance organizational goals.
- **Simple and clear.** "What will not be simple—simply will not be." Measures should be clear, simple, and easily measured.
- **Based on the satisficer approach.** Measures should be satisfactory and not necessarily perfect or optimal. Implementing performance measures in an organization is not simple, and, therefore, it is advisable to proceed gradually. The desire to implement a set of perfectly accurate measures may prove too difficult and lead to abandoning the process.

- **Founded on easy and simple data collection.** It is desirable to use data from existing databases in the organization and have the users of the measures be the ones collecting the data.
- **Customized to the organization.** The attempt to adopt as-are measures that have succeeded elsewhere may end up in disappointment. The organization must gradually build its own appropriate measures or properly adapt others.

THE SIX GLOBAL PERFORMANCE MEASURES

We present a set of six generic performance measures that can be expanded or reduced according to each organization's needs. The first three measures were defined by Goldratt and Cox (1992), and the others, by Eden and Ronen (1993). The global performance measures presented in Table 13.1 represent output measures, input measures, and process measures.

Throughput (T)

Example: The throughput (effective output) of traffic police is reducing the number of accidents and improving traffic flow. It is not the number of tickets issued.

Throughput—the **effective** output of the organization.

Table 13.1. THE SIX GLOBAL PERFORMANCE MEASURES

1	Throughput (T)
2	Operating expenses (OE)
3	Inventory (I)
4	Response time (RT)
5	Quality (Q)
6	Due date performance (DDP)

In **Business** organizations, the throughput is defined as the **cash flow** generated from sales—more specifically, total **actual sales** minus **real variable costs** of **those** sales.

Actual sales—sales that were actually carried out, minus returns and cancelled sales.

Example: A hospital OR should monitor the number of procedures and surgeries performed or the corresponding incomes, not hours of OR utilization. The focus should be on output, not input. Throughput is the contribution volume of the procedures.

Example: A company is committed to deliver every month 100 units of product A, 100 of product B, and 100 units of product C at a selling price of \$10 per unit. The company has no work-in-process (WIP) inventory, and there is no finished goods inventory at the beginning of the month. The real variable costs for each unit are \$4. The company decided to produce 200 units of A, 150 units of B, and no units of product C. This is a seemingly strange decision. If there are well-defined demands, why not produce accordingly? In reality, firms frequently do not produce according to market demands and justify their actions on grounds of economies of scale (i.e., reducing per-unit cost), savings in additional administrative work, or savings on additional machine set-ups. Sometimes the measure is the number of units produced with no regard to market demand, which results in inappropriate production decisions.

To calculate the throughput of the system for the previous example, let us look at the data in Table 13.2.

The throughput calculation is

$$T = 100(10-4) + 100(10-4) + 0 = \$1{,}200$$

Table 13.2. PRODUCTION DATA

	Product A	Product B	Product C
Demand (units)	100	100	100
Selling price per unit (S)	10	10	10
Real variable costs per unit (\$)	4	4	4
Actual production (units)	200	150	—

The output from products A and B is calculated based on 100 units that were sold (the surplus units will be counted in the inventory measure). In our example, production is 350 units (compared to a demand of 300), but the throughput is only $1,200, which is less than the full throughput of $1,800 (if the plant would have produced and sold what the market demands).

It should be noted that in many places, middle management is occasionally measured by the number of units produced; this is occasionally the organizational language. Such organizations still talk about units sold, tons, and so on. In the insurance industry, the measure of production (total new premiums sold in a period) is still abundant. This may lead to accepting orders that will result in losses.

Measuring throughput in monetary units (dollars) sends a message throughout the organization that "we mean business" and helps to meet due-date performance vis-à-vis customers by focusing everybody on creating effective output. In one organization, the authors encountered a department manager who successfully implemented the philosophy and refused to produce surplus by saying, **"This will not give throughput to the firm."** This reflects a successful implementation of measures that become part of the organizational language.

Example: Both public and business-oriented hospitals have very large fixed costs, mainly on personnel. The variable costs are only 10% to 15% of the budget. We should focus on throughput as the generator of contribution.

To summarize, the throughput of an OR can be measured monetarily (as discussed above) or by the number of patients operated on. In the ED, throughput can be measured by the number of patients with a discharge or hospitalization decision. The throughput of an MRI unit is the number of patients who completed the test (including interpretation).

Operating Expenses (OE)

These expenses include.

Real variable costs—raw materials, components, subcontractors, commissions, and so on.

Operating expenses—the sum of all **fixed** expenses of the organization during the measurement period.

- Direct labor.
- Indirect labor.
- Rent and other fixed expenses.

Another definition of operating expenses states that the operational expenses are the fixed costs for converting inventory into throughput (Goldratt and Cox, 1992).

These expenses are **fixed expenses** of the organization in the short and medium term. Fluctuations in demand only marginally affect the direct labor costs. The operating expense approach requires looking at the whole organization and evaluating whether expenses increased or decreased. Any suggestion for change or improvement should be evaluated by the manager to determine whether operating expenses will increase or decrease as well the impact on throughput.

Example: A large enterprise hired the services of a consulting firm. After analyzing some data and comparing the enterprise to similar ones in the market, the consultants advised a cutback of 10% in the costs of indirect labor. The CEO summoned the division managers and instructed them to cut 10% of indirect labor costs. This was immediately implemented despite the tense labor relations between the workers' union and management. How as this achieved? Very simply—some of the indirect workers were reclassified as direct labor. It is obvious that operating expenses did not decrease nor were any savings achieved.

Inventory (I)

Inventory is generally classified into three different categories that require different treatment:

- Raw materials inventory.
- WIP inventory.
- Finished goods inventory.

These three categories are important and should be managed and measured. In healthcare organizations, WIP inventory reflects patients in the system, whether waiting or being cared for. In treating patients, we should only measure WIP (e.g., patients in the ED, patients on a waiting list for kidney transplantation, patients in a waiting room of an outpatient clinic).

Response Time (RT)

Response time is a general term for various time measures that include lead time, cycle time, time to market, and response time. For more accurate definitions, refer to the *APICS Dictionary* (Cox and Blackstone, 1998) and Cox and Spencer (1998). We will simply relate to system response times by one term: "response time." The organization must identify its main processes and measure their response times.

An appropriate measure of response times is one that looks at the process from the perspective of the **customer**. The measurement should include the actual response times, without special allowances for the responsibility of "someone else." For example, a patient is concerned with the total time he spends in the system including various waits. He does not care who is responsible for a longer-than-usual wait.

Quality (Q)

Measures of quality contribute to organizational enhancement. Every organization must define its relevant quality measures. Examples include:

- Percentage of procedures performed without complications the first time.
- Costs of nonquality (e.g., readmissions to the ED, repeated surgeries).
- Customer satisfaction.
- Specific measures of clinical quality.
- Number of customer complaints.

Due-Date Performance (DDP)

Due-date performance reflects the organization's reliability in meeting deadlines.

Due-date performance can be measured in several ways:

Percentage of on-time performance: Measuring the percentage of patients or tests that were completed on time. For example, on-time performance in many EDs is set for four hours. The percentage of patients who met this standard is the measure for DDP. Even though this is a very simple measure, in situations with a high variability in the length of treatment, this measure can distort reality by encouraging the caregiver to select the simpler cases. In such cases, the treatments should be classified into groups of treatments, and DDP should be measured for each group separately.

CALCULATING PROFIT

We can conceptually define the profit of the firm using the previously presented measures as below.

"**Profit**" of the firm equals the **throughput** of the firm **minus** the **operating expenses.**

The importance of this relation is that it forces decision makers in an organization to think globally. Saving two labor hours in some activity or seven minutes of service time are not necessarily relevant. The important issues are the impact of decisions on global performance measures—the throughput or operating expenses—and, as a result, on profit. Therefore, in organizational decision-making processes, the following questions must be asked:

- Will organization throughput increase as a result of the decision?
- Will the operating expenses decrease as a result of the decision?
- Will the decision increase the difference between the throughput and the operating expense?

Long-term decision-making must also consider the impact of decisions on investments and tax issues.

EXAMPLE: ADAPTING GLOBAL PERFORMANCE MEASURES TO AN OR

A system of performance measures must be adapted for every organization. Let us consider an OR in a hospital. We will first relate to the six global measures.

Throughput: The number of operations by patient mix or operation type. In a for-profit hospital, the throughput of the OR can be measured by monetary contributions (revenues for surgeries minus real variable costs).

Operating expenses: Rent for the OR and payment for surgeons, anesthetists, nurses, administrative and cleaning staff. On the other hand, the costs associated with temporary seasonal workers or workers of a subcontractor who do not work on a regular basis (where the number of workers can be changed in response to workloads) are considered real variable costs.

Inventory: Number of patients waiting in the OR itself, plus number waiting in the preparation room.

Response time: Time from summoning patient from the ward to the end of surgery, or time from when patient enters the OR until leaving for the recovery room. In situations where the surgeon, anesthetist, or the OR itself is the bottleneck, the recommended measurement is the time from the end of "stitching" one patient until the first incision on the following patient.

Quality: Two measures—clinical quality and service quality. Typical clinical quality measures are the number of repeated surgeries and number of acquired infections.

Due-Date Performance: Percent of procedures performed within hospital standards (e.g., percentage of cataract surgeries).

The six global measures form a good starting basis. As appropriate, we may delete some of them and/or add others.

Note: In nonprofit organizations, there is a tendency to do extensive and seemingly endless research on finding appropriate performance measures. They should adopt a satisficer approach. First, start with two to three acceptable, yet not ideal, measures so we can start measuring right away. Then, as time goes by, measures can be refined or others added. There is no sense in delaying measurement until the "perfect" measure is determined. The lost time translates into inferior performance.

Example: There are not many agreed-upon measures for clinical quality in the ED. We can start for example by measuring the percentage of patients returning to the ED and/or the percentage of patients that spend more than six hours in the ED.

THE MEASUREMENT PROFILE AND GLOBAL DECISION-MAKING

The measurement profile is a tool to aid global decision-making (GDM). The tool examines alternative decisions using the organizational global performance measures. The use of the measurement profile examines alternative actions by the six global measures previously presented. In this two-dimensional matrix, the columns present the different alternatives (including no action), and the rows present the performance of the measures, as outlined in Table 13.3.

Table 13.3. THE MEASUREMENT PROFILE		
	Alternative A	Alternative B
Throughput		
Operating expenses		
Inventory		
Response time		
Quality		
Due date performance		

The measurement profile presents a succinct picture for each alternative and thus enables an easy comparison of the impact of each alternative on the various dimensions of organizational performance. A use of this profile across the organization contributes to the decision-making process by having everyone speak the same common and understandable language.

The six global measures are not the only measures useful for decision making. As seen by the OR example, some of the six measures can be deleted (if not relevant) and others added.

The following chapters will present some uses of the measurement profile in various decision problems.

COMMON MEASUREMENT PITFALLS

People behave and make decisions according to the way they are measured. We have seen examples where reliance on local performance measures can lead to suboptimization, which does not serve the organization well. Moreover, even if we use correct measures, there are situations where measurement fails.

People do not like to be measured. However, if they are, here are some things to look out for:

1. People try to define measures that are always fully correlated with the goal. Finding such measures is nearly impossible, therefore the satisficer approach is warranted.
2. People frequently want to be measured in a way that only serves their own responsibility, while ignoring the responsibility of others in the process. This can be very harmful.
3. People expect the measures to work for every possible scenario. For example, a measurement that will be appropriate for winter as well

as summer, namely, for a market constraint as well as for a resource constraint.

4. People look for fairness or equity in measures they use, and they are not always such.

CHAPTER SUMMARY

Performance measures are a control tool for guiding and navigating managers in an organization. In many situations, an appropriate change of performance measures can bring upon fast and significant improvement in organizational performance and enhancing organizational value.

The global performance measures presented in this chapter help the organization focus on activities that improve performance and thus better achieve the goal of the organization.

CHAPTER 14
The Effects of Variability and Uncertainty

OBJECTIVES

- Understand why variability is one of the biggest enemies of healthcare systems and why we need to manage it.
- Why traditional approaches to managing variability have failed and how new approaches can better manage it.

VARIABILITY

The uncertainty related to level of performance, malfunctions, faults, and disruptions is referred to as "**variability**". This will serve mainly as a general term for all the seemingly unexpected situations of problems, malfunctions, interruptions, and disturbances.

Murphy's Law says that if something can go wrong, it will, and it will cause the maximal damage at the most inconvenient time.

The law is occasionally phrased as the "bread and butter law." If a buttered slice of bread can drop to the floor, it will. If it drops, it will fall butter-side down, damaging the new carpet.

Some would add that is the slice falls butter-side up, we had spread the butter on the wrong side.

The O'Toole principle adds that "Murphy was an optimist."

Our approach to dealing with variability is based on Deming (1986), Goldratt and Fox (1986), and the authors' experience in dealing with variability in healthcare organizations. At the end of this chapter, we will describe Litvak's complimentary approach (Litvak, 2005).

Sources of Variability

Variability can be classified by its source:

1. Variability in demand.
   - Seasonality.
   - Technological changes and changes in preferences.
2. Variability in capacity.
   - Variability of work rates.
   - Variability in setup times, both physical setups and mental ones.
   - Malfunctions: device failure, computer crash, and so on.
   - Employee absenteeism.
   - Scheduling and timing problems.
   - Incomplete kits.
3. Variability in quality.
   - Unexpected failures.
4. Variability in the availability of materials.
   - Problems with quality of materials.
   - Delays in supply.
   - Supply problems (less than ordered, different from what was ordered, etc.).

Example: Variability in the emergency department (ED) of a hospital includes:

- Uncertainty in the case mix and arrival rate
- Unavailability of consultants/specialists
- Unavailability of operating rooms
- Unavailability of critical resources
- Uncertainty of demand (seasonality)

ACCUMULATING VARIABILITY IN A PROCESS

Consider the planning of a new line of services, products, or development. This is depicted in Figure 14.1.

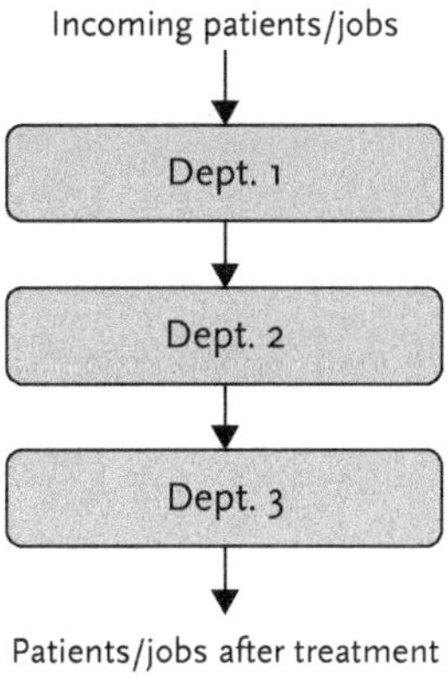

Figure 14.1:
Description of the planned process

Every task that enters the system (e.g., a patient receiving treatment, a request to develop a smart patient record, assembly in production) must go through stations 1, 2, and 3.

Let us assume that $15M has been targeted for creating this process. The developers are faced with three alternatives for buying equipment, each costing $15M. Figures 14.2 to 14.4 present the three alternatives using a cost-utilization diagram. The CUT diagram presents, as we have seen before, the **average** utilization of the resources.

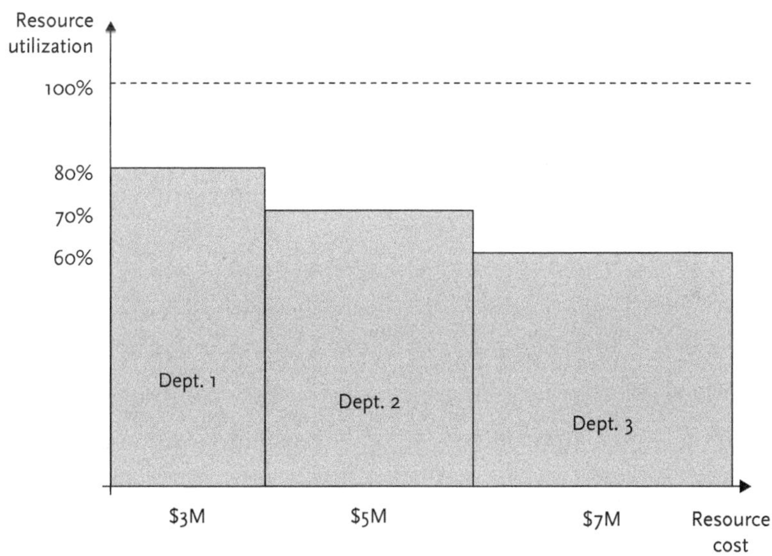

Figure 14.2:
Cost-utilization diagram for alternative A

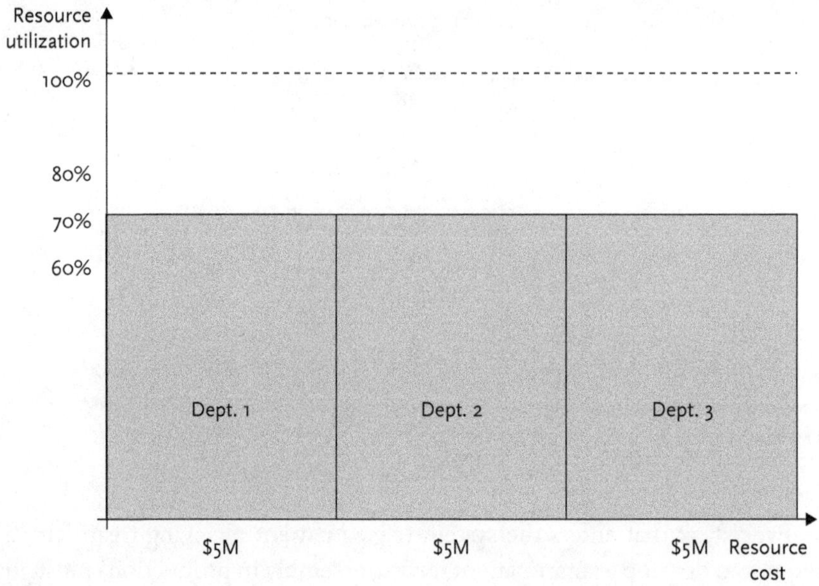

Figure 14.3:
Cost-utilization diagram for alternative B

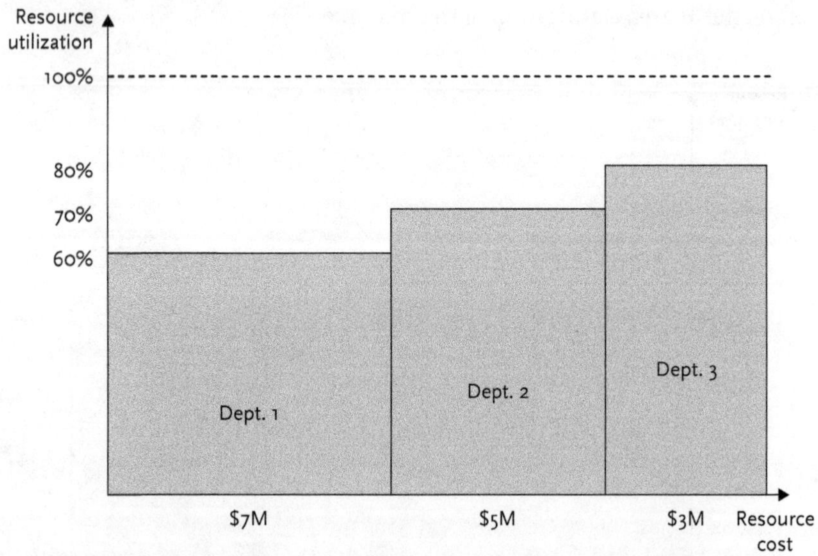

Figure 14.4:
Cost-utilization diagram for alternative C

Seemingly all three alternatives provide a reasonable solution. All seem to have excess capacity. However, the CUT diagram presents just the average utilization of the resources. In reality, utilization is not constant and varies due to fluctuations. Hence considering only average utilization can lead to worse decisions.

VARIABILITY IN UTILIZATION

There are two types of variability:

- Internal variability.
- Cumulative variability.

Internal Variability

Internal variability of a station comes from the **station itself** and affects its performance. Internal variability can result, for example, from a computer crash at the station, idling the station for a while and increasing the work rate the rest of the time. Other sources of variability can be worker absenteeism, quality problems, or having a "good day" with above-average achievements.

Cumulative Variability

The cumulative variability of a station results from **performance in preceding stages** of the process. Consider, for example, a group of hikers marching in a single file. Where would you rather be: at the head of the line or at the end of the line? The average speed at the head of the line is seemingly the same as that at the end of the line. However, experience shows that those at the end will occasionally have to run to keep up and occasionally halt as a result of the cumulative variability of all the hikers ahead of them. The standard deviation of a walker at the end of the line is bigger than at the beginning of the line. This is described in more detail by Goldratt and Cox (1992). Variability in a process is similar: the further a resource is from the beginning of the process, the higher is its cumulative variability.

Let us now examine the CUT diagrams of the three alternatives where the diagrams present both the average and variance of the capacity resulting from the internal variability of the stations and the cumulative variability of the preceding stations (Figures 14.5–14.7).

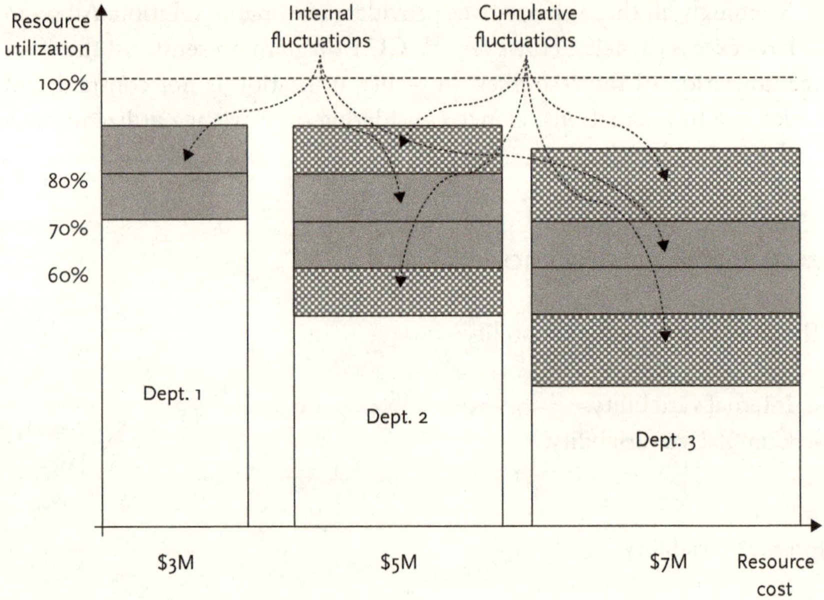

Figure 14.5:
Alternative A with internal and cumulative variability

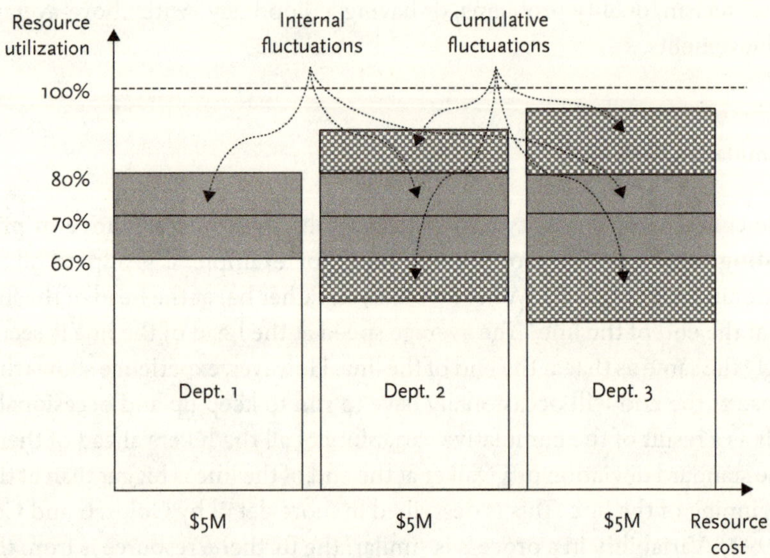

Figure 14.6:
Alternative B with internal and cumulative variability

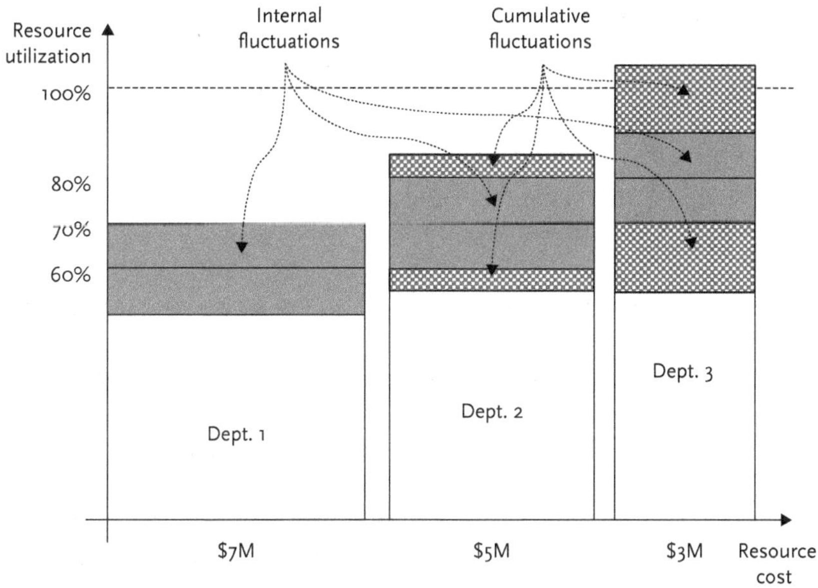

Figure 14.7:
Alternative C with internal and cumulative variability

Looking at the three figures, it is clear that alternative A is the preferred choice because even at peak utilization, there is no bottleneck despite the cumulative variability.

With alternative B, there is almost a bottleneck part of the time, and the system should be treated as if there is an actual bottleneck during these times.

The cumulative variability sometimes creates a bottleneck at station 3 of alternative C. This situation is typical for activities such as discharge from a ward, testing, evaluation or calibration, or other stations situated at the end of processes. Due to delays in earlier stations, such stations are underutilized most of the time. However, when a bulk of work arrives, there is a shortage of resources, and the station becomes the process bottleneck. Even though, on the average, such stations have adequate capacity, they become a bottleneck during most of the time. The following sections of this chapter will present ways to overcome this situation.

We will also present other ways to protect against cumulative variability, such as building a buffer in front of department 3, which might become the system bottleneck.

CATEGORIES OF CAPACITY

Capacity can be broken down into three categories:

1. Nominal capacity of the resource.
2. Protective capacity of the resource.
3. Excess capacity of the resource.

The **nominal capacity of the resource** is the average capacity required for performing its tasks.

The **protective** capacity **of the resource** is that part of the capacity that is targeted to **overcome** the internal and cumulative **fluctuations** in the load of the resource. These fluctuations result from changing demand, availability of personnel, availability of raw materials, from malfunctions, and so on. This capacity protects the system against routine fluctuations. It is not intended to protect against large and unexpected fluctuations that are rather rare, such as hurricanes, ongoing strikes, and so.

The system bottlenecks are usually expensive or scarce resources; thus, the system has difficulty in creating a protective capacity for them. However, systems must create **protective capacity in noncritical resources.** This will assure that bottlenecks will not be idle because of delays of workflow in the noncritical resources.

The **excess capacity of the resource** is that part of the maximal capacity of the resource that is not used—not used during routine operations and not even during increased utilization as a result of fluctuations.

Several conclusions emanate from this analysis:

1. During the planning stage for services, products or development, it is not enough to consider the nominal capacity. Planning according to averages can be compared to the situation of the statistics professor who drowned in a lake with an average depth of 12 inches.

   Demand should be by seasonality. For example, in an ED there is an obvious difference between the pressure during the day and during the night. A system analysis should consider two separate EDs—a day ED and a night ED.
2. In situations of large fluctuations during peak times, the system must be planned to meet the peaks, and to find ways to "sell the excess capacity" during off-peak times. For example, a restaurant whose primary business is during evening hours can try to increase sales during lunch by offering "business lunch" menus.
3. A system needs protective capacity. On a local level, this can be viewed as excess and waste. However, from a global perspective, the protective

capacity protects the throughput of the bottlenecks and assures achieving maximal output for the whole system.
4. Resources with a capacity utilization exceeding 85% are considered bottlenecks and must be managed accordingly.
5. While planning a service or production, we need to arrange sufficient protective capacity. The Japanese, for example, tend to build service and production systems with an average utilization of 70%.
6. The concept of "line balancing" is not consistent with reality, which has fluctuations in the system. Experience shows that a service or product line consists of resources with differing costs, some being scarce or expensive. We should maintain adequate protective capacity for the cheap resources so they can operate continually and allow focusing on bottlenecks.

THE FOCUSED MANAGEMENT APPROACH TO MANAGING VARIABILITY

Variability must be managed and not responded to when it happens, in an **effective** manner on the one hand and with **minimal costs** on the other.

We distinguish between two ways of managing and dealing with variability:

1. Protecting against variability.
2. Reducing variability.

Protecting against Variability

Creating protective capacity is just one of several methods to protect against variability. The various approaches are:

- **Building a buffer ahead of the bottleneck.** Building a buffer and managing it using the drum–buffer–rope (DBR) approach is a simple and effective way to reduce variability. The uniqueness of this approach is the building of one buffer and not spreading the WIP across the entire system. This brings quick results in terms of increasing output and reducing response times.
- **Creating protective capacity.** Creating this protection is immediate. Protective capacity can be achieved through by implementing TOC or Lean, reducing the garbage time, the purchase of resources, or through agreement with sub-contractors.
- **Building an overflow buffer after the bottleneck.** One should arrange overflow space and facilities after the bottleneck. This will allow keeping the bottleneck working when there are delays in stations that follow it. For example, the recovery room serving the OR is an overflow buffer that should have all the required protective capacity.
- **Building a buffer of materials.** Building a buffer of materials protects the system against the possible variability in their supply.

Protection against variability by creating excess capacity, protective capacity, or by creating the right buffers in the right places can be achieved rather quickly. The impact of these protective measures, specifically the right buffers and the DBR mechanism, is immediate and yields short-term results. The problem is that this improvement, as big as it may be, is a one-time achievement. After the initial results, further improvement in protective methods against variability is slow and lengthy and must be accompanied by activities to reduce variability.

Reducing Variability

There are several mechanisms to reduce variability. While the implementation of protection against variability is immediate and brings quick results, the reduction of variability is usually a slow process whose impact is realized in the medium and long term. For example, the approaches for managing quality and process control according to Deming (1986) are approaches that require a change in the thinking of most people in the organization. Implementing such approaches and observing significant results take considerable time, even years. Let us now examine approaches to reduce variability:

- **Reducing response time.** Reducing system response time allows for better prediction of demand which, in turn, allows significant reduction of variability in the system. In addition, the shorter the response time of the process is, the smaller its standard deviation is. For example, purchased goods arrive on the average every eight weeks, with a standard deviation of, plus or minus, one week. The firm can protect against a late arrival of materials by creating a week's safety inventory through ordering a week before the original order. If response time is reduced to 8 days, purchases would arrive on the average every 8 days with a standard deviation of, plus or minus, one day. Variability will naturally be smaller and so will the required level of safety stock.
- **Sharing information with customers and suppliers.** Sharing information reduces uncertainty. A customer providing her supplier with the demand forecast, reduces the supplier's uncertainty, and allows her to obtain raw materials, plan personnel, and so on. Even a forecast that will materialize only 70% but will be periodically updated may provide important value to the supplier. Improving the performance of the supplier contributes to the customer by reducing her variability.
- **Ability to create a common core for several products or services (the "mushroom effect").** Producing or providing service for every product or service separately, as depicted in Figure 14.8, requires separate planning of resources (and raw materials) for every line. Creating a

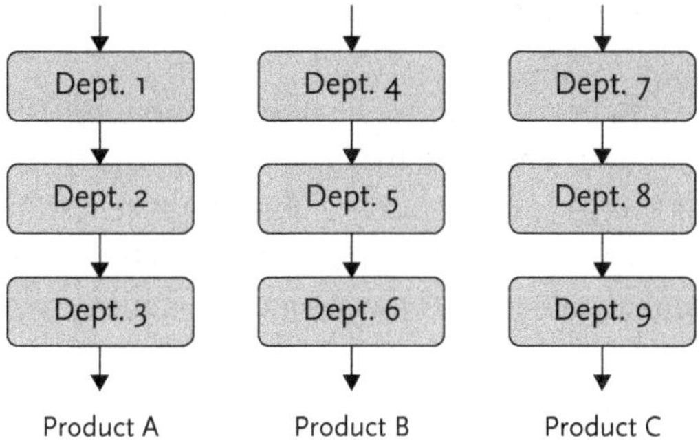

Figure 14.8:
A separate line for every product

common core for several products (the "mushroom effect"), as shown in Figure 14.9, allows reducing the variance in the planning of resources and raw materials. In service organizations, this translates into a more flexible and versatile service.

- **Standardization of components and kits.** Standardization of kits and components used by the organization will reduce the variability in work processes and will also allow lower levels of their inventory.
- **Using a single buffer for the entire project using the critical chain approach.** Using a shared buffer for all project activities, reduces, on average, the response time of the project along with the variance of the finishing date.
- **Quality improvement and process control.** Quality improvement and process control contribute significantly to reduction of variability. These methods are presented in chapter 18.
- **Working in smaller working batches, working packages, and transfer batches.** Using smaller work packages and transfer batches allows for a more continuous process, with less WIP, a shorter response time, and, as a result, smaller variability.

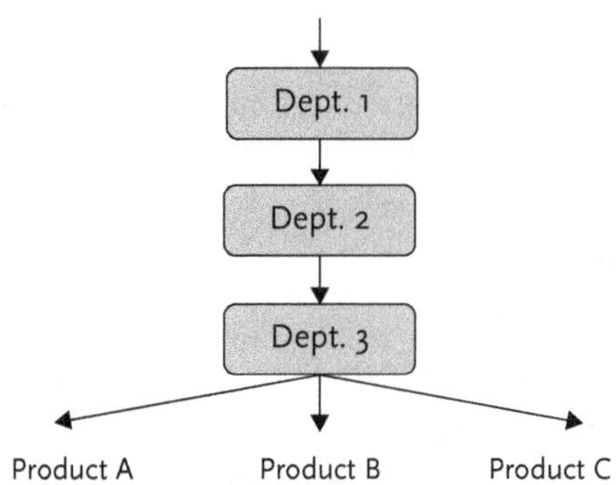

Figure 14.9:
Creating a common core for several products—the "mushroom effect"

LITVAK'S APPROACH TO MANAGING VARIABILITY

Litvak (2005) differentiates between **natural variability** and **artificial variability**. Natural variability stems from the process of arrival of patients to the ED. It has three types of sources: clinical presentation, patient flow, and professional expertise. They are random by nature and, in the case of the first two, patient driven. Litvak claims that natural variability can be neither eliminated nor even reduced. Instead, it must be optimally managed. In general, managing natural variability means creating homogeneous patient subgroups based on patient acuity and other criteria. Such solutions are group technology solutions discussed in chapter 11. Artificial variability is nonrandom, nonpredictable, and driven by priorities given by individuals. Unlike natural variability, artificial variability should not be managed; rather, it must be identified and eliminated. For example, artificial peaks in patient demand remain a major roadblock to increasing patient throughput and, therefore, to increasing hospital revenues.

IMPLEMENTATION CONSIDERATIONS

Variability can be managed by protection and reduction activities.

There is no doubt that reducing variability, especially using quality management and process control, contributes to the output of the organization and to enhancing its value. However, its implementation is more difficult, and the results are achieved only in the medium or long term, while requiring the involvement of most players in the system.

It is not surprising that many quality improvement programs do not achieve their goals because of these difficulties. On the other hand, **protecting** against variability, especially through approaches of management by constraints, is not sufficient, even though results in this case are obtained in the short term.

Combining both approaches seems to be the right solution: starting the implementation of improvements via management by constraints and, in parallel, building the infrastructure for the implementation of quality management approaches. In the case of implementing these improvement steps, it is safe to say that "quality comes second."

CHAPTER SUMMARY

Managing variability is an important issue that management must consider both for planning a service or producing a process and for the routine operation of the organization's resources. Variability that is not properly managed may turn noncritical resources into bottlenecks, thus increasing response time, decreasing throughput, and increasing the amount of work in process.

CHAPTER 15
The "Evils" of Traditional Cost Accounting

OBJECTIVE

- Discuss why traditional cost accounting may lead organizations to inadequate decisions.

LOSS OF RELEVANCE OF TRADITIONAL COST ACCOUNTING

Traditional cost accounting lost relevance back in the 1980s (Goldratt, 1990; Goldratt and Cox, 1992; Johnson and Kaplan, 1987). Traditional cost accounting methods were developed in the 1920s in leading U.S. firms and were suitable for the production environment of those days: labor-intensive mass production of a limited number of products, utilizing economies of scale, and learning curves. Direct labor wages were a major component in costs and were considered true variable costs, taking into considerations the labor relations at that time. The indirect costs were low, and assigning them to products based on direct wages (or another volume-based variable like machine hours) was a reasonable approximation for making business decisions such as continued production of a product, investment decisions, make or buy, and so on.

For example, the costing of one unit of product A was:

Materials	$10
Direct labor	$4
Overhead allocation	$2
Total product cost	$16

In the business environment of the past, the traditional cost accounting allowed the breakdown of business outcomes at profit centers by individual product and preparing a balance sheet for each product or service separately. One could make decisions about **one product or service** (e.g., increasing/decreasing production, using subcontractors) without **concurrently checking the impact of the decisions on other products or services.** This is the **separation principle,** which created a convenient decision-making tool for management.

Decisions regarding a product or service, based on the separation principle, required knowing the data relevant only for this specific product or service. For example, if the market price for product A was only $13, then a decision about ceasing its production was obvious (compared to a production cost of $16). If a subcontractor would be willing to produce the product for $12, the make-or-buy decision would again be easy. In another situation, if the market price would be $22 per unit, then traditional cost accounting, which is based on the product cost, provided a good answer for decision makers.

Several factors are responsible for the loss of relevancy of traditional cost accounting.

Changes in the Relative Weight of the Indirect Costs

When the traditional cost accounting was created in the 1920s, indirect costs were 5% to 10% of production costs. Today, the indirect costs (i.e., overheads) constitute 20% to 80% of the total cost of the product. The bulk of this increase comes from costs related to operations support (e.g., planning, operations control, scheduling, legal staff, quality assurance), IT, the marketing force, and the managers of finance and human resources. The weight of the traditional fixed indirect costs of production (e.g., depreciation, insurance, property taxes) has remained stable over time.

Changes in the Character of Labor Costs

In the **past**, direct labor costs were a **variable expense. Today,** direct wages are mainly a **fixed cost** in the short and medium terms. However, it is still customary in accounting to assign the indirect costs based on direct wages, causing severe distortions.

Expanding the Variety of Services and Products

Today's services and products are congruent with customer needs and preferences. Technological development, along with the desire to adapt services and products to customers, brought a large increase in the variety of products, services, and treatments available today. The competitive need to expand the variety of services and products presents a managerial challenge: how to expand the variety while maintaining the advantages of the organization whose operations are focused. The cost accounting systems must provide support with relevant information. Traditional cost accounting does not provide answers to the challenge of production complexity, development of prototypes, and providing a variety of services.

Distinguishing between Bottlenecks and Noncritical Resources

Today there is a clear distinction between resources that are bottlenecks and noncritical resources. The noncritical resources have built-in protective capacity that should protect the system against external fluctuations in demand and internal fluctuations resulting from malfunctions and so on. Traditional cost accounting does not recognize this distinction.

The Dominance of Financial Accounting

The sophistication of capital markets and the stricter rules for financial reporting have brought in recent decades a drive for research and regulation in financial accounting, with emphasis on financial reporting. On the other hand, managerial accounting remained virtually at a standstill and is considered only a supportive system of secondary importance. When resources are channeled into managerial improvement, the financial manager (who is frequently also responsible for the information systems) will usually prefer to invest in financial accounting tools needed for reporting to the stock exchange or the Internal Revenue Service, rather than investing in managerial accounting tools (e.g., decision support measurement systems).

LOSS OF RELEVANCE OF TRADITIONAL COST ACCOUNTING—EXAMPLES

"It Costs Us More"

A large pharmaceutical company bought a new machine at a cost of $2 million. This machine replaced an old, very labor-intensive, line. It produced a high-quality product in very short response times and in sufficient quantities to meet fully local market demands, all this at a capacity utilization not exceeding 60%. The return on investment was less than two years. The cost of producing a unit of the product was calculated by the accountants as:

Raw materials	\$10
Direct labor	\$2
Overhead	\$8
Total cost	\$20

A foreign customer wanted to purchase this product for \$16 per unit, in quantities corresponding to additional 10% of the machine's capacity. Even though the customer was from a totally different geographical region and even though he agreed to sell the product under a different name and for a different use, management refused to sell, claiming "it costs us more" and "we can't sell a product at a loss." The situation of considering costs that are not relevant for making decisions is well known and has been discussed in the literature for decades. However, many managers still use total cost data for decision-making.

"Big Batches"

The new CEO immediately pushed to reduce the product cost. The average production batch size (which was congruent with the market) was 10 units. Production resources were at excess capacity. Setup time was two hours, and the marginal time to produce one unit was 15 minutes (1/4 hour). The average time to produce one unit in a batch size of 10 is:

$$T(10) = (2 + 1/4*10)/10 = (2 + 2.5)/10 = 0.45 \text{ hours/unit.}$$

To reduce the cost per unit (which is a local measure that has no business meaning), management decided to work with batches of 100 units to capitalize on economies of scale:

$$T(100) = (2 + 1/4*100)/100 = (2 + 25)/100 = 0.27 \text{ hours/unit.}$$

Indeed, significant savings were achieved: the cost per unit decreased.

Note, however, that production costs did not decrease at all. Due to increased WIP inventory, the indirect costs increased along with finished goods inventory, with all their ramifications.

"Efficient Production"

A public company decided to make production more efficient. They realized that the overhead multiplier is 6.2 (for every dollar spent on direct labor in production, there is an overhead of $6.2). The product cost was:

Raw materials	$40
Direct labor	$10
Overhead	$62
Total product cost	$112

The desire to make production efficient brought a drastic reduction in direct labor and interfered with the company's bottleneck. After a 30% reduction in direct labor, the cost of the product was:

Raw materials	$40
Direct labor	$7
Overhead	$43.4
Total product cost	$90.4

The company was thrilled with their "savings" despite the reduced production throughput. Moreover, they shared the "cost reduction" with the customers by offering them an additional 10% discount.

"Savings"

A certain department in a company had a temporary manpower shortage. The manager of the department asked her colleague, the manager of another department with excess personnel, for help. The colleague agreed to transfer some people for the needed time but demanded compensation for the full cost of the people. The manager eventually decided to hire outside help at a lower cost.

The result—the company increased its expenses while the excess workers remained idle and received full pay.

CHAPTER SUMMARY

Classical cost accounting lost its relevance because the underlying assumptions that are its base are no longer valid, as seen in Table 15.1.

Table 15.1. LOSS OF RELEVANCE OF THE ASSUMPTIONS UNDERLYING TRADITIONAL COST ACCOUNTING

	Beginning of 20th century	Today
Overhead (indirect expenses)	<5%	20%–80%
Direct labor	Real variable cost	Fixed cost
Resources	Ability to adjust personnel	Coexistence of bottlenecks and noncritical resources (having excess capacity)

Conclusions from the analysis are:

1. The assumptions of traditional cost accounting, which were relevant at the beginning of the 20th century, are usually no longer valid, for analyzing costs of industrial, healthcare, and service organizations.
2. To allow better control and to assist decision-making, improvements should be made by focusing on performance of operations, marketing, sales, development, and service provision and not on the accuracy of data for costing products and services. The use of traditional cost accounting as a basis for decision-making can lead to wrong managerial decisions.

For proper decisions, other tools are required. Chapter 16 will present alternatives to traditional cost accounting that are appropriate for the modern business environment.

CHAPTER 16

Global Decision-Making

OBJECTIVE

- Explain how global decision-making (GDM) methodology can be used as an effective tool for decision making.

To deal with the irrelevancy of traditional cost accounting and to aid managerial decision-making, two approaches have been developed in recent years.

ACTIVITY-BASED COSTING

The activity-based costing (ABC) is a cost accounting method that is actually a refinement and improvement of classical cost accounting and was first introduced by Cooper and Kaplan (1988). Activity-based costing analyzes the indirect costs and allocates them in sophisticated and precise routines across the various services or products.

We feel that ABC only partially aids decision-making processes and that, in fact, using cost allocation is somewhat arbitrary and not relevant (Eden and Ronen, 2002). Moreover, Kaplan and Anderson (2004) admitted, "Many companies abandoned activity based costing because it did not capture the complexity of their operations, took too long to implement, and was too expensive to build and operate."

THE ORIGINS OF GLOBAL DECISION MAKING

GDM is a method derived from contribution accounting that was introduced in the 1940s, and throughput accounting offered by Goldratt (1991) as a managerial decision-making tool. In this chapter, we will discuss GDM

(Geri and Ronen, 2005) and other simple tools that will aid in managerial decision-making.

The resources of the organization must be taken into consideration in decision-making processes regarding pricing, investment, make or buy, and so on. One has to distinguish between two situations:

- Decision-making in a resource constrained environment (resource constraint).
- Decision-making in an excess capacity environment (market constraint).

DECISION-MAKING IN A RESOURCE CONSTRAINED ENVIRONMENT

Today's competitive business environment is usually an environment with excess capacity in operational resources or services, and the market is a "buyers' market." However, there are many situations, especially in healthcare organizations, where the organization is constrained by a bottleneck. There are also situations of bottlenecks resulting from a shortage of a very expensive resource, shortage of skilled professionals, peak or seasonal periods, and events of temporary or continual shortage of raw materials or critical resources.

In a resource constrained environment, managers face several decision problems.

Problems of Product and Service Mix

A resource constrained environment cannot allow the production of **all** products possessing market potential or deliver **all** possible services to the customer. System capacity is limited by its constraints, and a resource constraint forces managers to decide on product or service mix: on the one hand, which products to manufacture and which services to sell and, on the other hand, which products or services to exclude.

Make-or-Buy Decisions

A make-or-buy decision is a common managerial decision problem. Decisions to use subcontractors or freelancer specialists require strategic and tactical judgment. The advantage of subcontractors is the elevation of the resource constraint, which allows the expansion of the effective service availability of the organization. The important decision is which jobs to perform in-house (make) and which to purchase from subcontractors (buy), while considering system resources.

Pricing Decisions

At which price should a product or service be offered to the market? How should we price a product that passes through the bottleneck and at what price should we sell a product or service that does not pass through it (free goods)?

Decisions on Terminating Production or Services

Decisions on terminating production or services must be taken through a global perspective of the entire organization while considering system constraints. As we have seen, decisions based on traditional cost accounting frequently lead to system failure.

Decisions to Introduce New Products or Service Lines

These decisions must be taken from a global perspective, making wise use of information regarding system resources and understanding the impact on the critical resources.

Investment Decisions

The best investment decisions are those that enhance the value of the firm. Decision-making with a global perspective supports the increase of throughput, the reduction of operating expenses, or the increase in the difference between them. In the case of a system constraint, controlled investments that increase the capacity of the bottleneck are usually the ones that will lead to increased profits and value enhancement for the firm.

Decisions on Bidding for Contracts

As we have seen before, managers that use traditional cost accounting do not distinguish between work hours of excess capacity resources and work hours of constrained resources. The strategic and tactical tools that will be presented in this chapter will help make decisions on bidding for contracts.

Decisions regarding Product Differentiation and Market Segmentation

Product differentiation and market segmentation are important marketing tools. In many industries (e.g., cosmetics, automotive) segmentation and differentiation have been customary for years. However, many organizations have yet to capitalize on the differentiation and segmentation potential. Smart use of the critical resource can enable better segmentation and differentiation decisions.

GDM TOOLS

Several tools will help decision-making processes with a global perspective. The following tools are suitable both for resource constrained environments and for those with excess capacity (market constraint):

1. The measurement profile.
2. Cost-utilization (CUT) diagram.

THE GLOBAL DECISION-MAKING METHODOLOGY

The GDM methodology (Geri and Ronen, 2005) is a simple and practical methodology for adding the global perspective to decision-making. The three steps of the methodology are:

1. Make a global economic decision from the perspective of the CEO.
2. Make strategic considerations.
3. Change, if needed, local performance measures.

Step 1—Global Decision-Making from the CEO's Perspective

The decision should be such that it would achieve the maximal contribution to the organization's value and should reflect the CEO's perspective. The decision will utilize two tools we have introduced:

- Measurement profile.
- CUT diagram.

Step 2—Strategic Considerations

Strategic considerations relate to the long run and to considerations that involve intangible benefits. Step 1 generates the economic decision. Now, the manager can add strategic considerations that may change the global economic decision and he can calculate what that strategic consideration would cost the organization. Decisions are frequently made without in-depth analysis, claiming it was a strategic decision. Adding strategic considerations by management is important, but they will be more effective when carrying a price tag.

Step 3—Changes Local Performance Measures

Dependence on local performance measures frequently distorts decision-making processes. A manager will occasionally prefer to make a wrong decision that would maximize her local or personal performance measures, rather than a decision that would better serve the organization but would not be as good for her performance measures. Hence, there is a managerial necessity to examine and adapt local performance measures to maximize the organizational objective function. The use of local measures such as the profit per product or service, cost per service or product, number of units produced or served, or efficiency measures, may distort decisions and should, therefore, be eliminated or changed.

DECISION-MAKING IN AN EXCESS CAPACITY ENVIRONMENT

The GDM methodology is valid both in a resource constrained environment and in an excess capacity environment (market constraint).

The following example highlights the use of the GDM methodology in make-or-buy decisions in situations of excess capacity:

The dilemma: A large health maintenance organization (HMO) operates a testing laboratory as an independent profit center. The lab has excess testing capacity. However, because of the criticality of having highly skilled and specialized lab technicians and staff, the HMO management is inclined to keep the existing lab staff and not to sell any of its equipment. The HMO plans to perform 1 million tests in the coming year, which would still leave the lab at excess capacity. The lab charges $3 per blood test. The HMO has an option of buying blood tests from a local hospital for $2 per test. The variable costs per test in-house are $0.50. The HMO decided to buy the tests from the local hospital because of the lower total testing costs and for long-term strategic considerations concerning the relationships with this and other hospitals.

The analysis: In a world of local performance measures, it seems reasonable for the HMO to turn over all the tests to the external hospital laboratory (a buy decision) rather than perform the task in-house (make). Seemingly, the HMO saves $1 million by making this decision. Actually, the HMO spent $2.5 million out of pocket, and the fixed costs of the lab it owns were not affected (variable costs would have been incurred in both cases).

Let us now examine the decision using the GDM methodology.

Make a Global Economic Decision from the CEO's Perspective

The CUT diagram for the testing laboratory is presented in Figure 16.1.

When the lab tests are done in-house, the situation is one of excess capacity. Table 16.1 presents the measurements' profile for the decision.

The throughput of an organization is defined as the actual sales minus the real variable costs of these sales. Thus, the costs paid to the subcontractor in a buy decision will reduce the firm's throughput by $2.5 million.

The operational expenses (in conditions of excess capacity in the HMO lab) will not change. The total cost for salaries, rent, and machine

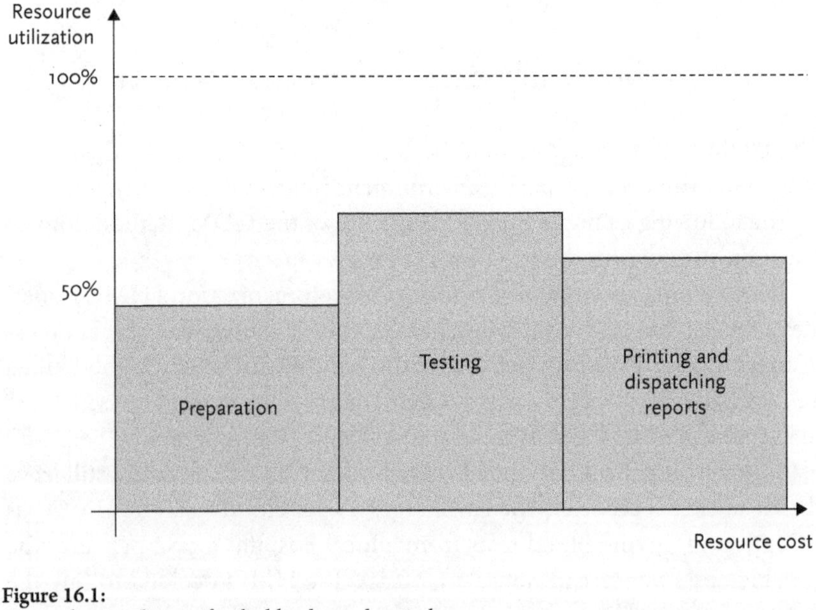

Figure 16.1:
Cost-utilization diagram for the blood tests done in-house

Table 16.1. MEASUREMENTS' PROFILE FOR THE MAKE-OR-BUY DECISION

Measurement	Make	Buy
Throughput	X	X–$2.5 million
Operating expenses	Y	Y
Inventory	?	?
Response time	?	?
Quality	?	?
Due date performance	?	?

maintenance will remain constant, whether the work will be done in-house or outside of the company. The bottom line is that giving the work to the subcontractor will reduce profits.

With respect to the other measures—every measure must be dealt with separately, considering its pros and cons for each alternative. It is clear from the measurement profile that if the last four measures (inventory, response time, quality, and due-date performance) are similar for the two alternatives, then the make (in-house testing) decision should be preferred to the buy (subcontractor) one.

Make Strategic Considerations

We must take into account long-term considerations and ones that relate to intangible benefits. On the one hand, the firm may have an interest in preserving a working relation with the external subcontractor because of the planned future growth of the company.

On the other hand, one must consider the negative strategic implications in using the subcontractor. A subcontractor may receive important information that may help it become a strategic competitor. At this stage, we know the financial implications of each alternative and thus are able to make the decision on economic grounds.

In many situations, the strategic consideration may include the following question: "Is a certain technology/facility/department really a **core competence** of the organization?"

Figure 16.2 presents the core competences matrix that assists in making the make-or-buy decision. It combines the strategic dimension of the technology and the efficiency dimension of the relevant department.

A department (or technology or facility) situated in quadrants 1 or 2 in the core competence matrix has strategic importance to the organization—this

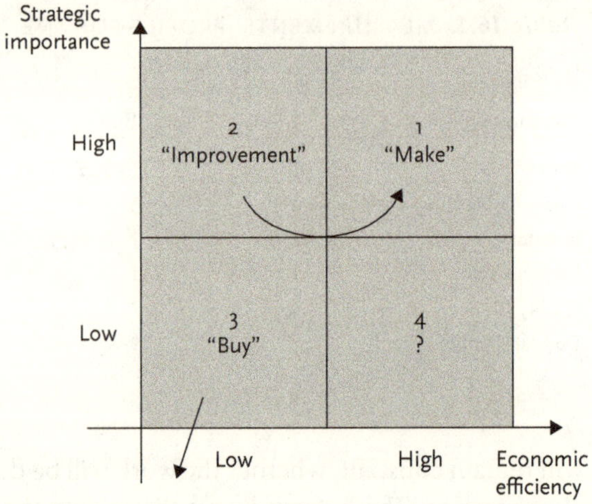

Figure 16.2:
The core competences matrix

is the **core competence** of the organization. Tasks of these departments should be performed in-house—for example, a department for development in a high-tech firm or project management in a company that overseas construction.

The tasks of departments in quadrant 1 should be performed in-house. Departments in quadrant 2 have core competence that should be kept within the organization, but they should not retain their low efficiency. One must find ways to improve the performance of such departments, making them more efficient and shifting them to quadrant 1.

Tasks of departments in quadrant 3 should be directed outside to a subcontractor or to outsourcing services: they do not have core competence and are not efficient as well—for example, dining or cleaning services in a hospital.

Decisions regarding departments in quadrant 4 will be evaluated individually according to the current strategy of the organization.

The decision to assign tasks to subcontractors is a strategic decision of management. An attempt to resolve the make-or-buy decision on local economic considerations may be detrimental to the organization. A decision based on the shaky economic wisdom of letting market forces dictate our actions encourages internal customers within the organization to prefer the buy decisions. This market forces approach allows management to disengage itself from the problem, perhaps leading to "drying out" of strategic technological departments. Such an approach will also prevent future investments needed to preserve the technological ability related to cutting-edge technology and information systems, which is so important for strategically critical departments.

A policy of performing tasks outside the organization only because of local economic considerations may bring about the loss of core competences and loss of clear strategic advantages.

Example: A hospital used subcontractors for all its IT needs, including billing and patient records. Over the years, the entire body of knowledge that related to these systems was totally lost. This created a strategic and economic dependence on subcontractors and limited the influence the hospital had on future development of IT products.

Example: A firm specializing in the production of testing equipment realized that the production of its products became rather standard. They outsourced production to a multinational firm in Asia, allowing considerable savings in production costs. The realized savings encouraged management to outsource sales and marketing as well, giving away strategic abilities to foreign hands, which resulted in a steep drop in sales and reaching bankruptcy.

Management and control are strategic capabilities in many organizations. Giving those abilities away make the organization vulnerable to deterioration of its business.

Change, If Needed, Local Performance Measures

Factors that prevent reaching the right decision in this situation are local performance measures such as the hourly rate and project profits. One must aspire to remove them. Measurement of project profit can be refined by using an external alternative transfer price. Another possibility is to make the production unit into a cost center (instead of a profit center), which management might want to keep in-house for strategic reasons (Horngren et al., 2000).

DECISIONS ON STOPPING PRODUCTION OR CEASING SERVICE

We will now apply the GDM methodology to a decision about stopping production of a product. The same technique can be used to analyze the cessation of some service.

Suppose management is wondering whether to stop production of a certain diagnostic kit. The production line used for this product is at excess capacity and in the coming year there is no planning for additional alternatives of use of this capacity. The market price of the kit is $4.00, and the production costs (by **traditional cost accounting**) are:

Raw materials	$2.00
Packaging	$0.50
Direct labor	$0.75
Processing	$0.31
Depreciation	$0.20
Indirect costs	$1.10
Total product cost	$4.86

Projected sales of the kit are 10,000 units per month. According to traditional cost accounting, the company is losing $0.86 on every unit sold. As a result, management is considering stopping production of this kit. It should be noted that the company will not lay off workers if they close the line as they are also needed for other tasks.

Let us examine the situation using the GDM methodology.

Make a Global Economic Decision from the CEO's Perspective

The CEO should draw the CUT diagram for the production line and consider the various alternatives. The CUT diagram reveals excess capacity.

Let us examine in Table 16.2 the measurements' profile of the two alternatives.

If the stop production decision is taken, throughput will be reduced by $15,000 compared to the continue production decision. This is because the selling price is $4.00 per unit, while the variable costs are $2.50 (10,000*[$4.00–$2.50] = $15,000).

Table 16.2. MEASUREMENTS' PROFILE FOR PRODUCTION EXAMPLE

Measurement	Continue production	Stop production
Throughput	X	X-$15,000
Operating expenses	Y	Y
Inventory	=	=
Response time	=	=
Quality	=	=
Due date performance	=	=

The real variable costs in the production are the raw materials and packaging. Some of the processing costs can also be considered variable (energy and parts). The manager may also consider other variables as needed.

The fixed costs are not about to change. Therefore, the economic decision should be to continue manufacturing. The contribution of sales in this case helps cover the fixed costs and hence should not be given up.

Make Strategic Considerations

By stopping production of the kit, the important strategic considerations are: Will the stoppage of production and sales of the kit negatively affect the firm's reputation? Will competitors capture the market share given up by the firm? In any case, step 1 of the methodology will clarify the financial consequences of each strategic decision to the management team.

Change, If Needed, Local Performance Measures

If a department manager is measured by a local balance sheet of a product line following the guidelines of traditional cost accounting, this measure must be changed. Performance measures that take throughput into account could be an appropriate substitute.

WHAT TO DO WITH EXCESS CAPACITY IN PRODUCTION AND SERVICE RESOURCES?

In the modern service and production environment there is an abundance of operational excess capacity. The question is what should be done with this excess?

Let us consider the following service mix example.

A private medical center is considering what price to charge for a new homeopathic service. The variable costs (mainly drugs) are $55 per visit. The other costs are fixed costs, and the medical center has excess capacity that allows serving 1 million customers annually.

The marketing consultants envision three scenarios for market demand as presented in Table 16.3.

The demand curve is represented graphically in Figure 16.3.

The natural solution is to choose the price that will maximize contribution. However, the maximal contribution will be reached if the service will be offered **at all three prices**: segment the market into customers A, who

Table 16.3. DEMAND AS A FUNCTION OF PRICE

Scenario	Price per visit ($)	Demand (patients per year)
A	100	100,000
B	80	200,000
C	60	500,000

are charged $100; customers B, charged $80; and customers C, patients, who are charged $60.

Let us examine this example using the GDM methodology.

Make a Global Economic Decision from the CEO's Perspective

We will first examine the problem using the measurements' profile as shown in Table 16.4.

The global economic decision is to sell the service at three differential prices. This will yield the highest contribution to the medical center, hence the highest profit.

Make Strategic Considerations

Long-term strategic considerations place several **threats on the organization** when selling at all three prices.

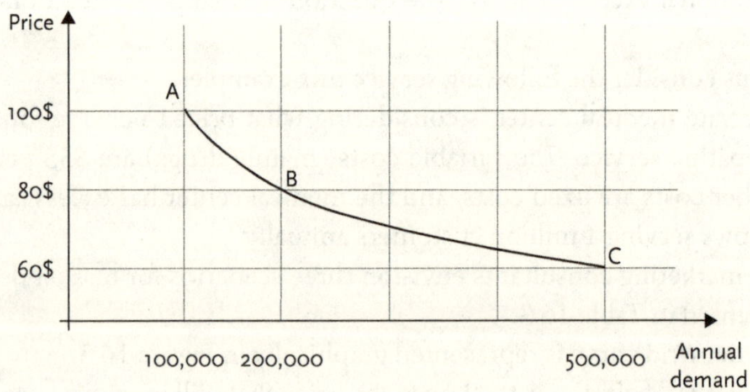

Figure 16.3:
Demand curve for service mix example

Table 16.4. MEASUREMENTS' PROFILE FOR SERVICE MIX EXAMPLE

Measurement	No service	Sell A	Sell B	Sell C	Sell at all prices
Throughput	X	X + $4.5M	X + $5M	X + 2.5M	X + $8.5M
Operating expenses	Y	Y	Y	Y	Y
Inventory	=	=	=	=	=
Response time	=	–	–	=	=
Quality	=	=	=	=	=
Due date performance	=	=	=	=	=

Falling Prices in the Market

- Selling the service to C type customers at $60 can lead to a **price drop** for customers A and B.
- The sales people, knowing that the margin of sales is only the variable cost, will sell the service in the future to all customers segments at lower prices (close to $55). Sales people always want to sell (occasionally at any price) and will justify price erosion by the positive marginal benefit to the firm.
- Customers A will find out that the service is sold to a market segment (customers C) at a lower price and will demand the lower price as well. In addition, Customers A will feel cheated.
- A and B customers may demand the lower rates even for their past visits. They may now demand lower prices for other clinic services.
- There is the danger that the excess capacity will quickly be filled up with services sold at cheap prices.

These dangers can be overcome by product differentiation based on market segmentation.

The services will be sold in different forms to different market segments. Each form will be priced at the perceived value to these segments. There are many industries that have specialized in market segmentation and product differentiation (e.g., the cosmetics industry, airlines), and there are other industries that have not done so. A passenger in first class on a flight may pay up to five times more than a passenger in economy class, and neither of them feels he is not getting his money's worth. Moreover, two passengers sitting next to each other in economy class probably have paid different prices for the same flight as their tickets may be of a different class, reflecting restrictions. The electronics industry differentiates products by performance or by brand names that reflect the perceived value of the products to the customers.

The high-tech industry differentiates products by performance, mainly by downgrading it. The automotive industry differentiates by model type (two-door, four-door, coupe, sedan, station wagon, etc.), by the number of features, type of transmission, manufacturer (e.g., GM has several brand names such as Buick, Chevrolet), and so on.

In most cases, the cost differential in providing differential services or producing differential products is small relative to the price differences customers are willing to pay. Therefore, the dimension of differentiation should include:

- Performance.
- Brand name.
- Size.
- Quality.
- Reliability.
- Quantity.
- Repetitiveness of service or product (e.g., one or frequent clinic visits).
- In-season or out-of-season.
- Packaging.
- Warranty.
- Service level.
- Geographic differentiation.
- Response times.

Correct product or service differentiation based on market segmentation can provide answers to the potential dangers of upper market segments, pushing prices down.

Change, If Needed, Local Performance Measures

Local performance measures such as price per unit may lead to policy failures that will prevent the organization from benefiting from product differentiation and market segmentation.

CHAPTER SUMMARY

The GDM methodology presented in this chapter is a simple and efficient tool for decision-making. It bypasses the need to determine product cost or product profit, whose use could be problematic or even misleading. This methodology is good for pricing decisions, make-or-buy decisions, pricing new products or services, stopping production or a service, determining transfer prices, bid pricing, determining product mix, and evaluating investments.

With all the benefits provided by this methodology, we must not ignore its big danger, which is the lack of threshold. Traditional cost accounting, with all its lack of common sense, provides a cost threshold. The disadvantages of a such a threshold are known: it is arbitrary and leads to loss of business opportunities. However, it provides a barrier to the pressure from sales people to sell more and more at any cost, while causing attrition in prices.

Management of organizations using the methodology must maintain a constant mechanism for determining a performance threshold by management for every product or family of products or services. This threshold will be determined by market prices, availability of resources, and strategic considerations. Such a mechanism requires a high level of management that enables differential treatment of products or services.

An organization that uses this methodology must have a common language among people in finance, marketing, development, and operations. Understanding the managerial approaches behind this methodology will result in better decisions, both at the strategic and tactical levels.

CHAPTER 17

Quality Management and Process Control

OBJECTIVES

- Understand the need to measure and improve quality.
- Break common quality myths.

One of the major breakthroughs in management over the past decades was in quality management and process control. Quality is today one of the most important factors in the competitive environment of any organization.

Bad quality has a very negative effect on the value of an organization by causing both a decrease in income and an increase in expenses. On the other hand, good quality has positive effects on income and expenses.

We view quality as an important value driver and as a tool for improving processes, products, and services. This chapter will present quality and process control in a goal-oriented **business approach**. We will show that good quality and a reduction of expenses can be achieved simultaneously.

WHAT IS QUALITY?

There are many definitions for quality. We will relate to the more prominent ones.

Operational Approach

The **operational approach,** characterized by Crosby (1979), states that quality means **conformance to requirements**. A product, service, or prototype has quality only if it conforms to the requirements dictated by the customer, the manufacturer, management, or standard. According to this definition, there is no quality difference between a new Rolls Royce that meets customer requirements or a Volkswagen Beetle (the older model) that was manufactured to meet all its required specifications. Service provided at a fast food chain like McDonald's can be considered of high quality if it meets standards of waiting times, service rules, and food preparation procedures as specified by the company. The first step in creating quality according to Crosby is to **define requirements.** We often come to realize that services or products do not have well defined requirements. Development of new products is occasionally done with incomplete specifications, resulting in many development cycles and delays in project completion.

Economic Approach

The **economic approach** to quality is defined by Schonberger (1986) in two dimensions that reflect quality of an organization and are closely related:

- Achieving a minimal garbage plant.
- Doing it right the first time.

"Garbage plant"—all activities that do not add value to the customer, the product, the service, or the process.

Performing a task **right the first time** means that **every** step in the process of performing a task was successfully completed the first time around without failures or quality problems.

These are the labor hours, money, and materials that are wasted on repairs, rework, errors, customer compensation for a bad service or product, and time devoted to solving these problems. This is also the noneffective time of specialists and marketing and sales personnel. The garbage plant are the nonconformance quality costs that take away dozens of percentages of workers' or managers' time.

Examples of garbage plants are:

- In the billing department of an health maintenance organization (HMO), it turned out that many of the billing people spend much time correcting billing errors.
- In the operating room of a hospital, much time of surgeons, nurses, and operating room staff was wasted because of patients arriving with incomplete kits, thus delaying or canceling operations.
- In a large hospital lab, several technicians spent most of their time looking for and correcting problems.
- The marketing personnel for a large HMO report that 40% to 60% of their time is ineffective due to repeat or canceled meetings and incomplete kits.
- The customer service department of a large insurance company reports that dozens of workers spend hours on the phone trying to resolve problems that arose from mistakes or ambiguities in insurance policies.
- In a certain restaurant, about 10% of customers received the wrong dish, simply because orders were not written down, and the waiter prefers to memorize them. This resulted in delays in food delivery, food that had to be discarded, wasted time of waiters and cooks, and unhappy customers, some whom will not return to the restaurant.

Much of the "garbage plant" can be avoided. We cannot always provide a service or produce a product with zero defects. However, by reducing the "garbage plant" from 50% to 30%, for example, one can achieve economic advantages and value enhancement for the organization.

When a task is performed right the first time, there is no need to redo any of the steps.

Centrality of the Customer Approach and Patient Centeredness

The **centrality of the customer** approach is derived from Juran's definition of quality (1989). Juran, one of the founding fathers of the quality theory, claims that one of the most important dimensions of quality is "fitness to use." This fitness emphasizes the centrality of the customer. The customer is the one that sets the standards; thus, the whole organization, including products, services, prototypes, and workers, should be subordinated to the customer's requirements. The product or service must be fit for the customer's use. Juran views the work processes as a chain of **internal suppliers that work to fulfill the needs and requirements of their internal customers**.

Alongside this, every element in the value chain of the organization should view itself as serving the **external customer**. In today's healthcare environment, **patient centeredness** is the focus of much attention.

Uniformity (Consistency) Approach

Taguchi, a Japanese engineer and one of the founders of modern quality theory, emphasized **consistency and minimal variance** as critical components of quality (Taguchi, 1986). According to this uniformity (consistency) approach, a service or product that is offered with minimum variation and a consistently uniform performance is testimony of a **controlled process.**

In **service organizations**, uniformity or consistency mean a **process** that repeats itself again and again with minimal variation over time.

In the healthcare system, consistency of waiting times in a clinic is considered a measure of service quality. If patients wait once for 10 minutes and other times for two hours, the resulting variation is problematic. If they have alternatives, such inconsistency in the level of service may drive patients to the competition.

In the McDonald's fast-food chain, consistency is one of the key parameters of quality. This means a repeatedly high level of service that conforms to requirements of time standards, performance, and service. In every McDonald's restaurant in the world, the customer issuing an order knows what to expect and will always get high-quality burgers and fries produced permanently by the **same** methods. This consistency is a value enhancer for the chain that produces a reputation that brings customers back again and again.

An example where lack of consistency had severely negative effects is the Howard Johnson's restaurant chain. For years, customers knew what to expect at any restaurant in the chain. At some point, variability among restaurants in the chain increased, such that the lack of consistency in what customers were receiving eventually led to the disappearance of this restaurant chain.

In **production,** consistency means having good control over a process or, in other words, the capability to produce the same product again and again, even thousands of times, regardless of other factors that may introduce **variability** into the system. Such factors include:

- Suppliers.
- Materials.

- Employees.
- Patients.
- Clinical guidelines.
- Equipment and computerization.

The fact that an organization maintains consistency and minimal variability despite these factors that introduce "noise" and changes is testimony that it is possible to achieve near-complete process control. This control assures the continual production of the same product at the same quality along time.

Other Approaches

We have presented four of the more popular definitions of quality. There are other definitions of quality that describe quality as meeting customer expectations or even **exceeding** them. Other definitions consider quality as being multidimensional: reliability, performance, perceived quality, response time, life cycle, and so on.

Eventually, as we shall see in the following discussion, improving processes of service, production, and development will yield improvement along any definition of quality. An organization that realizes that quality will enhance its value will soon implement quality improvement actions.

STAGES IN MANAGING QUALITY AND PROCESS CONTROL

There are three main stages in quality management and process control.

Stage A: The Organization Has No Quality Management and Feedback

Organizations in this stage are usually monopolistic organizations that lack customer awareness and feedback mechanisms for process control and improvement. At this stage, the organization is "doing its best" and solves problems in an ad hoc manner. Customer complaints are usually answered by "We worked by the guidelines" or "The customer does not understand, is not right, and is responsible." More serious complaints are solved by apologies, gifts, or compensations.

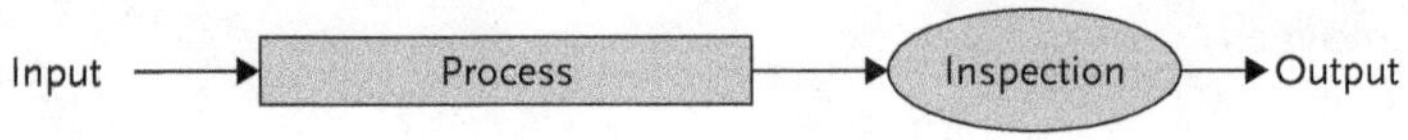

Figure 17.1:
Adding inspection at the end of the line

Stage B: Inspection—Quality Control at the End of the Process

At this stage, the organization adds a function of **quality control (inspection) at the end of the process** run by the quality control department, which is an independent body. These inspectors examine the final products and screen out the defective ones, as seen in Figure 17.1.

There is no doubt that being in stage B with inspection (quality control) at the end of the line is preferable to being in stage A, as there is some control over the outcome of the process. However, experience shows that inspection, as good as it may be, does not screen all defects. Moreover, the mere existence of a quality control department relieves responsibility from the operations people who see the quality control people as being responsible for quality. There is also the undesirable tension between personnel in the two areas. Because no preventive measures are introduced, the "garbage plant" continues to produce defective services and products. This open loop control approach, depicted in Figure 17.1, indeed identifies most current problems but usually does not prevent future ones.

Stage C: Process Control

Every organization wishing to survive in today's competitive environment must reach this stage, and the sooner, the better. This stage is also referred to as Deming's theory (Deming, 1986). At this stage, we have closed loop control, which is control with feedback at constant and short intervals as seen in Figure 17.2.

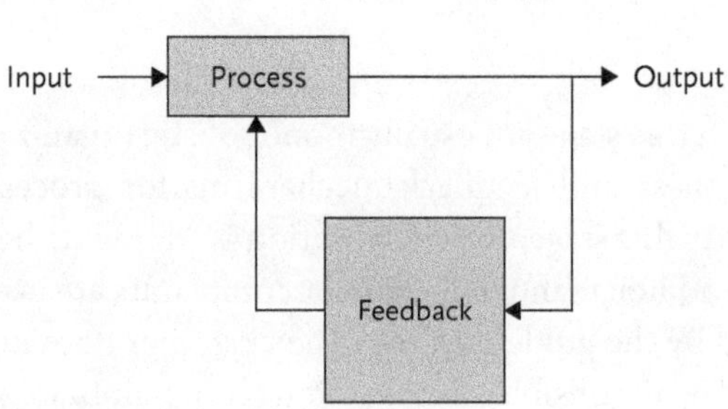

Figure 17.2:
A closed loop control system

The Principles of Process Control

The goal is continuous improvement of organizational value

This improvement will usually manifest itself in increasing the throughput of the organization.

Continuous quality improvement

This reflects continuous improvement of processes. Many managerial cultures focus on the short term and on achieving immediate and one-time results. Short-term improvement and advantages achieved by an organization will usually also be achieved by competitors after a short while. To establish a continuous competitive edge, there must be a continuous improvement of service processes, marketing and sales processes, production processes, engineering processes, and so on.

Emphasis on process improvement

Quality is achieved through correct processes.

The **85/15 rule** states that 85% of failures are caused by inappropriate processes and are the responsibility of management. Only 15% of failures are the responsibility of workers.

Processes that are under management responsibility include, among others, selection, recruitment, and training of employees; setting and measuring work processes; measuring and rewarding employees; working with complete kits; and processes of sales, marketing, pricing, and costing.

When a problem occurs in an organization, everybody is mobilized to solve it. However, in an organization that did not undergo the conceptual change in the spirit of Deming's theory, right after the problem has been solved, the unavoidable hunt for those responsible begins.

In contrast, the process control approach suggests that, after solving a problem, the following question must be addressed: "What was wrong in the **process** that caused the failure, and what can be changed in the process so this failure will not recur in the future?"

Example: One of the co-authors of this book was seen in the emergency department of a large governmental hospital where he arrived with severe abdominal pains. After spending a while in observation, he was discharged home despite a high white cell count. He was not even examined by a surgeon. Two days later he was rushed to another hospital, in a CT scan a ruptured appendix was revealed, he was rushed to emergency surgery and luckily survived to co-author this book! The failure was not the human error of missing the high white cell count, but it was a process failure under the responsibility of management. It is not the fault of an incompetent physician but that of management that assigned only an intern and a resident for that shift.

Example: In a certain regional airline, planes collisions with birds were a major cause of plane crashes. When the process was investigated, it turned out that bird migration repeats itself with amazingly high precision every year. As a result, corrective measures were taken to significantly reduce the number of crashes resulting from birds.

Prevention rather than fixing

The major focus should be on correcting the design of the process and on actions to avoid failures.

Example: A large HMO is interested in investing more in prevention rather than in treatment of preventable conditions. As a result of this strategic decision, the HMO initiated a campaign promoting healthier lifestyles and physical activity. They initiated free screening clinics for various conditions, and they financed sessions of aerobic exercises and other sports activities.

Use of data

Process control and improvement is possible only if the organization routinely collects data on what is happening with the process and analyzes them. ("In God we trust. All others should bring data.")

Use of graphical tools

The recommended control tools are process control charts, Pareto analysis, and use of various graphical tools (Deming, 1986). These tools enable focused and effective analysis of the data and identification of negative phenomena that require intervention and corrective measures. The continuous improvement in work processes achieved in this way will obviously bring about value enhancement.

Quality management and process control by the workers themselves

The modern approach to quality management and process control states that a person doing a job is also **responsible for its quality**. This requires setting initial conditions and an appropriate work environment:

- One must clearly define what is considered a "good" product or service.
- Workers and managers must be given the tools needed to evaluate the quality of a service or product.
- One must specify rules and procedures that will clearly define what should be done when a failure or a defective product or service is detected.

The "10 times rule"

The later the stage that a problem is detected, fixing it is 10 times more expensive.

Example: If a certain medical condition is diagnosed early at the community clinic, the consequences could be minor. If the condition is only detected after the patient is brought into the emergency department, the consequences, both clinical and financial, could be magnified 10 times. If the problem is only detected while the patient is hospitalized or during surgery, another tenfold harm can be expected. If the patient is discharged and the problem reappears later, the consequences could be grave (literally speaking).

Similarly, if a defective component in a medical device would have been detected while inspecting the incoming shipment, fixing it would be one-tenth the cost of fixing the problem if detected during production, and one-hundredth of the cost needed to fix the problem if detected during final quality control inspection.

This rule is presented graphically in Figure 17.3.

The conclusion is that most emphasis of control and inspection must be shifted toward the **beginning** of the process, rather than to the end (as is customary in stage B of quality control).

Participation of managers and employees

A quality product service or development is achieved by a quality process when the employees and managers are part of the process and are actively involved in the process design and control. They should also feel ownership over the

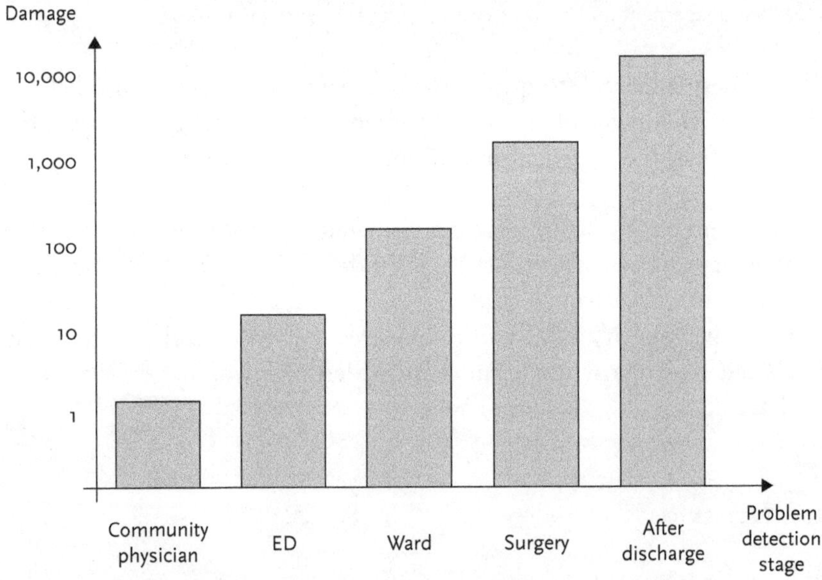

Figure 17.3:
The 10 times rule

process. Workers should be encouraged to be involved and more responsibility for the quality of the work should be delegated to them so they will feel part of the process and more committed. Evaluating, recognizing, and rewarding workers for their accomplishments is a quality improvement engine.

Team work

Process improvement is accomplished by team work that identifies problems, solves them, and prevents their recurrence. Experience shows that many problems are interdepartmental (i.e., between internal suppliers and internal customers), and multidisciplinary teams are very effective in solving such problems.

Commitment of management

Management must be committed to quality improvement, and process control must be involved. Quality improvement is not a standalone project but rather part of the tasks of the organization that affect the budget of the organization, the work plan, and routine control, as well as the use of the resources and tools of the organization.

Centrality of the customer

The customer must be the focus of attention of all levels of the organization. In an era of excess capacity in services and production, alongside fierce competition, there should be "subordination to the market" in all decision-making.

Working with a small number of quality suppliers

When looking globally at the long-term cycle cost of products and services, we realize that quality processes save money. One must work in cooperation with suppliers in a way that is based on problem identification and good will on both sides to solve them. This kind of cooperation can be achieved only by working closely with a small number of quality suppliers.

It should be noted that the approach of developing mutual long-term relations with a small number of suppliers might contrast with the obligation and the statutory responsibility of most public organizations to publish tenders or offerings for bids before any substantial agreement is signed. The bidding approach can reduce costs in the short term, but it makes it difficult for the organization to maintain and assure a quality service or production process. The resulting savings in costs are frequently offset by losses resulting from poor quality. On the other hand, we do not recommend going to the other extreme and "put all the eggs in one basket" by working with a single contactor. This exposes the organization to commercial and economic risks.

IMPLEMENTING QUALITY IMPROVEMENT PROCESSES WITH LEAN AND THE THEORY OF CONSTRAINTS

The implementation of quality improvement processes in organizations should be done using a business approach, in combination with the implementation of additional managerial approaches. The purpose of quality improvement in nonprofit organizations is to improve organizational performance, and in business organizations, it is enhancing their value.

Implementing only partial or limited quality improvements, confined to areas of operations (service, logistics, or production), will yield limited improvement in performance. Customers indeed want a high-quality product or service, but they also want fast response, reliable supply times, good performance, and services and products that are congruent with their needs, all this with competitive prices. In other words, management must evaluate the organization in a global manner as one complex yet integrated entity whose components must function better. Moreover, in most organizations, profit increases achieved by improving marketing, development, and engineering are more significant than profit increases achieved by improving production processes. Unfortunately, many managers equate quality improvement to improvements in production processes or improvements in service.

Management must focus on the important issues of the organization. Identifying critical issues must be done by adopting a global perspective. Managing the critical issues should utilize effective and efficient management tools. In other words, a successful implementation of quality improvement implies combining quality improvement using Deming's approach together with approaches such as management by constraints, Lean, managerial measurement and control, the complete kit concept, and advanced strategic approaches. Experience shows that applying just one managerial approach yields only partial success.

Quality improvement should be implemented **gradually**:

1. At first, improving operational systems by implementing Lean approaches, management by constraints, measurement and control, and the complete kit concept. This step provides fast results of increased throughput, reduced response times, and quality enhancement (mainly through the reduction of work in process).
2. Applying quality improvement processes and process control methods, working with departmental and interdepartmental teams, implementing process control charts.
3. Extracting strategic advantages following quality improvement: the ability to turn to markets that pay more for better quality, to increase prices in certain markets, and to compete with lower prices in other markets. This is possible through implementation of quality work processes, reduction of variable costs (especially raw materials), and increased throughput.

This approach can be called "**quality comes second**" (implementation-wise).

THE THROUGHPUT WORLD AND THE COST WORLD

The objective of quality improvement is to increase organizational profits, mainly through increasing throughput, namely, by increasing contributions from increased sales and better use of raw materials. Deming believes that the objective is to increase profits and to create more jobs by increasing market share, reducing response times, and adapting the product or service to the customer and high quality (Deming, 1986). This philosophy, which focuses on increasing the throughputs of the organization, is referred to as the **"throughput world"** (Goldratt, 1990).

In contrast to the throughput world, there is a different philosophy whose focus is on cost reduction. This quickly translates into a desire of management to reduce the size of the work force. This is known as the **"cost world,"** and it occasionally conflicts with the objectives of quality. In organizations that do not have job security for workers, it will be difficult for management to involve the work force while introducing improvements. In many cases, the "big money" is not made by reducing costs but rather by increasing throughput or improving quality.

QUALITY IMPROVEMENT MYTHS

Quality management and process control, according to Deming (stage C), break several **myths** that relate to quality management:

- **Myth—"Quality Work Takes More Time." Reality:** Quality work requires a **good and structured process**, and then it takes **less time**. For example, working with a complete kit in a development, sales, or production process will require less cycles in the process and naturally a **smaller time investment** and **shorter cycle** time.
- **Myth—"Quality costs more money." Reality:** In fact, high-quality work and quality processes cost **less money** as they result in less rework and fewer cycles, and they **reduce the "garbage plant."** Thus, quality costs less and generates a **higher contribution** to profit. Many customers are willing to pay a premium for quality services or products.
- **Myth—"It is not possible to provide a quality service or quality product in large quantities or in large organizations." Reality:** It is possible to provide quality service and produce a quality product even in **large quantities**, if processes are **good, consistent, and reliable**. For example, customers of a cell phone company may receive quality service if the company **develops a quality process:** a good software system that supports workers in the call centers and provides answers to most queries and a quality process of selecting, training, and controlling the employees.

CHAPTER SUMMARY

Quality improvement and process control are means that an organization must employ to survive and exist in a competitive environment.

Organizations that will not meet the required quality standard, which is raised year after year, will not survive. Organizations that will use quality improvement as a competitive tool can enhance their value.

Quality improvement, in combination with approaches detailed in previous chapters (management by constraints, JIT, the complete kit, Pareto rule) can all enhance organizational value without substantial (if any) financial investments and enable the organization to do more with the existing resources.

CHAPTER 18

Creating Value for Healthcare Organizations

OBJECTIVE

- Understanding the value-focused management (VFM) approach to increase the value of a business organization by increasing its cash flow, or in a not-for-profit organization to improve its performance.

One of the major problems faced by managers is how to initiate the process of enhancing value or improving performance and what priorities to set on the various possible improvements. For example, should they first perform improvements in the emergency department (ED), the operating rooms (OR), or perhaps in the laboratories or imaging services? Should management focus on improvements in the internal medicine wards, or should they focus on logistics or purchasing?

A manager in a healthcare organization cannot afford to spend more than 10% of his time on pursuing improvements. This is a result of the nature of his role that makes him spend most of his time on managing current and emergency situations, occasionally involving human life at risk. The complexity of management and technology inevitably forces the manager to spend most of his time on current issues.

There is no doubt that the manager of every ward or department (e.g., ED, OR) can and should perform significant improvements in their area. However, the major problems of the organization are interdepartmental problems, and only proactive efforts by management can lead to improvements. For example, improvements in the ED cannot be done only by the chief of that department because the work process also involves imaging and laboratory services, consultants and the inpatient wards.

VALUE CREATION FROM MANAGERIAL ACTIVITIES

This chapter will present a holistic and global approach to where management should focus based on the importance of the improvement and ease of implementing it.

The goal of the organization is to increase its value for the shareholders. The goal of the management, therefore, is to bring about a constant creation of value for the shareholders, and it is therefore incumbent upon management to constantly strive to achieve this goal. It is quite common that increasing shareholders' value brings upon better job security, financial benefits, and self-fulfillment for the employees, as well as value to the community. Value creation can arise from activities in two areas:

- Value creation from financial activities.
- Value creation from other managerial activities.

Creating value from financial activities focuses mainly on changing the capital structure, mergers and acquisitions, and distributing dividends. This activity is carried out almost entirely at the level of the firm's management and board of directors.

In this chapter, we focus on the creation of value from nonfinancial activities, because they have a significant potential to increase firm value and because this subject had been addressed to a lesser extent in practice and in academic research. Such value creation is caused by exploiting strategic changes, changes in business or organizational structure, increasing throughput in operations and logistics, improvement in quality, improvement in inventory levels, improvement in the information systems, and shortening of development times. Similarly, changes in cost accounting and performance measures, or improvements in decision-making processes, can contribute substantially to improving firm value.

Moreover, as we have seen in previous chapters, the "blind" use of traditional cost accounting and the use of local performance measures can lead to a decrease in the value of firms and organizations. Also, some decisions concerning investments as well as business, organizational, and operational changes do not contribute to improving the value of the firm. In many cases, this is caused by the **absence of a global perspective and lack of knowledge and an organized methodology for improving the value of the firm**. As a result, the firm's resources are utilized ineffectively, its value is not increased sufficiently, management's time is wasted, and its attention diverted from matters that are important for the firm. If these issues had been properly addressed, the organization could increase its value. In the sequel of this chapter, we deliberate on the subject of firm value and the various methods of assessing it. We will develop a focused model that will facilitate creating a link between changes in the various areas of the organization and increasing its value.

ASSESSING THE VALUE OF THE FIRM

Firm value is a concept commonly used by investors, managers, owners and boards of directors. Its use is particularly prevalent when the firm is being bought and sold, during mergers, when partners are co-opted, and in dealings with interested parties. There are several approaches to assessing firm value:

- **Market value**—the value as assessed by the stock market. This immediate assessment is of course relevant to traded public firms. However, experience shows that when the level of trade is low, a substantial gap may be created. It is the gap between the "true" value of the firm, as reflected in purchasing transactions or the transfer of control and its value according to the latest stock market prices reflecting low and insignificant trading.
- **Value according to actual transactions**—the value can be determined by transactions carried out in fact, in raising capital and co-opting partners in the firm, by exchanging shares and/or by mergers and acquisitions.
- **Asset value**—the asset value or worth of the firm's equity is the worth of the assets minus the worth of the liabilities.
- **Value according to discounted cash flow**—the basic assumption of discounted cash flows is that the worth of the business is the **present value of the discounted cash flows over time**. The firm's operational assets and the components of the working capital are needed to attain the cash flows, and their worth to the business is expressed in the discounted cash flow. In analyzing value, the present value of the unleveraged free cash flows is assessed. This amount represents the value of the activities. We must add the value of the "available" assets, which are not required to create cash flows (e.g., investments in real estate that are not done for purposes of the firm's operations, or cash surpluses). From this result, we subtract the worth of the net financial liabilities to the day of the valuation, to finally obtain the worth of the firm to the shareholders.

Academically, this method is considered more acceptable and correct. It is suitable for measuring the contribution of management to improving firm value, enabling the measuring of cash flows arising from the activities of the different sectors of the firm and their sources of finance.

The approach of this book in general, and of this chapter in particular, is to enhance the economic value of the firm, as it is reflected in the cash flow along time. We believe that in the long run the economic value of the firm will level out at its market value.

ENHANCING THE VALUE OF THE FIRM: THE VALUE-FOCUSED MANAGEMENT METHODOLOGY

We propose the VFM model for increasing organizational value (Geri and Ronen, 2005). The VFM model helps managers focus on those places in which the potential for increasing firm value is greatest, bearing in mind the limited management resources. The model is based on the principles of value-based management, as presented by Copeland et al. (1996), along with additional managerial insights.

The VFM model boasts the following two dimensions:

1. It details the action items required in the "field" for creating value.
2. It focuses managerial attention on the important activities that give the highest value, considering the organization's limited resources, particularly the managerial resources in short supply.

The stages of implementing the VFM model are as follows:

1. Determine the goal.
2. Determine the performance measures.
3. Identify the value drivers.
4. Decide how to improve the value drivers.
5. Implement and control.

Determine the Goal

The goal of the firm is to increase shareholders' value. This should be clear to all the managers and employees. The goal can be sustained over time if the interests of the employees, the suppliers, the customers, and the community are borne in mind at all times.

Determine the Performance Measures

The performance measures include the financial statements and the global performance measures of the system (see the six measures in chapter 13).

Identify the Value Drivers

A **value driver** is defined as an important factor that significantly affects the value of the firm (such as increasing sales, increasing throughput, shortening response time, reducing inventories).

Identify the Relevant Value Drivers

Four approaches are used to identify the relevant cost drivers.

Balance sheet and profit and loss statements approach

Sections of the balance sheet and the profit-and-loss statement are reviewed one at a time to identify potential firm improvement against the ease of carrying out the improvement, using the focusing matrix (as described in chapter 7).

The functional approach—bottom–up

The major functions in the organization are reviewed systematically and examined for the existence of relevant value drivers. Such functional areas may include:

1. The organization's strategy.
2. Marketing and sales.
3. Human resources.
4. Information systems and information technology.
5. Finance.
6. Technological innovation.
7. Clinical quality.
8. Service quality.
9. Logistics and purchasing.
10. Operations of wards, labs and other departments.
11. Cost accounting and measuring.
12. Organizational structure.

13. Risk management.
14. Customer service.

The review of the functions is carried out by interviewing the management and key personnel in these functions, touring the premises, perusing the financial and management statements, interviewing customers and suppliers, and comparing with other similar organizations. Attention is then directed to the important value drivers from among those selected, with the help of the focusing matrix. The importance of each value driver is measured according to the incremental value it affords the firm.

The global performance measures approach

The global performance measures (see chapter 13) are reviewed one at a time, and the potential increment to the firm's value originating from improving them is examined.

Identifying the core problems (top–down)

After collecting the data in stages 1, 2, and 3, undesirable effects are mapped and the core problems are identified using the focused current reality tree approach (see chapter 7).

The relevant value drivers (up to 10) are collected using some combination of the four previously mentioned methods. Using the focusing table and the focusing matrix, an examination is made of the potential for each value driver to add to the firm's value and the difficulty of implementation. This process ends with the selection of the value drivers to be used for improving the firm's value.

Decide How to Improve the Value Drivers

A detailed implementation plan for improving each of the value drivers is prepared, usually by teams of managers and employees, using the innovative managerial techniques described earlier in this book.

Implement and Control

The implementation of the plan and its control are the responsibility of the management.

STRATEGIC VALUE DRIVERS

Strategy is the path that the management of an organization takes to reach the goal. An organizational strategy should express the directions of the organization in the following dimensions:

- What are the firm's products and services, and what should be their market positioning?
- What is the market where the organization is competing?
- What are the organization's core competences, and how can they be preserved?
- What are the weaknesses and vulnerabilities, and how can the organization protect itself from them?
- What is the firm's strategic breakthrough plan?
- What is the organizational policy regarding prices and quality of its services and products?
- What is the desired growth rate of the firm?
- What investment level is needed?
- What are the strategic elements that may produce sustainable competitive advantage?
- What is the market segmentation and service/product differentiation potential for the firm's products or services vis-à-vis the competition?
- Where should the firm's constraint be located?
- What should the capital structure of the firm be?
- What should the business and organizational structure of the firm be?

The answers to these questions and others shape the functional strategies in the areas of marketing, sales, finances, technology, information systems, operations, service, logistics, quality, human resources, and risk management of the firm.

Some of the value drivers that can enhance the value of a healthcare organization are considered **strategic value drivers**. Such value drivers can be:

- Changing the strategy of the organization from a high variety service provider to a specialty or a more focused one.
- Moving from a nonprofit organization to a for-profit one.
- Privatization of a public hospital.
- Creating profit centers in public health care organizations.
- Decentralization of a health maintenance organization (HMO).
- Adopting a prevention strategy rather than a treatment one.
- Changing the organization attitude and focus to serving customers (instead of "treating patients").

CASE STUDY: QUEEN MEDICAL CENTER

We will now examine a case study for value enhancement in a large nonprofit hospital.

The Hospital

Queen Medical Center (disguised name) is a 1,500-bed hospital, employing over 4,000 workers including about 800 physicians. The hospital has an ED, a surgical division that includes ORs and inpatient wards, a gynecological division with ORs and inpatient wards and departments for internal medicine, ophthalmology, and all other departments common to a large hospital.

The hospital is considered the leading and best in the region and enjoys reputation and prestige in all areas of operation. It is a university teaching hospital, and its physicians train dozens of medical students and physicians every year. The hospital meets its budget. Its main customers are four large HMOs which provide coverage to the entire regional population. The hospital is known for its technological innovation and its tendency to be a world leader in adopting new diagnostic and therapeutic approaches.

The hospital is professionally managed by a group of physicians with extensive managerial training and experience. The hospital has laboratories and imaging services amongst the best in the world and enjoys a stable work force with low employee turnover. The hospital is proud of being a technology leader and is very open to innovation.

The hospital operates outpatient clinics that serve about 350,000 patients per year. There are 700 deliveries annually and 26,000 operations per year. The ED serves about 111,000 patients per year.

Let us now examine the enhancement potential of the hospital using the VFM approach. As mentioned in the beginning of this chapter, increasing value of a nonprofit organization is improving its performance measures vis-à-vis its goal.

Determine the Goal

The goal of the hospital is to increase its value by providing high quality medical service and treatment to as many patients as possible within short response times, while maintaining a balanced budget.

Determine Performance Measures

The performance measures are:

- Clinical quality measures.
- Service quality measures.
- Strategic innovation measures.
- Throughput.
- Response time.
- Cash flow.
- Annual profit.
- Customer satisfaction.
- Worker satisfaction.

Identify the value drivers

Identifying Value Drivers from Relevant Sections in the Hospital's Financial Statements

There is high profitability in the outpatient clinics. Thus, analyzing the potential of the outpatient clinic, a potential value driver could be increasing the outpatient clinics throughput.

Using a Bottom–Up Approach to Identify Functional Value Drivers

To be able to identify the functional value drivers for the hospital, let us review the functional area one by one:

1. **Hospital strategy**—The hospital provides a varied array of services and is considered the best in its region. The hospital strategy is based on providing the best clinical service, using advanced technologies and attracting renowned specialists to improve the relevant quality. The hospital management has a business orientation and finances some of its expenses by building support services on the hospital campus: a hotel for patients' families, restaurants, a shopping center and parking lots. The hospital is also investing in advanced technologies and is a partner in various start-ups.

A strengths–weaknesses–opportunities–threats (SWOT) analysis for the hospital is presented in Table 18.1.

Table 18.1. SWOT ANALYSIS FOR QUEEN MEDICAL CENTER

Strengths	Weaknesses
• A variety of services • Excellent reputation • High clinical level • Innovative and dynamic management • Professional management and business oriented • High technological capability	• High managerial complexity • Management expertise of wards not sufficient • Employee dissatisfaction • Unstructured processes in the wards • Local and sectorial optimization
Opportunities	**Threats**
• Developing business ventures of services in the hospital • Purchase of new technologies and techniques • Development of new technologies and techniques	• Competitors may close the clinical and technological gap • Excess capacity in other hospitals in the region may lead to price wars • Tight contracts with the main customer

2. **Marketing, sales and business development**—Performs extremely well.
3. **Human resources**—The employees are dedicated, but there is a sense of alienation between management and employees. Most of the department heads are superb professionals in their specialty, but they lack management vision and training. The physicians have an inherent conflict between their own interest (private practice) and the hospital goal.
4. **Information technology**—The hospital has very good management information systems that enable it to exercise control over budgets and timetables. The hospital is running a pilot of implementing an electronic patients' records system, using advanced technologies.
5. **Finance**—The hospital is financially sound.
6. **ED**—During day hours the ED is managed professionally and patients receive quality treatment both clinically and from a service perspective. In the afternoon and evening hours the situation is different with resulting long queues. The average wait is four hours. There is no systematic and structured scheduling and prioritization. The ED relations with the hospital (on-call and specialty consultants) are not congruent with the load. During the evening and night hours, there is a severe shortage of specialists in emergency medicine and general and orthopedic surgeons. There is great potential to reduce the long waits.
7. **ORs**—The clinical quality of the surgical procedures is high, and the technological know-how is very advanced. There is an obvious segmentation (surgeons, anesthetists, surgical nurses). There are idle times in

the ORs, and the anesthetists are the bottleneck. Too many people are involved in managing the ORs (head surgical nurse, head of the division of surgery, head of the anesthetics department). There is insufficient integration of management methods, and the scheduling of operations does not meet the needs. The bottlenecks are not sufficiently utilized, and the logistics department is not involved enough.

8. **Outpatient clinics**—They serve about 350,000 patients annually. There is potential to increase this number by improving efficiency and effectiveness and enhancing marketing.
9. **Management of the wards in the hospital**—There is no doubt that there is room for improvement in the wards. The main concern and the potential value driver is the managerial quality of the management team. During the hospital evaluation process, it was decided to focus on the departments with the highest potential for enhancement. At this stage, management will not direct improvements in the wards, as it seems that the potential is not as large as in the ED, the ORs and some other areas. Any department heads wishing to make improvements in their departments, at their initiative, will receive management support and appropriate budgets.
10. **Technology and innovation**—Queen Medical Center is one of the world leaders in technological innovation, both in equipment and treatment.
11. **Quality**—Clinical quality is measured systematically and meets world standards. Service quality is excellent in some departments and there is room for improvement in others.
12. **Logistics and purchasing**—The logistics are complex due to the large variety of services provided in the hospital. Logistic problems in the OR cause occasional delay due to shortages in some items. There is a need to shift towards standardizing OR equipment, and careful preparation of kits there. Purchasing costs are relatively high and there is potential for price and inventory reduction.
13. **Pricing and costing**—Most decisions are taken by top management using a global view, taking resource capacity and marginal profitability into consideration. However, the approach by mid-level management is that of the traditional cost-accounting.
14. **Organizational structure**—The organizational structure is based on divisions which consist of the several departments. The current structure is somewhat problematic, but management decided to first treat the "low hanging fruits" that will bring upon immediate improvement, and only later will discuss changing the organizational structure which is difficult to perform and whose contribution is questionable.

15. **Risk management**—There is a separate department that manages medical risks in a professional manner.
16. **Customer service**—There is a department handling customer complaints and trying to identify process improvements.

Through this summary and with the use of the focusing matrix, the following potential value drivers were identified:

- Reducing waits in the ED.
- Increasing throughput in the ORs.
- Increasing throughput in the outpatient clinics.
- Improving logistics and purchasing.

Identifying Value Drivers Using Global Performance Measures

A review of the various performance measures identified the following potential value drivers:

- Establishing due-date performance in the ORs and adhering to it.
- Reducing response time in the ED.
- Increasing Throughput in the ORs.

Top–Down Approach to Value Drivers

At first, the following relevant undesirable effects for the hospital were identified:

- Value is not sufficient: the hospital does not fulfill its potential.
- Insufficient revenues.
- Critical resources not fully utilized.
- Sense of manpower shortage.
- High level of complexity.
- Insufficient managerial expertise in some departments.
- Complicated organizational structure.
- The outpatient clinics do not meet their potential.
- Operating rooms are not fully utilized.
- Local and segmented optimization.
- Alienation between management and employees.
- Processes are not sufficiently structured.
- Conflict of interest between the personal welfare of physicians and the welfare of the hospital.
- Long waits in the ED.

The focused current reality for the hospital that contains these undesirable effects is presented in Figure 18.1.

The focused current reality tree facilitates the identification of the core problems of the hospital. The core problems are potential value drivers. Thus, dealing with the core problems will enhance the value of the hospital.

Choosing the Relevant Value Drivers

After reviewing the list of potential value drivers, management decided to focus on the following drivers:

1. Increasing OR throughput.
2. Reducing waits in the ED.
3. Increasing the throughput in the outpatient clinics.
4. Reducing purchasing costs.
5. Cultivating human resources.

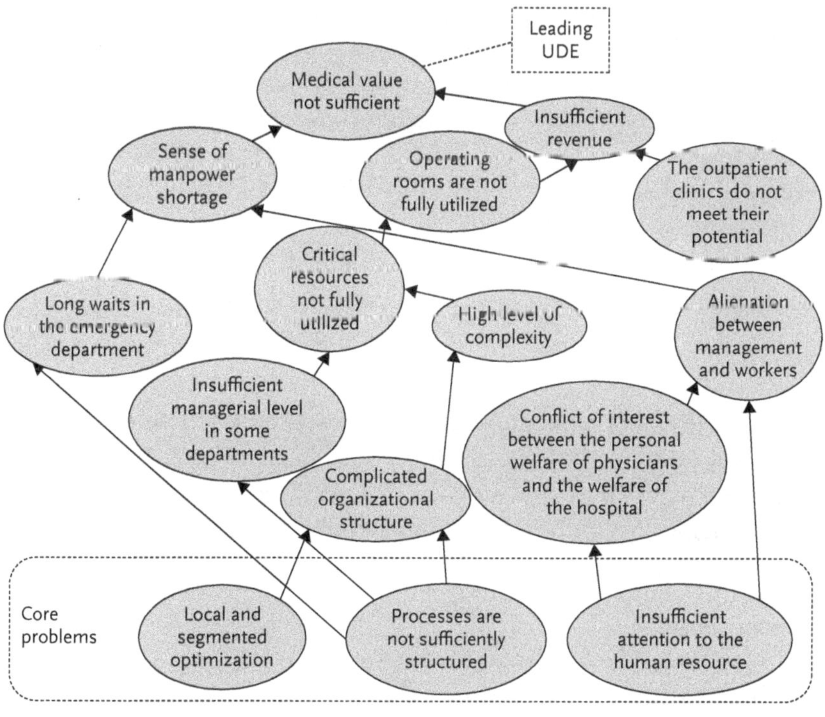

Figure 18.1:
The focused current reality tree for Queen Medical Center

Decide How to Improve the Value Drivers

Decisions to improve the value drivers are detailed as follows.

Increasing OR Throughput

Increasing OR throughout will be carried out by taking the following steps:

Exploiting the constraint

The constraint (bottleneck) is the anesthetists' time. In various measurements that were taken, it was determined that the ORs are utilized only 60% of the time, mainly due to inefficient time of the anesthetists:

- Operations start late. Even though all the resources are available at 8:00 AM, the first operation does not begin before 8:30 AM or even 8:45 AM. Measuring the start time of surgery and making sure that the first one starts early may help solve most of this problem.
- Operations end early. The shift ends at 4:00 PM, so surgeons refrain from starting long operations in the afternoon. A change in the OR scheduling where the long operations are scheduled at the beginning of the day and the short ones at the end of the day, may solve this problem.
- Long set-up times between operations. Shortening the various steps of transporting patients into the OR, administering initial anesthesia, immediate removal to recovery, and rapid cleaning can all contribute to increasing anesthetists and OR utilization.
- Canceled operations because of incomplete kits.

Elevating the constraint

Analyzing the labor content of the anesthetists revealed that because the hospital is a teaching hospital, the number of residents is relatively large in comparison to other general hospitals and to university hospitals in particular. Reducing the number of residents can help increase OR throughput.

Better scheduling

Scheduling patients using the drum–buffer–rope approach (chapter 5) can contribute to constraint exploitation. Some of the scheduling can be done by the wards and some through central scheduling and appointments.

Integrating OR management

In the OR, there are too many managers (head nurse, head of anesthesia, and head of surgical division-in charge of scheduling). Appointing a "plant manager" for the OR complex, making her in charge of the site, the scheduling, and the logistics, may help solve the problem.

Incorporating logistics

Preparing kits ahead of time and introducing new processes of team work can help increase the number of operations and their quality.

Results

All the previous steps can increase the number of operations by 20% in six months with the current mix of operations.

Note: The existing mix of operations can be (partially) changed, but management has decided not to do so because of the public nature of the hospital.

All the previously described activities can be done with minimal investment. The difficulty of performing these steps is 3 on a 1 to 5 scale: it is rather easy to exploit the constraints, but the need to coordinate several departments that are not subordinated to one another makes the task more difficult.

To get a better feel for the importance of increasing OR throughput, let us examine this through profitability calculations.

The current expense structure of the surgical division is:

Sales	100
Variable costs	10
Fixed costs	85
Profit	5

After increasing throughput by 15% with the same resources, the picture is:

Sales	115
Variable costs	11.5
Fixed costs	85
Profit	18.5

Thus, the potential for enhancement exceeds 300% (!).

Assuming that the profits from the increased throughput are mostly invested in the hospital (with the minority used to reward physicians or as dividends for the government who owns the hospital), this improvement withstands any standard of the objective function of the hospital.

Hence, this value driver will be rated a 5 on the importance scale (very important).

Reducing Waiting Times in the ED

Wait times in the ED will be reduced by the following steps.

Improving scheduling, ordering, and follow-up

The improvement approach will be through a proactive and dynamic buffer management.

The first step is identifying the causes for the waits. Using the Pareto approach, the major causes are:

1. Waiting for X-rays and other imaging services.
2. Waiting for a surgical consultant.
3. Waiting for the discharge letter.

A team consisting of the ED chief along with representatives of hospital management can help resolve these problems.

As a second step, management will define the maximal accepted wait for 95% of patients (e.g., four hours). Every patient will have her arrival time recorded, and after the first hour follow-up will be conducted by three buffer zones ("traffic lights"):

Green zone—ED time between zero and two hours: In this zone, only the patient status will be monitored.

Yellow zone—ED time of two to three hours: In this zone, they will collect statistics on the reasons for delay.

Red zone—Waiting of three to four hours: In this zone, the supervising nurse will initiate an expediting process, and will record statistics on the cause for the delay.

The hospital management will convene with the ED management once a week and will use a Pareto diagram or focusing matrix to analyze the reasons for delays and will take corrective actions.

This approach yields three outcomes:

- Introducing order and priorities in managing ED time.
- Expediting actions when needed.
- Identification of the real problems, using a global perspective, and taking corrective actions.

Changing the organizational structure of the ED

The idea is to form autonomous units of emergency medicine specialists, thus reducing the dependence on outside ED consultants. This can be done by recruiting nonoperating general and orthopedic surgeons (e.g., retired from operating). Hospital management decided that this step will be considered six months after implementing the previous step.

The ease of implementation of this step—4.

Importance for value enhancement—5.

Increasing Outpatient Clinics' Throughput

Outpatient clinics' throughput will be increased by negotiating with the major customers (the four HMOs), exploiting the competitive advantage of high clinical quality, excellent reputation, fast response times, and attractive prices. These actions can increase outpatient clinics' throughput by 5%.

Ease of implementation—4.

Importance—4.

Reducing Purchasing Costs

Purchasing costs will be reduced by classifying suppliers into A, B, and C groups and focusing on Group A suppliers. Seven suppliers were identified, accounting for 65% of purchases.

In parallel, the purchased items were classified, and 75 items were found to account for 85% of purchasing costs.

By focusing on these items and suppliers, better negotiations with them, and careful analysis of the needed quantities, it is possible to achieve a 5% savings in purchasing costs.

Ease of implementation—4.

Importance—5.

Dealing with Human Resources

The alienation felt by the workers vis-a-vis management ("us vs. them") brought upon mistrust and frustration. This requires immediate attention.

Dealing with human resources will be done at several levels:

1. The hospital CEO and a team of top management will meet with all employees of the hospital in departmental and divisional meetings.
2. Initiating team forging activities for the entire hospital, in addition to activities in each department.
3. Building a permanent process that will monitor worker feelings and their comments on a monthly basis.
4. Allocating some of the CEO's time to random interviews with employees and to attempts to resolve some of the problems that cause alienation.

Ease of implementation—2.
Importance—4.

The previous five value drivers are presented in the focusing table of Table 18.2.

Let us now map the improvement potential using the focusing ("easy-important") matrix of Figure 18.2.

The Improvement Implementing Process

Management decided to start working on the following value drivers: increasing OR throughput, reducing ED waiting times, and dealing with human resources. Though difficult to deal with, management has considered the human aspects to be important, and has decided to deal with it as soon as possible. The other value drivers will be dealt with at a later stage due to insufficient management time to be devoted to the change process

Table 18.2. FOCUSING TABLE FOR QUEEN MEDICAL CENTER VALUE DRIVERS

Value driver	Importance	Ease of implementing
A. Increasing operating room throughput	5	3
B. Reducing waiting times in the ED	5	4
C. Increasing outpatient clinics' throughput	4	4
D. Reducing purchasing costs	5	4
E. Dealing with human resources	4	2

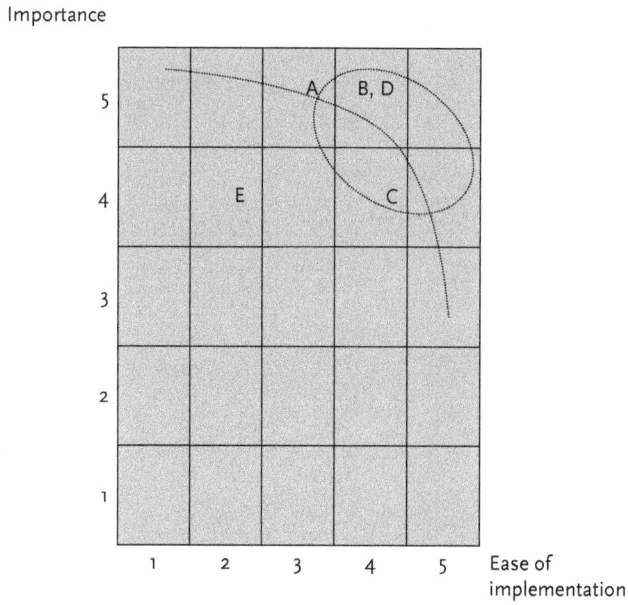

Figure 18.2:
Focusing matrix for value enhancement in Queen Medical Center

and the organizational inability to absorb too many changes in the short period. These steps will be postponed to a later stage, which will begin in about six months.

CHAPTER SUMMARY

Enhancing an organization's value is the goal of its managers. In this chapter, we presented a practical approach to increase the value of the firm, especially through dealing with managerial issues and measuring the contribution to the value of the firm.

The VFM methodology, presented in this chapter, enables managers to examine where they should devote their time and energy and in which areas the contribution will be marginally small. The methodology fits both for-profit and nonprofit organizations.

CHAPTER 19

Implementation and the Process of Ongoing Improvement

In the process of improving organizational value, three questions must be addressed (Goldratt, 1990):

- What to change?
- What to change to?
- How to make the change?

What to change? The goal is to enhance the value of the firm or improve performance in nonprofit organizations. We will exploit the value drivers to enhance the value of the organization on the one hand and treat the **value inhibitors** (policy constraints, dummy constraints, weaknesses, and threats) on the other. The idea is to focus on a small number of factors that we will try to improve. It is simply impossible to properly focus on too many issues simultaneously.

What to change to? We will want to utilize the value drivers and enhance the value of the firm along time.

How to make the change? This is the key question. The principles discussed in this book seem simple, but it takes time to fully implement them in an organization. This is a result of the need to change the minds of many people in the organization and create a work environment that is open to new ideas and their implementation.

THE PROCESS OF CHANGE

The process of change has several stages.

The Business/Functional Diagnosis of the Organization

The business/functional diagnosis of the organization will be done by identifying the business environment it is operating in and identifying value drivers. These will be performed as follows:

- In-depth interviews with employees and managers.
- Examining financial reports, marketing reports, operational and development reports.
- Examining other improvement endeavors (external and internal) done by the organization.
- Collecting external information on the organization.

Once the value drivers have been identified, they are prioritized so we can focus on the more important ones.

Drafting an Implementation Plan

After the business/functional diagnosis has been completed, a draft is prepared for a value enhancement implementation plan.

Training and Knowledge Transfer

Knowledge about new and novel management approaches and tools that were described in this book will be transferred to top management through an interactive workshop lasting several days. During this workshop, management identifies the value drivers and prepares a detailed implementation plan. Later, the knowledge will be transferred by workshops to middle management and all other employees.

The guiding principle is that implementing a change will be done by the management and workers themselves. This reduces resistance to change as it is done internally and not by external agents.

Establishing Value Enhancement Teams

Management should establish several value enhancement teams, each of which will deal with one of the various value drivers. The value-enhancing process is carried out in the spirit and tools presented in this book.

Performance, Monitoring, and Control

Management serves as a steering committee for the project. Its role is to oversee and manage the work of the value enhancement teams, meet with them on a regular basis, and approve their findings and recommendations for implementation.

PRINCIPLES OF INTRODUCING CHANGES AND REDUCING RESISTANCE TO CHANGE

Several principles should guide management when it plans to enhance the value of the organization or improve its performance:

1. Implementation should be performed by people within the organization.
2. The role of an optional external facilitator will be to introduce methodology, transfer knowledge to management and workers, and facilitate the implementation process.
3. The value enhancement teams will include rank-and-file people of the organization.
4. The number of teams should be small. They will be responsible for suggesting changes and for the actual implementation.
5. Areas for enhancement will be chosen by their contribution to value and the difficulty in implementing them, using the focusing matrix.
6. Value enhancement plays a central role of the duty and work of management and is not a side project.
7. All the organization's workers should gradually join the knowledge transfer circles.
8. Follow-up and control of the implementation of value enhancement will be done using the tools presented in this book.

THE ROLE OF INFORMATION TECHNOLOGY IN THE CHANGE PROCESS

Information technology plays a central role in the change process. However, the idea that implementing an information system will, in itself, solve the organizations' problems needs clarification. Implementing an information system in an organization should be done according to a two-stage model (Ronen and Pass, 1997) as follows.

Changing the Managerial Approaches and Processes of the Organization

First, there is a need to implement approaches such as management by constraints, the complete kit concept, the value-focused management model, the three-stage model for decision-making, global measuring and control, project management methodology, and more.

Designing an Information System that Will Support the Prescribed Approaches

After the work processes have been redesigned and the managerial approaches have been implemented, information technology must be adapted to support these newly established approaches. The resulting information system, designed according to the satisficer frame of mind, will be highly effective, yet simple. Building such information systems to support these approaches is a necessary condition for a continuation of value enhancement processes along time.

THE 3–1–1 MODEL FOR IMPLEMENTING CHANGE IN HOSPITALS

Hospitals are highly complex organizations with multiple entities, with many interactions among them, as can be seen in Figure 19.1, which is an oversimplification of the real environment.

When facing daily distress and pressure, managers seek solutions and very frequently believe that purchasing or developing the right software will provide remedy. Acronyms such as EMR, MRP, ERP, CCPM, HIM, and PACS[1] float around and are thought of as possible solutions. However, even good IT does not solve managerial problems. It cannot substitute the necessary change in management. We need simple solutions. Some managers feel that the way to proceed is to improve each of the departments depicted in Figure 19.1 independently thus relieving distresses. This approach is indeed better than doing nothing, but it does not consider the global system view presented in chapter 2. Independent treatment of all departments provides equal importance to all elements of the system, which is, obviously, not the case. Management cannot spread its attention equally across

1. The acronyms as defined as follows: electronic medical records (EMR), material requirement planning (MRP), enterprise resource planning (ERP), critical chain project management (CCPM), health information management (HIM), and picture archiving and communication system (PACS).

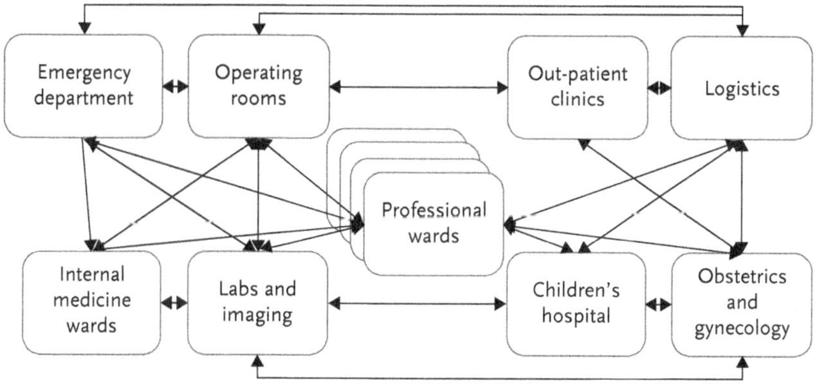

Figure 19.1:
The complex hospital

all departments. Management attention is a real bottleneck while trying to introduce significant managerial changes hence a more focused attention is required.

We present here the 3–1–1 model that simplifies the complex model depicted in Figure 19.1. The 3–1–1 model helps organizations to focus on and navigate through the needed managerial changes. This model is schematically described in Figure 19.2. The "3" (in 3–1–1) represents the three critical elements of hospitals that need attention: the emergency department (ED), the operating rooms (ORs) and labs and imaging. The first "1" represents the most critical issue of synchronization between the ED and the internal medicine wards. Lastly, the second "1" relates to hospital-specific issues (e.g., intensive care unit).

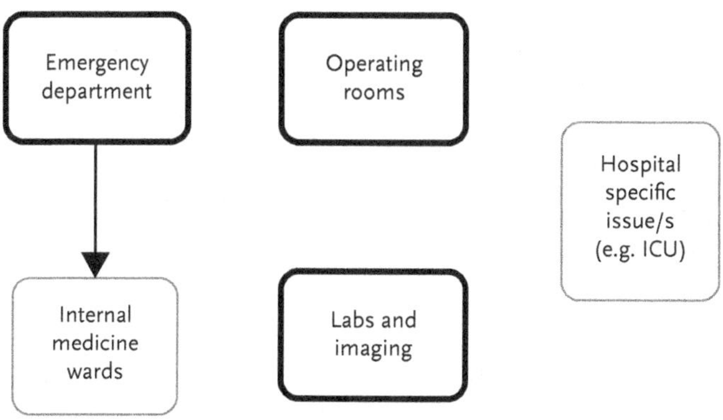

Figure 19.2:
The 3–1–1 model

The ORs are in many ways like production plants. Each OR is independent and is loosely coupled with other ORs. ORs are relatively easy to improve, and the improvements provide high value both in the medical domain and the financial domain. We have demonstrated in earlier chapters how to apply the seven steps of the theory of constraints (TOC) to reduce the "garbage plant" and increase throughput in the ORs. Other useful tools for OR improvements are the complete kit concept, strategic gating, and tactical gating by the drum–buffer–rope approach. Expected results are 20% to 100% improvements in throughput, 50% to 80% reduction in response times, and significant quality improvement.

The labs and imaging serve the entire hospital and are therefore very important. The focus should be on response time reduction. The labs and imaging services are relatively easy to improve. The recipe for improving lab throughput and response times is working in small batches and small transfer batches. Imaging improvements will be achieved utilizing the seven steps of the TOC, and the Superzoufing method. Response time improvements can be as high as 50%.

The ED is very tough to deal with but incredibly valuable. It is very complex, demanding, and stressful for all parties. It is highly dependent of other components as consultants, imaging units, laboratories, the ORs, and bed availability in wards, especially internal medicine wards. The 10 times rule is very applicable to the ED as every delay or error results in a tenfold magnified negative consequence down the road. Running some shifts with junior staff only rather than senior staff will be very detrimental downstream. The useful tools for improving ED operations include the seven focusing steps of TOC, buffer management by using the "traffic lights" system introduced earlier in this chapter, and offloading ED physicians with phlebotomists, nurses, paramedics, and physician assistants. Other important changes should include having an emergency medicine expert available 24/7 and offering a walk-in ED clinic (according to the group technology approach).

Following the treatment of the three most critical components of a hospital, we must consider synchronization issues. Synchronizing between departments is a most critical issue. For example, in many healthcare systems, the most critical linkage is between the ED and the internal medicine wards. The problem stems from overcrowding in the internal medicine wards, resulting in interruptions of admission to these wards from the ED, leading to long boarding times and ED overcrowding. A remedy can be found by synchronizing discharges from wards with discharges from the ED. Most discharges from the internal medicine wards occur in the afternoon, but discharges from the ED are spread throughout the day. The problem can be resolved by introducing a policy of discharging at least three patients from each internal medicine ward before 11:00 AM and admitting

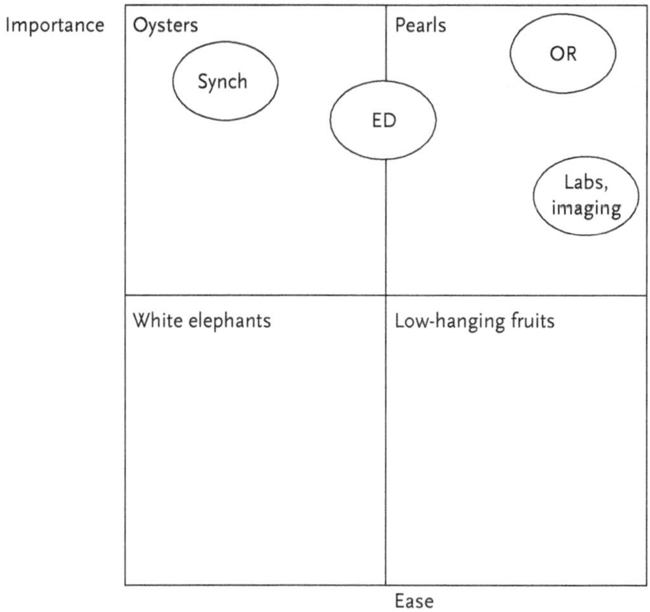

Figure 19.3:
The conceptual focusing matrix for the 3–1–1 model in a typical hospital

at least three new patients before 3:00 PM. Other effective tools are subordination of the ward routines to the discharge process, assigning a discharge nurse in each internal medicine ward, establishing a ward control center for follow-up and expedition, and offloading the bottleneck (in this case the expert physicians in the ED and internal medicine).

The last element of the 3–1–1 model is hospital specific and relates to specific units (e.g., intensive care unit, outpatient clinics). Approaches should be tailored to the specific needs and problems of the units.

Figure 19.3 presents a conceptual focusing matrix for a characteristic prioritization within the 3–1–1 model of a typical hospital (see chapter 3). "Synch" in the figure represents the synchronization between the ED and internal medicine wards.

In summary, the 3–1–1 model presents a holistic approach, uses simple and focused solutions, does value leveraging, and tailors a set of solutions for each hospital.

THE PROCESS OF ONGOING IMPROVEMENT

The idea behind the process of ongoing improvement (POOGI) is that improvement is not a one-time project but rather a continuous process.

This is in a way similar to the notion of continuous improvement in quality management.

During the first improvement round, management and the organization tackle the highest priority issues according to their potential for value creation. As soon as the solutions for these first priority issues are implemented successfully, top management and local managers are ready to look for the next round of improvement, tackling issues with lower yet substantial potential for value creation.

THE "TRAFFIC LIGHTS" SYSTEM AND THE PROCESS OF ONGOING IMPROVEMENT

The buffer management "traffic lights" system (see chapter 11) is a twofold mechanism for managing units like EDs:

1. It serves as a tactical tool used by physicians and nurses to prioritize the treatment of patients in the department thus preventing long stay of patients in the system.
2. It is a strategic tool for managers to identify the causes that prevent the department from meeting the agreed-upon completion times.

Causes of patient entrance into the red and the black zones are systematically recorded. The data regarding the causes for delays are periodically analyzed using a Pareto analysis. The Pareto analysis allows one to focus on the major causes for delays. This might serve as the engine for improvement in the process of ongoing improvement.

CHAPTER SUMMARY

Though the concepts and tools of focused management are intuitive and simple, the implementation process is not trivial and requires a great deal of management attention. This chapter presented the 3-1-1 model for hospital improvement that points out what to change and what to change to. It provides a recipe for the change process, including training and knowledge transfer and a process of ongoing improvement.

CHAPTER 20
Success Stories

The tools, methods, and philosophies of this book were very new and novel 15 years ago, and there weren't many documented successful applications. They are still novel and not widely used. However, the last decade witnessed a surge in applications. Many of them are based on the Lean approach. The authors of the book have taught the focused management approach to over one thousand students, mainly in the United States and in Israel, and many nice and successful implementations developed from participants' projects in these courses. The authors also led nearly twenty improvement implementations in healthcare organizations and in over 150 other nonprofit and for-profit organizations. We present here a series of successful implementations in the United States, United Kingdom, and Israel. For some of the successful results, we do not know what specific tools from the arsenal presented in the book were used. We present here several examples of successful implementations of the methods and tools based on our personal involvement with many organizations, projects of our students, and personal communication with implementers in the United Kingdom.

A GENERAL HOSPITAL, UNITED KINGDOM

Objectives

- Discharge patients from the emergency department (ED) in less than four hours.
- Reduce delayed admissions (trolley waits) that exceeded 12 hours.

Results (within One Year)

- 35% improvement in less than four hours throughput in the ED.
  - 2002: 68.0% patients discharged in less than four hours.
  - 2003: 92.2% patients discharged in less than four hours.
- Zero over 12-hour trolley waits.
- 91% reduction in trolley wait times exceeding four hours.

TWO HOSPITALS IN BUCKINGHAMSHIRE, UNITED KINGDOM

Objective

- Increase the percentage of patients who wait less than four hours in the ED

Results

- Hospital A percentage increased from 74% to 92%.
- Hospital B increased from 71% to 89%.
- Average patient stay time in the ED reduced to three hours.

HOSPITAL IN OXFORDSHIRE, UNITED KINGDOM

Objective

- Reduce length of stay of geriatric patients.

Results

- In a period of four months, average length of stay was reduced from 48 days to 10 days.

This seems a rather striking, nearly infeasible result. Our hypothesis is that in the process of applying focused management tools, some patients with excessive lengths of stays were discharged. These excessively long stays had a big impact on the average length of stay. It would have been wiser to focus on the median length of stay.

OTHER HOSPITALS, UNITED KINGDOM

Objective

- Reduce ED throughput time.

Result

- Reduced ED throughput time from 50% less than four hours to 80% within two months.

THE NUCLEAR CARDIOLOGY LAB—A REGIONAL MEDICAL CENTER, NEW JERSEY

Objectives

- Improve nuclear scan quality (decrease the number of false positive scans).
- Improve service quality to patients and physicians.
- Decrease backlog of patients waiting for testing.
- Decrease duration of testing.
- Increase laboratory availability.
- Improve patient, physician, and employee satisfaction.

Results

Table 20.1 summarizes the pre- and postintervention performance measures.

A LARGE PRIVATE HOSPITAL, TEL AVIV, ISRAEL

Results

- Number of operations increased 20% within nine months.
- Profits nearly doubled (variable costs accounted for 20% of costs so additional operations were very beneficial).

Table 20.1. PRE- AND POST-INTERVENTION PERFORMANCE MEASURES

	Pre-intervention	Post-intervention
Response Time (hours)	5.5	3.3
WIP (points)	10	8
Quality of service		
% False + Tests	~25	~5
Patient satisfaction	poor	good
Physician satisfaction	fair	very good
Capacity	16	27

- Waiting times for operations decreased by 20%.
- Queues for operations and imaging tests decreased by more than 20%.
- Improved clinical quality and service quality.

According to the CEO of the hospital, the three tools with the highest impact were eliminating dummy constraints, using specific contribution for prioritization, and working with complete kits.

A SMALL PRIVATE HOSPITAL, ISRAEL

Objectives

- Increase throughput in ORs
- Increase quality

Results

- Number of operations doubled in one year (2007 vs. 2006).

The tools used included the seven focusing steps of the theory of constraints, complete kits, and specific contribution.

OPHTHALMOLOGY ORs—A PUBLIC HOSPITAL, ISRAEL

Results (within Four Months)

- Throughput—Up 43%.
- Operating expenses—Unchanged.
- Waiting time for surgery—Decreased 41%.
- Response time—Decreased 14.5%.
- Quality—Up 20%.
- "Garbage time"—Decreased 16%.

MEDICAL IMAGING CENTERS: THE CT UNIT, ISRAEL

System Goal

- Enhance value by maximizing profits while maintaining high clinical value and high service quality.

CT Unit Goals

- High-quality CT imaging while maintaining patient satisfaction.
- Address bottleneck: CT scanner, 50% ineffective time.
  - Causes:
    - Lack of dressing room.
    - Undefined distribution of tasks.
    - Patients late arrivals
  - Dummy and policy constraints:
    - Every worker is entitled to a taxi ride until 10 PM. Since they wanted to save money, they decided to end the shift at 9:30 PM.
    - Dressing room was not used because lack of lead protection. CT room served as dressing room.

Results

- Pre-intervention: six patients per hour.
- Post-intervention: 7.5 patients per hour (25% improvement within two months; goal: 9 patients per hour).

A PUBLIC HOSPITAL, TEL AVIV, ISRAEL

Objective

Reduce trolley waits (boarding times) in the ED

- Increase percentage of patients who spend less than four hours in the ED.

Results

- Percentage of patients staying in the ED for less than four hours increased from 55% to 67% in one year.
- Trolley waits decreased significantly. This was mainly achieved through better synchronization with the internal medicine wards' discharge process, by having the wards discharge two patients before 11:00 AM.

REFERENCES

Albanese, C.T., D.R. Aaby and T.S. Platchek, 2014. *Advanced Lean in Healthcare.* North Charleston, SC: GreatSpace Independent Publishing Platform.

Black, J., and D. Miller, 2008. *The Toyota Way to Healthcare Excellence: Increase Efficiency and Improve Quality with Lean.* Chicago: Health Administration Press.

Coman, A., G. Koller and B. Ronen, 1996. The Application of Focused Management in the Electronics Industry—A Case Study, *Production and Inventory Management,* Second quarter, 65–70.

Cooper, R. and R.S. Kaplan, 1988. Measure Costs Right: Make the Right Decisions, *Harvard Business Review,* 66(5), 96–103.

Copeland, T., T. Koller and J. Murrin, 1996. *Valuation—Measuring and Managing the Value of Companies.* New York: John Wiley and Sons.

Cox, J.F. III, and J.H. Blackstone, 1998. *APICS Dictionary* (9th ed.). Falls Church, VA: APICS, The Educational Society for Resource Management.

Cox, J.F. III, and M.S. Spencer, 1998. *The Constraint Management Handbook.* Boca Raton, FL: St. Lucie Press.

Cox, J.F. III,, M. Robinson and W. Maxwell, 2016. Unconstraining a Doctor's Office: TOC's Buffer Management Can Help Solve Core Scheduling Problems. *Industrial Engineer,* 48(2), 28–33.

Crosby, P.B., 1979. *Quality Is Free.* New York: McGraw-Hill.

Committee on Quality Health Care in America, Institute of Medicine, 2001. *Crossing The Quality Chasm: a New Health System for the 21st Century.* Washington, D.C., National Academy Press.

Deming, W.E., 1986. *Out of the Crisis.* Cambridge, MA: MIT Center for Advanced Engineering Study.

Dettmer, H.W., 1998. *Breaking the Constraints to World-Class Performance.* Milwaukee, WI: ASQ Quality Press.

Eden, Y. and B. Ronen, 1993. Improving Workflow in the Insurance Industry: A Focused Management Approach, *Journal of Insurance Issues,* 16(1), 49–62.

Eden, Y., and B. Ronen, 2002. Activity Based Costing and Activity Based Management, *Articles of Merit 2002 Competition, FMAC Award Programs for Distinguished Contribution of Management Accounting, International Federation of Accountants.* New York: National Federation of Accountants, 47–58.

Gawande, A., 2011. *The Checklist Manifesto: How to Get Things Right.* New York: Metropolitan Books.

Geri, N. and B. Ronen, 2005. Relevance Lost: The Rise and Fall of Activity Based Costing. *Human Systems Management,* 24, 133–144.

Goldratt, E.M., 1990. *The Haystack Syndrome: Sifting Information Out of the Data Ocean*. Croton-on-Hudson, NY: North River Press.

Goldratt, E.M., 1994. *It's Not Luck*. Croton on Hudson, NY: North River Press.

Goldratt, E.M., 1997. *Critical Chain*. Croton on Hudson, NY: North River Press.

Goldratt, E.M. and J. Cox, 1992. *The Goal: A Process of Ongoing Improvement* (2d rev. ed.). Croton-on-Hudson, NY: North River Press.

Goldratt, E.M. and R.E. Fox, 1986. *The Race*. Croton-on-Hudson, NY: North River Press.

Grosfeld-Nir, A. and B. Ronen, 1998. The Complete Kit Concept: Modeling the Managerial Approach, *Computers and Industrial Engineering*, 34(3), 695–701.

Gupta, N. 2003. Constraints Management: Recent Advances and Practices. *International Journal of Production Research*, 41(4), 647–659.

Hillier, F.S. and G.J. Lieberman, 2002. *Introduction to Operations Research* (7th ed.). New York: McGraw-Hill.

Horngren, C. T., G. Foster and S.M. Datar, 2000. *Cost Accounting—A Managerial Emphasis* (10th ed.). Englewood Cliffs, NJ: Prentice-Hall.

Institute of Medicine, 1999. *To Err Is Human: Building a Safer Health System*, edited by Linda T. Kohn. Washington, DC: National Academy Press.

Institute of Medicine, 2003. *Crossing the Quality Chasm*. Washington, DC: National Academy Press.

Johnson, H.T. and R.S. Kaplan, 1987. *Relevance Lost: The Rise and Fall of Management Accounting*. Boston, MA: Harvard Business School Press.

Kaplan, R.S. and S.R. Anderson, 2004. Time-Driven Activity-Based Costing. *Harvard Business Review*, 82(11), 131–138.

Karp, A., and B. Ronen, 1992. Improving Manufacturing Operations: An Entropy Model Approach, *International Journal of Production Research*, 30(4), 923–938.

Knight, A., 2014. *Pride and Joy*. Herts, UK: Never Say I Know.

Lawal, A.K., T. Rotter, L. Kinsman, N. Sari, L. Harrison, C. Jeffery, M. Kutz, M.F. Khan and R. Flynn, 2014. Lean Management in Health Care: Definition, Concepts, Methodology and Effects Reported (Systematic Review Protocol), *Systematic Review*, 3, 103. Published online September 19, 2014. doi: 10.1186/2046-4053-3-103.

Leshno, M. and B. Ronen, 2001. The Complete Kit Concept—Implementation in the Health Care System, *Human Systems Management*, 20(4), 313–318.

Litvak, E, 2005. Optimizing Patient Flow by Managing Its Variability. In *From Front Office to Front Line: Essential Issues for Health Care Leaders*. Oakbrook Terrace, IL: Joint Commission Resources, 91–112.

Livne, Z. and B. Ronen, 1990. The Component Chart: A New Tool for Purchasing and Production, *Production and Inventory Management*, 3, 18–23.

Maayan, E., B. Ronen and A. Coman, 2012. Assessing the Performance of a Court System: A Comprehensive Performance Measures Approach, *International Journal of Public Administration*, 35(11), 729–738.

Mabin, J.M. and S.J. Balderstone, 2000. *The World of the Theory of Constraints: A Review of International Literature*. Boca Raton, FL: St. Lucie Press.

Mabin, V.J. and S.J. Balderstone. 2003. The Performance of the Theory of Constraints Methodology: Analysis and Discussion of Successful TOC Applications, *International Journal of Operations and Production Management*, 23, 568–595.

Pass, S. and B. Ronen, 2003. Managing the Market Constraint in the Hi-Tech Industry, *International Journal of Operations Management*, 41(4), 713–724.

Ronen, B., 1992. The Complete Kit, *International Journal of Production Research*, 30(10), 2457–2466.

Ronen, B., A. Coman and E. Schragenheim, 2001. Peak Management, *International Journal of Production Research*, 39(14), 3183–3193.

Ronen, B. and S. Pass, 1997. Manufacturing Management Information Systems Require Simplification, *Industrial Engineering*, 24(2), 50–53.

Ronen, B. and J.S. Pliskin, 2006. *Focused Operations Management for Health Service Organizations*. San Francisco, CA: Jossey-Bass.

Ronen, B. and Y. Spector, 1992. Managing System Constraints: A Cost/Utilization Approach, *International Journal of Production Research*, 30(9), 2045–2061.

Ronen, B. and M. Starr, 1990. Synchronized Manufacturing as in OPT: From Practice to Theory, *Computers and Industrial Engineering*, 18(8), 585–600.

Schonberger, R.J., 1986. *World Class Manufacturing: The Lessons of Simplicity Applied*. New York: Free Press.

Schragenheim, E. and B. Ronen, 1990. The Drum–Buffer–Rope Shop Floor Control, *Production and Inventory Management*, 31(3), 18–23.

Schragenheim, E., J. Cox, and B. Ronen, 1994. Process Flow Industry—Scheduling and Control Using Theory of Constraints, *International Journal of Production Research*, 32(8), 1867–1877.

Shingo, S., 1996. *Quick Changeover for Operators: The SMED System*. Cambridge, MA: Productivity Press.

Shoemaker, T.E. and R.A. Reid, 2005. Applying the TOC Thinking Process: A Case Study in the Government Sector, *Human Systems Management*, 24, 21–37.

Simon, H.A., 1957. *Models of Man*. New York: John Wiley and Sons.

Smith, K., 2004. *Eastern Financial Florida Credit Union: Creating a Competitive Advantage in the Mortgage Lending Business*. Paper presented at TOC World 2004 Conference, Uncasville, CT, April.

Suzaki, K., 1987. *The New Manufacturing Challenge*. New York: Free Press.

Taguchi, G., 1986. *Introduction to Quality Engineering: Designing Quality into Products and Processes*. Cambridge, MA: Productivity.

Zidel, T.G., 2012. *Lean Done Right: Achieve and Maintain Reform in Your Healthcare Organization*. Chicago: Health Administration Press.

INDEX

Tables and boxes are indicated by an italic *t* and *f* following the page number.